Peter Bazalgette is chief creative officer of Endemol International. He has worked in television for twenty-five years, creating internationally successful formats such as *Ready Steady Cook* and *Changing Rooms*. He was nominated as one of the *Daily Mail*'s ten 'Worst Britons' for bringing *Big Brother* to the UK.

BILLION DOLLAR GAME

How Three Men Risked It All and Changed the Face of Television

PETER BAZALGETTE

TIME WARNER
BOOKS

TIME WARNER BOOKS

First published in Great Britain in April 2005 by
Time Warner Books

Copyright © Peter Bazalgette 2005

The right of Peter Bazalgette to be identified as the Author of this
Work has been asserted in accordance with the Copyright, Designs
and Patents Act 1988.

A CIP catalogue record for this book
is available from the British Library.

HB ISBN 0 316 73109 9
CF ISBN 0 316 72915 9

Typeset in Sabon by M Rules
Printed and bound in Great Britain
by Clays Ltd, St Ives plc

Time Warner Books
An imprint of
Time Warner Book Group UK
Brettenham House
Lancaster Place
London WC2E 7EN

www.twbg.co.uk

For Hilary

CONTENTS

Foreword   1

PART I

1 Absolute Beginners   7
2 Closer to Reality   18
3 Everything Is Changing   37
4 Unpopular Ideas   52
5 Ideas Won't Keep   78
6 The Worth of a Man   112
7 Put Me on Television   135
8 Deals Are My Art Form   152
9 To Withstand the Highest Bidder   176
10 A Very Good Case   200

PART II

11 Civilisation As We Know It   225
12 Trash Heroes and Pantomime Villains   237
13 Sex Rears its Head   245
14 Bimbos, Bans and Boycotts   260
15 Vote Early, Vote Often   272

Postscript   283
Big Brother Transmissions Worldwide, 1999–2005   287
Acknowledgements   291
Bibliography   293
Index   295

FOREWORD

'You can't do that. You can't do it, no you can't. This is awful.'
That was the response *Big Brother*'s creator got when he first
mentioned the television format to his closest colleague. 'Whose
was the sick mind which infected all the others? Because this
does seem to be an infectious disease – worse than BSE.' That
was how Germans responded to *Big Brother* when it appeared
in their country. The man behind this outrage, warned off by his
peers and condemned as sick, was John de Mol. One moment he
was a successful television producer in Dutch television, the next
he was internationally demonised. His idea earned charges of
Nazism in one country, caused a constitutional crisis in another
and a confrontation between Islam and the CIA in a third. And
John de Mol had created *Big Brother* merely as an entertainment
show to make money. As it happens it did that too, in prodigious
quantities.

In 1999, after the very first series of *Big Brother* had only
been on air for two weeks, John de Mol was made an offer that
rated his production company at more than a billion pounds. He
was visiting the world television market at Cannes, in the South
of France. The mighty publishing and television combine
Pearson came on the line. They offered to merge their TV company with de Mol's. They were even agreeing to de Mol's own
valuation of his business. This would create a vast, multi-billion
dollar, international company of which he would own a full 25
per cent. A rich deal by anyone's standards. At this moment

de Mol looked up. At the front of his company's sales stand he could see a queue of television executives forming. Ten a.m. was a strangely early hour for a species that rarely emerged before noon. They were all desperate to secure the rights to *Big Brother* for their territories, even though it had yet to prove itself in its first country of transmission, Holland. De Mol had a big decision to take. There were billions of pounds riding on it either way. Was it too early to sell out? Or would tomorrow be too late?

John de Mol had a fifteen-year track record of producing entertainment shows. He relished doing it. But there was something he liked more – making a deal. And there was one thing he loved above all else – taking risks. To get real satisfaction, this chain-smoking businessman – single-minded to the point of monomania – needed to gamble. In Cannes that autumn Monday morning the conditions were perfect. An instant decision was required. He paused, took one more look at the queue, and announced to Pearson: 'The deal's off.' When asked why, when they had agreed to all his terms, he simply replied: 'The time's not right.' De Mol's own colleagues, who had been negotiating for months, were flabbergasted and depressed.

Within six months they would find several pressing reasons to be cheerful again. By then *Big Brother* had indeed sold rapidly across the world. But, more crucially, with its linking of television, the internet and telephones in one entertainment package it established de Mol and his company as a hot stock. They were catapulted up into the final, frenzied days of the dotcom boom. By March 2000 Pearson's offer was to seem puny, insulting even.

In 2000 de Mol was to triumph again by achieving the unthinkable for a European. He conquered the American television market. In this quest he had to compete with two British men, each also intent on creating the most successful television format ever. Paul Smith launched *Who Wants to Be a Millionaire* the year before *Big Brother*. Charlie Parsons got the desert island challenge, *Survivor*, away in the US the year after. But the fortunes of these three were linked more intimately still. In the mid-nineties de Mol had tried to buy Smith's company. He narrowly failed to grasp a half share in what would become the most cash-generative property the television industry has ever seen – *Millionaire* was, tantalisingly, created just a few months later. And Charlie Parsons was to sue de Mol up to the highest court in Holland, alleging *Big Brother* was nothing more than a crude copy of his own format, *Survivor*. Billions of pounds of revenue were to hang in the balance as the Dutch judges deliberated. Of this triumvirate of aspirants de Mol would make the most money, Smith would win the most viewers and Parsons would issue the most writs.

I brought *Big Brother* to Britain. By good fortune I acquired the rights to the format having decided, with my colleagues, to join John de Mol's production company in 1998, just a year before the show took off. I was able to experience at first hand the unparalleled obloquy *Big Brother* and its producers earned wherever it was made. I had previously produced many popular TV shows that were roundly and regularly condemned by critics. These were the people for whom television should be, it seemed, a cross between an educational facility and an improving enema. They reacted to entertainment rather as one suspected they did to sex or rich food – Anglo-Saxon distaste (that is, guilt) for something done purely for pleasure. But *Big Brother* was different. This wasn't just a show they attacked. This was one they wanted stopped. And the more extreme the debate became, the more John de Mol enjoyed the outrage. To him it was another sort of gamble, and just as attractive as the risks he took in business. I witnessed the entire adventure at first hand.

Billion Dollar Game is about one man and his show – the P. T. Barnum of modern television. John de Mol eventually hit the biggest jackpot in the history of television production. This is the story of how he did it.

Peter Bazalgette
January 2005

PART I

CHAPTER ONE

Absolute Beginners

As for the boys and girls, the dear young absolute beginners, I sometimes feel that if they only *knew* this fact, this very simple fact, namely how powerful they really are, then they could rise up overnight . . .

COLIN MacINNES

John de Mol looked out of the window. Photographers were lurking in the bushes. They wanted to grab a picture of him, or his lover or, preferably, both of them together. At twenty-one de Mol was just a television producer. But his name was well known. Not only had he been a successful disc jockey in his teens but his father ('the Dutch Sinatra') had been a star. Now, in 1976, he had moved into the apartment of his girlfriend. Not that scandalous, even in the seventies, surely? But the blonde Willeke Alberti was Holland's most popular female singer of the time. And the real spice was that she was nine years older than de Mol. Everyone loves a story with the promise of cradle snatching.

Anyone aged twenty-one would be unprepared for such scrutiny. De Mol – shy in public situations – disliked the personal exposure. But another side of him relished the provocation. Let them write what they like, let them be scandalised. De Mol was already extraordinarily tough-minded and driven by an overwhelming ambition. His contemporaries put it down to his combative relationship with his father as a boy. If he scored one goal in football he was asked why he had not scored two. He was meant to go to college to become a lawyer or, failing that, a sports teacher. Not to leave school at seventeen to be a disc jockey. De Mol had other ideas and, in the end, his father had relented.

Despite the unwelcome attentions of the press de Mol and Willeke managed to sustain their relationship and were married in 1976. They had a grand wedding, organised for them by one of Holland's leading theatre impresarios, Joop van den Ende. Willeke often starred in live shows that van den Ende promoted. He treated the nuptials like one of his big productions and capped it by making the best man's speech. Van den Ende was first to become de Mol's deadliest business rival, then his closest ally in a quest to dominate the European entertainment industry. They would both become billionaires, at the same time, in the same deal.

In Spain the following year the future architect of that deal, a young man called Juan Villalonga, was just beginning his first job. As yet he knew nothing of the media. He had gained a master's in business administration at Barcelona's Instituto de Estudios Superiores de la Empresas. Now he was entering the Banco Central, founded by his uncle, Ignacio Villalonga. Villalonga junior was already a man with contacts. Not least among them was his school friend José Maria Aznar. Aznar was later to become Prime Minister of Spain, gaining all the powers of patronage that go with the post. Villalonga's business career was now up and running.

Even in his early twenties de Mol had status in Dutch television. He was the unusually youthful producer of the chart show on the public channel TROS. In the days before pop splintered into a rainbow of niche genres, the weekly chart show was a unifying television event which captured huge audiences. It was a

plum job and de Mol ran the show with the confidence of someone twice his age. On one occasion he had a top Dutch band on
the show called Earth and Fire. The lead singer was chatting in
the studio reception when a pimply, stick insect of a fifteen-
year-old youth approached her for a radio interview. His name
was Ruud Hendriks. De Mol grabbed him by the scruff of the
neck and personally propelled him out of the studio on to the
street. Not a very auspicious start to their relationship. Twenty-
five years later de Mol would rely on Hendriks to milk the
internet boom to their mutual advantage.

De Mol rose rapidly in Dutch television. But the entertainment programmes he was producing – chart shows, beauty
contests – were conventional fare. The future creator of *Big
Brother* was unaware of a controversial 1968 play on BBC2
called *The Sex Olympics*. This imagined a soporific audience
being fed a diet of television porn, enlivened by a new idea: 'The
Live Life Show'. A family was sent to live in a remote croft
under twenty-four-hour camera surveillance. They were set certain diabolical challenges by the all-controlling production team
and several deaths resulted.

The Sex Olympics had merely imagined a family being filmed
round the clock. The following year it happened when a
Canadian documentary maker, Allan King, shot *A Married
Couple*. He filmed one family for ten weeks, intimately charting
the relationship of Billy Edwards and his wife Antoinette as it
deteriorated. Then, in 1972, it happened again. The US director
Craig Gilbert followed a Californian family for a year. Ten million viewers tuned in to each documentary, witnessing Bill and
Pat Loud gradually grow apart until, in the final episodes, they
agreed to divorce. And in 1974 *The Family*, another year-long
saga, appeared on the BBC. These three projects had one thing
in common: in each case the featured couple split up. Was the
scrutiny too much? In its bid to reveal human intimacies had
television caused rather than merely followed the drama? There

was no clear answer because then the trail went cold. No comparable television show would appear in the next twenty years.

The man who would later capture this territory, John de Mol, became a senior executive producer at TROS at just twenty-three. To his contemporaries he was shy, even aloof, and relentlessly determined. At this point, in 1978, he looked around him: 'Jesus Christ – all my colleagues are forty or fifty years old. I'm not going to wait for that.' De Mol was displaying the same impatience with Holland's public broadcaster that he had with school: 'About every six months or so I would get a letter saying, it is an honour to tell you you have been promoted and you now go from grade 6A to 7 or 8 or whatever.' He decided to leave and become a freelance producer. He was an absolute beginner again. At the time there were six public broadcasters delivering programming to two channels. Everyone worked for them in-house. Freelance producers were unheard of. So de Mol was taking a big risk that the broadcasters would still use him. And to begin with they didn't, so he needed to generate his own living.

The hugely popular American singer John Denver was due to tour Europe the same year. The pageboy haircut, the pubescent spectacles, the wholesome tunes ('Rocky Mountain High', 'Annie's Song') – all these went down particularly well in middle-of-the road Holland. De Mol decided he would televise one of his concerts, but he needed the agreement of Denver's manager. He discovered this was Jerry Weintraub, at the time the most powerful music promoter in the United States. He had worked with all the top talent, from Elvis Presley through Bob Dylan to Led Zeppelin. Undaunted de Mol made an appointment to visit his office. This was in Los Angeles so he had to borrow a thousand guilders to buy an economy flight to the US West Coast.

John de Mol landed at LA International Airport late one night with the Dutch tour promoter in tow. The usual knot of autograph hunters was hanging around the arrivals hall where the biggest names in entertainment at the time – Robert Redford, Jane Fonda, Warren Beatty – routinely emerged. No one gave the insignificant Dutch pair a second glance.

The next morning they went to Jerry Weintraub's office for a ten o'clock meeting. The US had by far the biggest music industry in the world. And what had Holland come up with? The Smurfs. De Mol did not register on Weintraub's radar and the meeting was taken by an assistant. De Mol explained that when John Denver came to Holland he wanted to make a television special. The assistant looked at this baby-faced, would-be entrepreneur and said, 'No, we're not gonna do that.' After a twelve-hour flight the entire meeting took just three minutes. De Mol then had to get back on the plane and fly another twelve hours home: 'The guy looked at me, like – who are you? Go away.' There would be something of a contrast in the same city twenty-one years later: a personal driver, the best hotel and network chat shows competing for the first interview. But for the moment, all doors were closed to him.

Despite his painfully wasted trip to Los Angeles de Mol did, in the end, get what he wanted. Back in Holland he called a friend at RCA Records, John Denver's record label. The friend introduced him to RCA's European boss and he did a deal with Jerry Weintraub on de Mol's behalf. He would, after all, televise Denver's concert. Showing a naivety he would not repeat, de Mol then offered to give the television show to AVRO, one of the public broadcasters, as long as they would let him work on it. AVRO counter-proposed that de Mol organise and produce the entire show and deliver them a completed videotape. 'Jesus Christ, how do you mean? How do I do that?' asked de Mol. He had to find out quickly, in the process hiring an office and assembling a team. By accident, de Mol had set up his first production company. He then produced several additional television specials in quick succession.

Now de Mol was the subject of more unwelcome publicity and, once again, the cause of it was his love life. He had married at the tender age of twenty-one a woman nine years his senior. Absolute fidelity may have been at the core of his marriage vows but it was an aspiration rather than a reality. John de Mol liked women. Women liked John de Mol. Willeke and he had had a baby son, named Johnnie (who was also genetically programmed to enter the entertainment industry in due course), but within two years de Mol had started a relationship with another singer, not as celebrated as Willeke but younger. There was a hugely successful female group at the time with the enticing name of Luv. All three were beautiful – one brunette, one redhead and one blonde. De Mol fell in love with the blonde, by the name of Marga Scheide. He had first met her when he was producing a pop show, *Disco Circus*, for TROS in 1977. Luv's manager had brought the girls into de Mol's office to perform in order to blag them on to the show. He succeeded. Now de Mol left Willeke and moved in with Marga. Once more probing long lenses were focused on his comings and goings. He hated it, but he was in love with Marga.

Up to this point the world's entertainment industry was dominated by television, radio and music companies. The first personal computer had not yet been launched and the mobile phone was so big that it needed two grown men to carry it. Even five years on from the first mention of an 'Internet', telephone companies were seen as mere providers of a speech-only service. But in 1978 one of the visionaries of the technological boom that was still to come started to formulate a powerful theory. The idea would eventually create trillions of dollars of value at the end of the twentieth century, albeit briefly. Nicholas Negroponte taught at the Massachusetts Institute of Technology in Boston. MIT is funded by industry. Negroponte found he could raise large sums from visiting executives when he started showing them three overlapping circles. One was labelled

'Broadcast and Motion Picture Industry', the next 'Computer Industry' and a third said 'Print and Publishing Industry'. He asserted that the three circles would, by the year 2000, converge and revolutionise the communications media. He had omitted the telephone industry which was eventually to lead the stampede towards convergence in the last decade of the century. But otherwise he was uncannily accurate. He had predicted the means by which John de Mol would make his fortune and the year in which he would do it.

Television commissions proved few and far between for John de Mol Productions. There was no developed market for programmes made independently, outside the public broadcasters. And what they did allow to be produced out of house tended to be material that would only run in the fringe of the schedules. It had little value. John de Mol Productions was a hand-to-mouth business with a permanent overdraft. Twice de Mol had to pledge his house against his company debt to stop the banks calling in their loans and closing him down. To keep his company afloat de Mol would do anything and everything. He found himself trying to turn kickboxing into a mainstream television sport. He shot commercials for local companies. There is even a promotional video of the time that proudly announces 'The John de Mol Productions Wedding Video Service'. More promising than the video service was his move into talent management. De Mol became the manager of a few television presenters and several bands. In 1981 he met Spargo, a Dutch group that had already had a number one hit in Holland, Belgium and Germany. Their record company advised them to get professional management and introduced them to de Mol.

They met him at his rented office – the attic of a garage attached to a suburban house in Hilversum. There they found just John and his secretary. She went home almost immediately because he could only afford to employ her a few hours a day. He gave them all a sales pitch about how he could improve their careers and make them money. He clearly had an affinity for the pop world from his days as a disc jockey. But Spargo were decidedly unimpressed. De Mol may have had big plans but he looked like a teenager and he was sitting in a suburban garage. He nevertheless managed to persuade them to return for two more meetings and they gradually softened. Spargo's bass player, Jef Nassenstein, remembers it as a combination of charm and ambition.

When de Mol had talked the group round he finally revealed that he wouldn't manage them personally. He was going to hire a singer from another Amsterdam group for that. De Mol showed them into what would be their new agent's office – an even smaller shack, a lean-to adjoining the garage. Spargo signed up and went on to have six further top ten hits across Europe. When their popularity waned a couple of years later, Jef Nassenstein then joined de Mol as a television producer and stayed with him for twenty years. From those first meetings with de Mol, Nassenstein remembers a man who did not appear to be particularly turned on by money or status. More someone who loved making a deal, someone who had to win and who was fixated by show business – live concerts, television shows, any event where there were risks attached and where the clamour of the fans was palpable.

Today it is hard to credit just how underdeveloped Europe's television economy was in 1982. TV entertainment adhered rigidly to about four genres that had emerged after the Second World War – sitcoms, dramas, soap operas and 'light' entertainment. Television channels were government owned or, at the least, heavily regulated. In the United States, by contrast, there was already multi-channel television. There was even a high-tech share index, the NASDAQ, for new technology and media companies. (Unnoticed, this index hit its lowest point, post-1980, in August 1982. It then started a seventeen and a half year bull run that would finally peak in March 2000. This would also be a highly significant month for John de Mol.) In Europe there were few opportunities for entrepreneurs such as de Mol to build a business. He needed to make more programmes. One man, who was intent on breaking up the Continent's staid media markets, now provided him with that chance.

Rupert Murdoch's News International company was extending into television via its Sky channel brand. This disrespectful Australian was challenging the cosy, European world of two-channel, government-controlled broadcasting. Holland was a promising territory because it already had a mature underground cable network delivering the television signal to much of the country. There was a great opportunity for a new service with some imported programmes. Sky's strategy was to roll out area by area. De Mol read in the newspaper that Sky would start in the south-west of Holland and that they were looking for a local show to help the launch. True to form, de Mol boarded an aeroplane and flew to London to see Gary Davy at Sky. Like Murdoch, Davy was an Australian. De Mol offered to make the local programme. The meeting lasted little longer than his encounter in Los Angeles four years earlier, but this time he had a deal.

John de Mol Productions made the show and then a series of further programmes each time Sky launched in a new area of Holland. De Mol was asked to find a female presenter who looked and felt Dutch but who was fluent in English. He screen-tested a hundred hopefuls without feeling he had found the right one. Then Jef Nassenstein, now working for John full-time, sug-gested John's teenage sister, Linda. Nassenstein had seen her host a stand at a trade fair to earn herself extra pocket money and he had been impressed by her charm and self-confidence. John was at first reluctant but in the end they tested her. She was by far the best. But de Mol's dilemma was that recommending his sister to Sky looked like small-town corruption. So he prepared a tape of three candidates, revealed only their Christian names and sent the tape to Sky. Davy called back swiftly and said with typical antipodean directness, 'John, good news, we want Linda'. 'I have a confession to make,' replied John. 'It's my sister.' And Davy said, 'I don't care if it's your mother or grand-mother. That's who we want.'

The launch show, and several that followed, were successful but they were only one-offs. De Mol still had little regular business and still had to live a hand-to-mouth existence. Nassenstein and he would creep into video editing facilities slackly managed by one of the public broadcasters. They sometimes edited an entire show there, using expensive equipment, and then stole out again. No one was any the wiser and, most importantly, no one ever invoiced them.

De Mol concentrated hard on keeping Sky, his one major client, happy. But a crisis intervened. After several difficult years, John de Mol's business appeared to be stabilising. He had a successful talent management division. He at last had recurring television commissions via his Sky contract. The company had outgrown the converted garage and taken larger offices on an industrial estate. As ever, he was very careful with expenditure – he managed to get cheap premises from a building contractor whose business was not prospering and who did not need the offices attached to his warehouse. De Mol also kept the number of staff to an absolute minimum. But, with his growing level of work, he had been strongly advised to employ a book-keeper. He found the cheapest one he could and, as a further economy, de Mol only allowed him to come in for a few hours a day. He used to sit in a little cubicle, chain-smoking. His chosen method of book-keeping turned out to be highly idiosyncratic. On the surface everything looked fine. But it emerged one day, when the bank contacted de Mol direct, that business was a good deal worse than it seemed. In fact the company was virtually insolvent. This time the debts were too big to be serviced by further mortgaging his home. More worryingly, he could not find a bank willing even to consider bailing him out. His company remained small. He was only twenty-eight and he looked a good deal younger. He presented too much of a risk. What the banks saw was a would-be businessman who had badly overreached himself and would probably do so again. On an obscure industrial estate, adjacent to a warehouse full of building materials, it looked as though John de Mol Productions was finished.

CHAPTER TWO

Closer to Reality

Television is actually closer to reality than anything in books.
The madness of TV is the madness of human life.

CAMILLE PAGLIA

In a last throw of the dice John de Mol contacted an old colleague from his radio days. Willem van Kooten was the most
famous disc jockey in Holland. He was also a shrewd and
wealthy businessman. He had a music publishing company
which gave him links to leading bands. He was able, at the time
quite legitimately, to play and promote these artists on his radio
show, driving the sales of their music. Every time a record was
played or sold his company collected the royalty on behalf of the
artist. Van Kooten remembered and liked de Mol. As a radio
man van Kooten knew nothing of television but was impressed
by de Mol's new ambitions. Fifteen years older, he recognised
much of himself in the younger entrepreneur. Unlike the bank
attempting to foreclose on de Mol, van Kooten was a genuine
risk taker. He decided to save John de Mol Productions.

Van Kooten agreed to invest £300,000, a huge leap of faith.
He now became de Mol's benign mentor. He was available
whenever de Mol wanted any business advice. He knew from his
own company that there was money in owning rights. De Mol
had a vision of creating and exploiting television formats which

van Kooten shared. There was only one condition – that de Mol hire a new book-keeper.

De Mol began to repay van Kooten's confidence in him quite soon afterwards. He was producing the launch shows for Sky but the daily programming, mostly music shows, all came from London. De Mol told Gary Davy he could make them more cheaply and won the contract. Linda de Mol was paired with a cat glove puppet and an English disc jockey, Pat Sharp, in the *DJ Cat Show*. They linked pop videos, much as the digital music channels do today. At rehearsals de Mol would sit on the studio floor rather than inhabit the control room. In an entirely casual industry he stood out. He wore a smart suit and tie, looking every inch the executive. Smoking was banned in studios, but de Mol had to smoke. So here, as in many places in the future, he negotiated a dispensation that allowed him to puff away. Everyone who worked there remembers him sitting in a haze of smoke with the fire officer beside his chair, monitoring the disposal of the cigarette butts. The show was broadcast daily. Sky soon added another daily show as well as a weekly programme. De Mol had finally achieved regular throughput for his company. And in Linda he had also discovered a presenter who would, in time, host many of his most popular formats in Holland and Germany.

The small circle around John de Mol now began to share his social life. They discovered that he was very restless, always wanting to go out to find excitement at gigs and parties. Nassenstein put it down to his ceaseless quest for female company: 'It's ladies. I think he has this from his grandfather, a band leader. As a performer I more than once talked to some of the older musicians in Holland. They always remembered grandfather de Mol as a ladies' man. Maybe it skips a generation to John. It was a game he played.' His colleagues also learnt what a typical social evening at home consisted of for de Mol. Dinner had to be followed by either a board game or cards. And de Mol always played to win. His favourite was the board game Risk. Simply put, it is a game of world domination. This was a concept for which he seemed to have an affinity. He particularly excelled at the deal making. One player makes a non-aggression pact with another player while he is weak. Then, when he has built up his armies, he overwhelms his former ally. More often than not, whatever the game, de Mol won: 'I love playing games. If you call me at 3 a.m. and say let's play, I'll say fine. I'll take a shower and be there in one hour. I'm very competitive. I like to win games.'

When Jef Nassenstein's music career was waning, and he first asked de Mol for a job, the same game-playing instinct was deployed. Nassenstein had been a star and a client. Would he settle down, with due humility, to be a faithful employee? De Mol told him he might have something but first asked if he could help a friend of his out. He told Nassenstein about a theatre producer who needed someone to drive a truck containing his sets. These then needed to be set up and taken down after each performance. This was the test: would the erstwhile pop star settle down to the life of a humble roadie with good grace? Would he put up with fellow roadies recognising him as the former star and asking why he was now performing such a menial task? Nassenstein passed the test and after three weeks de Mol gave him a job on the production team of an American format for which he had acquired the Dutch rights – a show called *Family Feud*. It had been created by Mark Goodson. This and other formats, such as *What's My Line?*, had made him rich.

In *Family Feud* two families competed to guess how the public answered a series of questions in an opinion poll. Nassenstein's new job was to help pick the families. It was a very significant commission for John de Mol Productions. They made the show for Vara and it lasted for six years. De Mol also managed to sell a second US property, *The Wheel of Fortune*, to a Belgian channel. It had been invented by another wealthy US programme creator, Merv Griffin. Griffin was a former singer who had had a number one hit in 1950 with 'I've Got A Lovely Bunch Of Coconuts'. He had proved, once again, that there was indeed gold in successful formats, particularly simple ones. Competitors spun a wheel which stopped on a number, dictating which question they had to answer for cash prizes. The American game shows that had spread across the world were all of a kind, with grinning hosts, coloured lights and big cash prizes. A manifestation of the American genius for fairground entertainment. These formats sold well because they had a proven track record, a sort of sales guarantee, from their country of origin. Crucially, they could then be remade elsewhere in a local language with that territory's own hosts and cultural nuances.

American formats had dominated the world for thirty-five years. Early on the US networks had strenuously sought to create mass audiences and did not have a conscience about producing shows whose sole aim was entertainment. All the formats relied on members of the public to participate. In some they were the grinning ciphers of a piece of vaudeville driven on by hyperactive hosts. *The Wheel of Fortune* and *Family Feud* were typical. Others were more inventive and contained distinct echoes of the reality shows to come by placing their participants in more revealing situations. *Candid Camera* started on ABC Television in 1948, the creation of Allen Funt. It was a remarkably innovative idea at the time, playing practical jokes on unsuspecting victims and recording the results on hidden cameras. The very first television programme had Funt disguised as a waiter in a restaurant that, it turned out, served only liver. Some were psychologically revealing tricks. They put six *Candid Camera* actors in a lift, all of them facing the wrong way. Would the one unsuspecting member of the public assert his common sense and face the lift door? Or would he be cowed into joining

the others? Time after time he joined the others. *Candid Camera*
also developed a shrewd line in embarrassment. One stunt
involved hiring the victim as a hypnotist's assistant and then
having a shapely female client strip, apparently while under hyp-
nosis. It was a very influential show which attracted such talents
as Woody Allen, who started by writing scripts for it. When the
format was sold to Britain's commercial channel in the 1960s it
was blessed by the whimsical inventions of Jonathan Routh. He
ran a car down a hill into a garage to complain it was not working properly. On examination the poor mechanic would discover
it had no engine in it. He concealed himself inside a lifelike tree
trunk and waited at a London bus stop. 'Does this bus go to
Sherwood Forest?' he enquired of a bus conductor. *Candid
Camera* placed people in completely ludicrous, unreal situations.
What then flowed from that false premise was undoubtedly
revealing and, in a sense, real. A parallel indeed with the 'reality'
shows that were to follow.

One key difference between these shows and the 'Family'
documentaries of the 1970s was that the latter were high-risk.
Formats were developed in order to give broadcasters certainty.
The producers of *An American Family* could pick the most interesting family possible but still not know what they were going to
shoot in advance or how compelling it would be. *Candid
Camera* and other hits, such as the biographical *This Is Your
Life*, were guaranteed to deliver a result every time. As the
number of television channels rose and with it the level of competition, demand for formats would grow and grow. John de
Mol wanted increasingly to create formats of his own. And his
inspiration was ideas such as *Candid Camera* and *This Is Your
Life*, which delivered narrative and emotion as well as competitions and cash.

The commission of *The Wheel of Fortune*, the first outside
Holland for John de Mol Productions, meant that the company
was getting closer to its one real competitor, Joop van den Ende

Productions. De Mol kept a very close eye on Joop van den Ende, the former theatre producer who had presided at his wedding. Van den Ende now had a thriving TV production company. He was more outgoing than de Mol, enjoyed a good relationship with the press and exuded an air of wealth and success. He already had two hit formats in Holland. The first was *The Surprise Show* which was a highly emotional, wish-fulfilment programme normally climaxing in large family gatherings and torrents of tears. The second was *The Soundmixshow*, one of the cleverest, simplest TV formats ever invented. Starstruck amateur singers were encouraged to dress up and sing like their musical heroes. It put a winning combination of classic songs and personal achievement into the heart of the Saturday night entertainment schedule. *The Soundmixshow* eventually sold across the world, including to Britain (*Stars in Their Eyes*) and the US (*Your Big Break*).

De Mol and van den Ende were seen as fierce rivals. It was true that they were. But they also kept up with each other – quietly meeting, unbeknown to anyone else, on Saturday mornings at van den Ende's house. There they would discuss the state of the market and how to extract better deals from the broadcasters. In this way de Mol learnt that van den Ende was buying his own TV studio. He immediately resolved to do the same, in order to house *The Wheel of Fortune*. Being de Mol, though, he found a cut-price approach. He managed to get temporary use of a derelict sports hall in which to shoot the show. He and Nassenstein enjoyed going there because the previous, bankrupt, owner had left behind a cellar of vintage wines. Shortly afterwards he also sold *The Wheel of Fortune* to a Dutch channel. This made the sports hall very busy and John de Mol Productions, at last, solidly profitable. But still he wanted to create his own shows rather than simply buy in American seconds. Van den Ende had done it. He had to do it too.

In 1984 de Mol made his first attempt. He decided, radically, that John de Mol Productions would produce a chat show without a host. The audience would ask all the questions of a celebrity guest, entirely unmediated. At the time people rarely challenged TV's already staid conventions and it was a difficult concept to sell. De Mol finally persuaded one of the public broadcasters to commission it.

The name of the show, '*Hemd Van Je Lijf*', means literally 'the shirt from your body'; it is a Dutch expression denoting persistent or extreme questioning. It was recorded in a Utrecht theatre owned by a Dutch comedienne and her husband whom de Mol also represented. It was organised in the round in a very intimate setting. The first show went very well. A well-known football coach of English origin, Barry Hughes, was an extrovert and considered automatically funny because of the appalling accent with which he spoke Dutch. The questions flowed from the audience and Hughes went through his well-rehearsed stock of footballing anecdotes. In the control room de Mol and Nassenstein were rubbing their hands. It looked like a hit. On the second day of recording they felt even more confident. Rob de Nijs, a successful Dutch singer, was the guest and he, again, coaxed a lively response from the audience. The new idea was working.

For the third recording they had booked an actor called Kees Brusse. He walked on to the stage to a ripple of applause. He sat down. But he didn't say anything. Whatever they may have planned beforehand, he was now entirely flummoxed. Ten seconds, twenty seconds – still he said nothing. He looked at the audience; they looked at him. Someone coughed. Thirty seconds, one minute, two minutes, still nothing. In the wings Nassenstein began to sweat. In the audience De Mol was thinking, 'Give me a rope and I'll hang myself.' He focused on Brusse and privately willed him to say something. Anything. Suddenly, finally, a middle aged lady in the audience piped up with a question. She was not even one of the audience who had been set up with a prepared question in advance. Out of desperation, Brusse latched on to this unrehearsed contribution as his lifeline. He got up from his chair and went to sit on the edge of the stage next to her seat. This put him completely out of range of the camera positions. The actor and his fan then started a banal dialogue. By now there was an incestuous conversation going on that was of no interest to the rest of the audience and invisible as far as the television production was concerned. The recording was junked and the series had to be completely overhauled. De Mol's next attempt at a format was to improve on this. It would not be difficult.

In 1984 a local record company collaborated with the Dutch edition of *Playboy* magazine to launch a new girl group called Centrefold. The deal was that the girls, three of them, appeared nude as the centrefold spread, and then exploited their naked notoriety by launching a musical career. The man who looked after them at the record company was Herman van der Zwan. He discovered that John de Mol had arranged for Centrefold to join his talent management business. Having secured all three of the girls de Mol also offered van der Zwan a job running his agency. De Mol had done many deals in the past with van der Zwan, knew him well, and had already contracted other bands of his, including the chart-topping Dolly Dots. Van der Zwan later became (after Nassenstein) the second of a long line of former clients recruited by de Mol. Today they see it as a power play – those to whom he had touched his forelock in a deal he later liked to employ. Once in the job, they found the relationship soon changed and it swiftly became clear who was the boss. Under de Mol's management the Dolly Dots went on to star in a succession of television specials and one movie. It was all done in the best possible taste. They were clothed, albeit partially, from now on.

John de Mol and his small team were close. They worked

hard and played hard. De Mol did not like starting first thing –
10 a.m. at the earliest. And he was best avoided before lunch.
But he would often work till the early hours of the morning.
This and his amorous nature made the maintenance of personal
relationships difficult. His colleagues were able to help de Mol
when Marga, the blonde singer from Luv, left him rather suddenly. De Mol returned home to their house one evening to find
that, without warning, Marga had departed, leaving little more
than the television set and some knives and forks. Nassenstein
and a few others had to help de Mol refurnish the house to
make it a home once more.

The Sky deal had given John de Mol Productions some sta-
bility. Later productions of foreign formats, such as *Family
Feud*, had enabled his company to grow. He had even been
involved in a strange international soap opera made in
Argentina. Then he managed to sell a hospital drama to a
Dutch broadcaster. *Medical Centre West* was a substantial
commission and a real breakthrough for him. He borrowed
the empty half of a working hospital. They shot the surgery
scenes in the actual operating theatres when they were empty
at weekends. The series became a big hit. The storylines were
deliberately provocative and began to stimulate a good deal of
controversy in the Dutch press. Unlike his love life, this was
controversy that de Mol relished. It was good for business. In
the United States soap operas stayed where they had started,
propping up the afternoon television schedules designed to
sell soap powder to bored, chocolate-eating mothers at home.
In Britain, by contrast, *Coronation Street* had already been
running in prime time for twenty-five years and the BBC had
launched a rival, *EastEnders*, in 1986. De Mol set out to challenge social issues with melodramatic storylines. *Medical
Centre West* created its first storm with a plot about euthanasia. It became a national talking point. Holland later became
the first European country to legalise assisted suicides. The

Dutch are often regarded as the most liberal race in Europe, with their gay soldiers, cannabis cafés and exotic sex shops. This is to misunderstand them. They are really quite conservative but will tolerate anything if it is regulated. Even golf. In Holland it is actually illegal to play golf without an official club handicap. So long as a law has been passed governing a particular vice the Dutch are content. The argument over euthanasia gave John de Mol an appetite for outraging the bourgeois consensus of his native country. He was to repeat this trick many times in the coming decade.

But most of all he wanted to create successful entertainment formats of his own that would sell abroad, rivalling the American formats he had been producing in Holland. Television is a hit-driven business. If you create a major hit you can derive income from it worldwide for as long as it remains popular. Someone once called this earning money while you sleep. The inventor of the US game shows *The Price Is Right* and *Family Feud*, Mark Goodson, had been doing that (and no doubt sleeping very soundly) since 1956. When he died in 1992 he was said to be worth $450 million. His great competitor, Merv Griffin, came up with *Jeopardy* as well as *The Wheel of Fortune*. He sold his company to Columbia Pictures in 1986 for $250 million. This was precisely the model de Mol and van Kooten wanted to develop. But, as yet, they were still buying other people's formats rather than selling their own.

In 1989 Ruud Hendriks, the youth ejected by de Mol from the studio, resurfaced. He had bought *The Price Is Right* franchise for Holland. RTL was a broadcasting group originally controlled from Luxembourg by a reclusive businessman called Albert Frere. He had exploited the liberal laws in Luxembourg to broadcast radio and then television services to other European countries. RTL decided to launch a commercial channel on to Holland's cable system. At last a proper market for programming was about to emerge in Holland. De Mol's struggle merely to survive was over. His struggle with Joop van den Ende's larger production company, however, was intensifying. RTL appointed Hendriks as their director of programmes. He wanted to ask Joop van den Ende to make *The Price Is Right*, but van den Ende was also trying to get a commercial channel off the ground and refused to sell programmes to those he regarded as his rivals. This presented a chance for his main competitor, John de Mol Productions. De Mol went to see Hendriks in his new office. Hendriks asked him if he thought they had met before. De Mol replied that they had not. 'So you don't remember physically kicking me out of your television studio when I was a teenager?' De Mol, in full-on selling mode, apologised. Hendriks said that, actually, he would have done the same. He outlined his need for a company to produce *The Price Is Right*. De Mol agreed on the spot and got the contract.

The Price Is Right had been running on American network television for more than thirty years. The basic game was that contestants had to guess the price of desirable consumer goods and the one who got the closest won the items themselves – washing machines, cars, holidays. Its wonderfully vulgar trademark was an audience whipped up into a frenzy of greed, four of whom were then asked to 'come on down'. Their reaction to this invitation shamed a Billy Graham conversion for its fervour. When the producers considered the show to be flagging somewhat they would pull off a stunt. A Texas farmer who won a grand piano was given a bonus prize of an elephant, the idea being that he would have an additional supply of ivory. The farmer was expected to take his bonus in cash value, but he insisted on an elephant in kind and one had to be flown in from Kenya.

John de Mol judged the format to be a little tired by this time and told the owners, the Goodson organisation, that he was going to introduce some new games for the Dutch audience. This he was expressly refused permission to do, so he decided to do it behind their backs. When the show launched on the new RTL4 channel it was an immediate hit so the Goodson executives had to accept the new elements. Hendriks then asked John de Mol Productions to come up with a magazine show, for five o'clock every afternoon. De Mol asked Hendriks how much money he had. Hendriks halved the amount he actually had available and named the sum. De Mol returned the day after and said they would make two hundred shows for that agreed budget. This made Hendriks very happy. He was even happier when the imaginatively titled *The Five o'Clock Show* also became a big success. Six years later, when Hendriks went to work for de Mol, he examined the company accounts and found that his new employer had made vast profits from *The Five o'Clock Show*. These were enhanced by some highly lucrative sponsorship deals with companies such as Unilever. After his early experiences de Mol was never again outmanoeuvred in a deal. He now had a growing and highly profitable company, but he had no single show that he had invented which could earn him money while he slept. This remained his next goal.

Radio Veronica had been one of the Dutch pirate radio stations. After being ruled illegal it managed to win a licence to be one of the public television broadcasters in Holland. It had become respectable, but not that respectable. By 1989 it wanted a populist, break-out format for its Saturday night schedule and asked John de Mol to provide it. He gathered a small group of his producers around him and brainstormed a series of ideas over several months. But de Mol never seemed entirely happy with what they had come up with. Finally they had refined an idea and gathered in de Mol's office (by this time a brick-built block on an industrial estate). They had to present to Veronica within a few days. He gave them a jolt: 'Guys, what we have here is just not good enough. It's OK but it won't do.' There was one element that did intrigue de Mol –

a sort of home video shot as contestants were followed around. He told everyone to concentrate on that but to give it a new purpose. One person in the room suddenly started talking about people who were infatuated with someone but too shy to say so. Another member of the team then mentioned the personal ads in newspapers and magazines in which people advertised for companionship, love and even sex. How could small ads be made to work on television? They quickly came up with the idea of recorded video messages being delivered, unannounced, to the intended recipient. What would the reaction be? They thought of a bus to drive the presenter around with the messages. And that they would pull all the participants together in the studio for a big, show-business finale. Finally, one of the brainstormers even came up with the title of the show: *All You Need Is Love*. Unusually, the entire format had fallen into place in two hours flat. They had already managed to compile a list of some other personal messages the programme might deliver: a divorcee's search for a new relationship, an apology to a wronged partner or, perhaps, a proposal of marriage. They left the room intoxicated with the idea and the number of possibilities that had arisen from it.

Veronica swiftly agreed to produce *All You Need Is Love*. Shortly afterwards they began broadcasting promotions asking for viewers to send in messages they would like the programme to deliver for them. The response was gratifyingly large. The bus was commissioned – a long, aluminium-grey American mobile home with the legend 'All You Need Is Love' tastefully emblazoned across it in pink, Beatles-era, pop art lettering. One early letter they received was from Maurits, a gay man. He had been in a relationship for eight years which, at times, had been very difficult. He wanted to thank his partner, Rob, for sticking by him. The team referred the letter to de Mol. He appeared to have no problem with the subject matter, but he was dubious about exactly what sort of item this would make for the programme. They explained they would find the partner and ask him into the studio as a normal member of the audience. There they would surprise him with Maurits serenading him in song. 'OK,' said de Mol. 'We'll do the item. But no handbags and no kissing.' Was he personally squeamish? Possibly. But it was 1989 and homosexuality was not exactly a regular theme on Saturday night game shows, even in Holland. In addition, it was for a public broadcaster which at least purported to be more high-minded than the newly emerging commercial channels. But this would not be the only time in de Mol's career that, in making a provocative entertainment show, he ended up challenging social attitudes.

Maurits was helped to write his song and rehearsed in secret. His partner, Rob, happily attended the sixties-style studio. The host, Robert ten Brink, sat down next to Rob – a genial looking character with cropped hair, moustache and a Hawaiian shirt. He asked him about his relationship and then revealed that Maurits wanted to serenade him. In a moment of inspired kitsch, Maurits bounded on to the stage and performed his song, with the assistance of three go-go girls in polka-dot dresses. The heartfelt lyrics applauded his partner for cooking dinner every night for eight years and for running his bath for him. In case anyone was in any doubt by this time, the song also pointed out there would be no baby in their house and they would never have a marriage certificate. But Maurits loved him and wanted all Holland to know. His lover was so overcome by this serenade that, at its conclusion, contrary to de Mol's express instructions, he gave his partner an enormous kiss. It was vulgar, touching and controversial all at the same time. They made it the cornerstone of the first programme. Satisfyingly, it created a storm.

Within two weeks the production team had, if anything, surpassed themselves. They astutely spotted that they had been

sent, by coincidence, two almost identical letters. They were
from female fans of an obscure local singer called Frans Bauer.
Both were infatuated by him and wished to send their local hero
a passionate video message inviting him out on a date. Better
still, they were both called Diana. The producers surprised Frans
Bauer at a gig and showed him one of the video messages. 'Yes,'
he replied 'I'd love to go out on a date with her.' He was then
invited to the studio to meet the sender. Here he was surprised
by a second video message, also petitioning for an intimate
evening. Now he was asked to make a choice, between Diana
the blonde and Diana the brunette. He was genuinely embarrassed by the dilemma but eventually chose the blonde. The
brunette started to cry. Then she started to scream. She followed
this up by shrilly abusing her blonde rival. Not to be outdone,
the blonde returned fire and an unseemly slanging match ensued.
After this the already positive ratings of *All You Need Is Love*
shot up. And Frans Bauer became the best-known singer in
Holland.

This was an interesting formula – a programme packaged to
look like an entertainment show with a format that fed off
people's emotions and amplified events from their own lives.
To this extent *All You Need Is Love* was a close relation of
This Is Your Life. But there was also a key difference. *This Is
Your Life* belonged to the world of traditional, post-war television: saccharine, ever-smiling and safe. Divorces were glossed
over and illegitimate children hushed up. In that world had
there ever been a brawl between two besotted pop fans it
would have been edited out. John de Mol left it in and promoted it as the highlight. Tasteless? Perhaps. Exploitative?
Certainly, like all television. More real, more true to life?
Arguably. Could the formula be repeated? It certainly could,
and within a year.

In 1989 an Englishman called Mickey Hayes approached
John de Mol with the germ of a television idea. Why not have a

programme in which real marriages took place? Hayes had failed to sell the idea in staid, conservative Britain, but de Mol agreed a deal with him and then worked with his creative team to turn the idea into a fully-fledged format. What emerged was a show in which three engaged couples participated. In each case the groom would record an emotional video proposal. Tears were not obligatory but very much encouraged. These clips were played into a typically glitzy de Mol studio. Here the couples would play games and answer questions in order to win an immediate wedding along with an armful of expensive wedding presents. The marriage itself was intended to be the finale of the show. De Mol sold the show, now named *Love Letters*, to his former employers TROS in 1990. They agreed that his sister Linda should present it. He applied to the company's local authority, Hilversum, for a special licence to hold a marriage in a television studio. It looked as though this would be granted. The video proposals were made and the studio booked. At the last minute the local authority got cold feet. They refused to issue a special licence. Their decision was leaked and, once again, a public storm ensued. Was it appropriate for the institution of marriage to be used as the basis for television entertainment? How could the couples themselves make serious vows in the circumstances? The management at the broadcaster held their nerve and the producers immediately applied for a marriage ceremony at the Hilversum registry office. This they were allowed.

In the first programme blonde Linda de Mol greeted viewers in a startling yellow and black Tyrolean dress. She said three couples were to compete for prizes, including a live wedding. She emphasised they would have this live wedding before the end of the show. Their relatives were in the audience already dressed for it. The three couples were then introduced via three stunt videos. Jeanine, a receptionist, surprises Will, an architect, by emerging from the back seat of a car parked near him (in full wedding regalia) and forces him to propose on camera. Then Rob and friends, dressed as Roman legionaries (for reasons best known to the production team), march through a city centre and invade an office block where Rob makes a passionate proposal to Dorine at the entrance. Finally, Lars is allowed to conceal himself in an aeroplane on which Alexandra works as a stewardess. He proposes over the captain's intercom and then pounces on her, mid-aisle, as she is dispensing gin and cashew nuts. Back in the studio, the three couples were guided through various games in which Rob and Dorine were eventually the winners. Cut to heavenly choir, white doves and the full wedding treatment presided over by a smiling lady registrar. So at the end of the studio recording the winning couple had been transported direct to the centre of Hilversum for their marriage. This was faithfully recorded on video and skilfully edited into the programme as though it had just happened. *Love Letters* went on air in December 1990. It was emotional and dramatic. The public loved it.

The only difference between this furore and the previous lather concerning *All You Need Is Love* was that this time it started before the programme went on air. This made *Love Letters* an immediate hit. Both shows continued through the 1990s commanding huge Saturday night audiences.

John de Mol coined a new name for this stable of programmes – 'emotainment'. In October 1992 he was quoted in the Dutch magazine *Privé*: 'What's new in the shows is that men don't hide their emotions. If you'd said this would've been on TV three years ago people would have said you were crazy.' The article pointed out that now ordinary people could become stars just by appearing on such shows. But it wondered how they could cope with such personal and painful confrontations. The burgeoning academic industry known as 'media studies' now started to produce learned papers on emotainment. Was it right to exploit emotions to make money? Were emotainment's critics mostly middle-aged men who had been brought up to abhor displays of emotion and who didn't understand this new, media-savvy generation? Was TV, once the province of expert journalists and actors, being democratised? De Mol was less concerned with analysing his property. He wanted to know where else he could sell it.

Armed with what he claimed to be a new television genre – emotainment – de Mol now returned to the West Coast of America. Surely now he could realise his dream and pull off a sale to the biggest media market in the world. In two trips de Mol was never once accorded a meeting with anyone senior enough at ABC, NBC or CBS, the major networks, even to contemplate buying his shows. At best the junior executives he saw were patronising, explaining how US television relied on sitcoms and dramas because that was what their viewers wanted. At worst they showed him the door before he had even explained the principle of emotainment. In the early 1990s John de Mol at last had two homegrown hits and a very healthy cash flow. But he remained marooned in a country with a population of fifteen million and much of his production relied on formats imported from America. Could he ever break out?

In Germany, since reunification easily Europe's biggest media market, the broadcasters were, in fact, paying careful attention to the potential of emotainment. Having heard of the break out of *Love Letters*, RTL executives came to Holland to watch a recording. They liked the format. They loved Linda de Mol, the presenter. So, to keep it in the family, Linda de Mol was employed to present it for them in Germany. She could already speak good German but a language coach was immediately hired for her to make her fluent in game-show German too. The deal for the show was somewhat naive, but this time it was in de Mol's favour. RTL, believing themselves to be taking a big risk, had given no thought beyond the first series. They had no option or price agreed for a possible second run. When, in 1991, *Love Letters* turned out to be as big a hit in Germany as it had been in Holland, RTL were in a position of weakness. This de Mol would exploit with characteristic ruthlessness.

CHAPTER THREE

Everything Is Changing

The medium, or process, of our time – electronic technology – is reshaping and restructuring patterns of social inter-dependence and every aspect of our personal life. It is forcing us to reconsider and re-evaluate practically every thought, every action, and every institution formerly taken for granted. Everything is changing . . .

MARSHALL McLUHAN
(QUOTED IN THE FIRST ISSUE OF THE US MAGAZINE *WIRED*)

In late 1991 and early 1992 calls came in to John de Mol's personal office from German broadcasters anxious to steal *Love Letters* away from RTL. Each time they would ask 'How much do you want for the show?' This was a most welcome question for de Mol. He was used to parsimonious Dutch broadcasters arguing every penny and demanding to see detailed budgets. Among the calls was one from Leo Kirch, the most powerful media owner in Europe at the time. He had control of Germany's biggest commercial satellite channel, Sat 1. His personal assistant announced, much as a royal chamberlain might, 'Mr Kirch would like to have dinner with Mr de Mol. The dinner will be in Munich.' When he heard the suggested date de Mol agreed but said he had to leave the dinner by 9.30 p.m. in order to catch the last flight back to Amsterdam. He had an important breakfast meeting the next day. The assistant called back. 'There is no need to foreshorten the dinner. Mr Kirch is sending his personal plane to pick you up and return you.'

On the appointed day de Mol and Nassenstein drove out to the old Schiphol Airport, now used by private jets. De Mol was quiet and apprehensive. He hated flying. They were greeted formally by a stewardess and served drinks. It was only a short flight but a turbulent one. This made de Mol even more apprehensive. He sent Nassenstein up to the cockpit to complain to the pilot. Nassenstein did as he was told though he knew it to be a Canute-like command to the elements. Forty minutes later they landed safely in Munich at six in the evening. As they walked to the chauffeur-driven car provided by Kirch, a uniformed airport official said, 'Remember, the airport closes at eleven o'clock tonight.' They then sped towards their meeting which was to be in a private room of an old restaurant in the mountains outside Munich. Both men had been in at the beginning of John de Mol Productions, in a converted garage. Now the most powerful man in European media wanted to do a deal with them.

Leo Kirch had started his business in the 1950s by acquiring the rights to a Fellini film, *La Strada*. It turned out to be a big hit and he was on his way. He then gradually acquired the rights to a huge number of other movies for which he made the broadcasters pay dearly. This enabled him to move into broadcasting. By 1992 he controlled one of Germany's two dominant commercial satellite broadcasters and some specialist pay TV channels. His companies were thought to be worth $5 billion.

De Mol and Nassenstein entered the restaurant. Nassenstein recalls Kirch lurking in his limousine until they had sat down so that he could make a dramatic entrance; De Mol places him at the table before they walked into the private room. Both remember an elderly man carefully perusing his special Braille menu – he was virtually blind. Kirch waited for his moment and then pitched in: 'John, I want *Love Letters* and I want Linda on my

channel. I will pay you one million Deutschmarks per show.'
These were eye-popping sums that bore no relation to the cost of
making the programme. It was exactly twice what RTL had
paid for the first series of *Love Letters*. For anyone else this
would have been a wonderful, irresistible offer, but de Mol was
now in full game-playing mode. Years of experience, late at
night, were now deployed. He was polite but cool. He chatted
noncommittally about what such a deal might mean. They also
talked about the European television business. Suddenly it was
ten o'clock. 'I'm sorry, Mr Kirch,' said de Mol, 'but the airport
is closing at eleven. I think we ought to leave now.' 'John,' came
the reply, 'the airport closes when I say it closes.'

They talked on. No commitments were made. De Mol and
Nassenstein finally reached the airport at 1 a.m. The same uniformed flunky was there, saluting this time and not daring to
complain about the hour. The next day de Mol called RTL and
began to leverage Kirch's offer as only a poker player can: 'I
wouldn't leave you for just another hundred thousand
Deutschmarks per show. You were the first ones to believe in the
show and to back Linda. But this is five hundred thousand more
per show. We have to talk about this.' RTL certainly did have to
talk about it. Kirch was their direct competitor. They arranged
to meet very soon.

One Friday morning shortly afterwards, Nassenstein and de
Mol set out from Hilversum at 9 a.m. to drive to RTL's headquarters in Cologne. Within three hours they were seated with
RTL's programme director Mark Conrad and two of the company's financial officers. Negotiation then began. At four o'clock
the following morning, sixteen hours later, they emerged with a
deal. RTL had undertaken to pay John de Mol Productions two
hundred million Deutschmarks (approximately £45 million) per
year for three years. The output deal would cover local productions of *Love Letters*, *All You Need Is Love*, *Medical Centre
West* and a number of other, as yet unnamed, programmes.

De Mol and Nassenstein drove home along the autobahn as dawn broke that Saturday morning. They were tired but elated. They had just cleaned up in the biggest game they had ever played. Nassenstein watched de Mol operate in amazement: 'What he always did, in negotiations, when the other guys think – now we're there – he gives it just one more turn. Always.' On this occasion, in a single night, they had catapulted their company into the position of being a major supplier of television content in Europe. De Mol continued to drive a three-year-old car and to live in a modest house. What mattered to him were the shows themselves and, even more than that, the deals. The fact that money flowed from both was pleasant but somehow secondary.

John de Mol came from a background of making entertainment programmes. He had now hit upon the idea of adding real events in people's lives, real emotions, into the mix. In Britain also, producers were experimenting with ways of turning real lives into revealing and reliable programming. Paul Watson was a documentary maker who, with Franc Roddam, had made the controversial series *The Family* for the BBC in 1974. Watson had gone on to make several celebrated one-off documentaries in which the participants often revealed far more about themselves than they had ever intended. He was a brilliantly perceptive and manipulative director. In 1992 he went back to making an extended series about a family. This time, instead of exploring a working-class British family, he seized upon a brash, arriviste Australian household in the suburbs of Sydney. The matriarch was a chain-smoking, hard-drinking, tempestuous, foul-mouthed, aggressive but intelligent woman. In other words, Noeline Baker was a star. Plant a camera near her and you could be sure that one incident would follow another. Likewise her partner Laurie with his racist opinions. The series, named after their opulent suburb – Sylvania Waters – was ruthlessly revealing about Australia's suburban society. And Watson had pointed the way towards what became known as the docu-soap. Establish a documentary team at a location where you are guaranteed frequent, strong stories – such as an airport, a vet's clinic or a cruise ship – and the broadcaster could be sure of a series of powerful narratives. It removed the risk of the documentary director setting out to make a single programme, unsure as to what the outcome might be.

In 1992, at the headquarters of MTV in New York, they wanted to inject the same human narratives into their music-driven schedule. At first MTV contemplated a soap opera but that turned out to be too expensive. So then they turned to Jonathan Murray and Mary-Ellis Bunim who were running a small production company. Murray came from a documentary background and Bunim had started in soap operas. They proposed something more radical than Watson's series. As fans of *The American Family* twenty years before, they suggested placing seven young New Yorkers in a Manhattan loft apartment and then following their life together. They would manipulate the shows to produce regular, reliable storylines. MTV bought and furnished the apartment. Bunim–Murray advertised for people to take part and carefully 'cast' the final seven participants. Without the invitation (and a daily allowance) they would never have been living together in this way, particularly with cameramen and lights present twenty-four hours a day. In that sense it was an entirely contrived idea. But they called it *The Real World* and it ran for six months, attracting seven hundred thousand viewers a week. This was a tiny audience for a major network but satisfactory for a cable station like MTV. They commissioned a second series. Television was now moving towards being less of an art form and more of a commodity. Producers were now having to make programmes less for themselves and more for the audience. *The Real World* represented the beginning of this trend but it had a good deal further to go.

Entertainment producers, with no loyalty to the documentary tradition, would prove the most groundbreaking.

The ultimate result, it was already being debated, would be an audience which could not only choose what to watch when they wanted to watch it but also intervene in the programming to determine its outcome. This speculation was occurring not in the television industry but in the world of computing. On 26 January 1993 the first issue of *Wired* magazine appeared in San Francisco. It was nothing less than a manifesto for a digital age. It offered an intoxicating blend of foresight and hyperbole that would characterise the insanely ambitious period up to the end of the millennium. Its founding partners, Louis Rosetto and June Metcalfe, had previously run an avant-garde magazine in Amsterdam called *Electric Word*. They started *Wired* with Dutch capital, but they launched it with some truly American hype: 'Why *Wired*? Because the Digital Revolution is whipping through our lives like a Bengali typhoon while the mainsteam media is still groping for the snooze button.' In case that was not enough they quoted good old Marshall McLuhan as well: 'Everything is changing – you, your family, your neighborhood, your education, your job, your government, your relation to "the others". And they're changing dramatically.' Rosetto rounded it off modestly by promising 'a revolution without violence that embraces a new, non-political way to improve the future based on economics beyond macro control, consensus beyond the ballot box, civics beyond government and communities beyond the confines of time and geography'. *Wired* took off rapidly and before the end of the year was being published monthly rather than bi-monthly.

Rosetto's was one of the first declarations of a philosophy that was shortly to seduce most computing, telephony and media businesses. Another founding contributor of *Wired* was Nicholas Negroponte. He had now discovered a wider audience for his three converging circles. Later in the same year Raymond

Smith, the chairman of the Bell Atlantic Corporation, a telephone company, announced a $33 billion merger with TCI, a cable TV company. In the end he failed to pull it off but his enthusiasm for television pictures coming down telephone wires was undimmed: 'The computer and the television and the telephone are merging into one . . . this industry transformation will transform [sic] not just the way Bell Atlantic behaves, but the way the public behaves – the way that we work, and the way that we play, and the way that we learn . . .' From now on that was to be gospel. Unbelievers beware. Viacom, a conglomerate that included cable and telephony companies, were believers. In 1993 Viacom bought the Paramount film studio for $10 billion. They were driven by the perceived need to secure film content for their network. And soon after Time Warner launched a pilot scheme for their cable television subscribers in Florida. The 'Full Service Networks' gave them interactive set-top boxes through which they could receive games, videos of their choice and online shopping. It was the brainchild of forty-five-year-old Jerry Levin. He had been regarded as a wunderkind nine years earlier when he had saved their HBO channel by making it the first US network to be delivered via satellite. Since then he had been desperate to prove he could once again deliver a step change in Time Warner's business. The Full Service Network never took off and was quietly dropped before long, but Jerry Levin remained determined to dazzle everyone with his brilliance. He was prepared to take risks to prove this. Eventually he would commit himself to a breathtaking gamble six days into the new millennium. From it would flow a rush of other deals, one of them featuring John de Mol. On Levin's office wall he kept a framed quotation from George Orwell's *Nineteen Eighty-Four*: 'The voice came from an oblong metal plaque like a dulled mirror . . . the instrument (the telescreen, it was called) could be dimmed, but there was no way of shutting it off completely.' Big Brother was already watching someone.

Three days before the debut issue of *Wired* appeared Marc Andreessen released Mosaic on to an early internet site. Andreessen was a computer science student at the University of Illinois. He was twenty-one and thought it ought to be simpler than it currently was to access the embryonic world wide web. Mosaic was the first, easy-to-use web browser. By the end of the year hundreds of thousands of people were using Mosaic to surf the web. It allowed them to post the first 'home pages' on which they could place photographs of themselves and their families. It also enabled pornography. Tim Berners-Lee, the Englishman whose brainchild the world wide web was, initially disapproved of such uses and criticised Andreessen for adding visual images to what had previously been only a text service. In 1993 web traffic increased by 350,000 per cent. Near the end of the year some of that new traffic was directed towards a web site at the Cambridge University Computer Laboratory. There a graduate, Quentin Stafford-Fraser, had developed a system for monitoring their coffee pot from anywhere in the building. A simple video camera, which updated the image every few seconds, let them see when the coffee needed replenishing. The image was programmed to appear in the corner of their computer screens. In November 1993, in a frivolous mood, they connected this image to the web. It was the first animated video image ever offered. This novelty attracted millions of hits from around the world. People were fascinated by being able to access something from another continent, even if it was only the surreal image of a coffee pot emptying and filling up from time to time. They enjoyed choosing when they could watch it rather than having it scheduled for them. It would not take long for people to think of other images that could be made available.

During the early nineties John de Mol saw a lot of Ruud Hendriks at RTL4. Being an intensely private person de Mol had few very close friends, but he was supplying RTL4 with many of their most successful shows and the two met often. They

reflected on their own attitudes to business and their relationships to the respective fathers who had shaped their outlook.
These were sometimes emotional conversations and they grew
closer. One day in early 1993 de Mol asked Hendriks if, with his
international contacts, he knew of a company that might like to
buy John de Mol Productions. He had pulled off some spectacular contracts with his programmes. Now the inveterate deal
maker wanted to put the crown jewels into play – his own company. De Mol was still living quite modestly on the salary he
paid himself and had decided it might be time to make some
solid capital too. He had previously asked the international
accounting practice KPMG to value his business. They had come
back with a figure of around £45 million. Hendriks immediately
suggested that RTL might want to be the purchaser. It would
give the company a greater degree of independence in producing
its own formats. He promised to get back to de Mol.

Hendriks took the idea to RTL Holland's managing director,
Freddy Thyes, a short and aggressive Luxembourger who had
come from the steel industry. He thought television was peopled
with self-indulgent fat cats. At a convivial dinner at Joop van
den Ende's house to honour his programmes and stars, Thyes
had stood up and said they were all too expensive and should
take pay cuts. One of the amply endowed presenters protested
by stealing up behind him and simply placing her breasts on his
head.

Thyes hated the idea of the acquisition. He told his programme
director that he did not want to pay the tough-negotiating de
Mol twice – once for his programmes and a second time for his
company. Hendriks countered with the argument that owning
John de Mol Productions would make RTL independent of the
other large production company in Holland, Joop van den Ende
Productions. Thyes replied that he liked playing them off against
each other. Within a year van den Ende and de Mol had merged
their companies. Hendriks was there when they told Thyes of

their plan: 'He looked like he'd had a heart attack. He was really pale and grey.'

One Saturday morning in the spring of 1993 John de Mol had driven, as he often did, to Joop van den Ende's mansion for one of their private chats about the state of the Dutch production business. They sat together over coffee, as usual. This time, though, van den Ende had a momentous suggestion to make: 'Why don't we merge our two companies?' De Mol was not remotely fazed and replied, 'Good idea.' They were both irritated at how the broadcasters tried to manipulate the rivalry between the two companies to their own advantage. They were trying to sell their formats to the same broadcasters abroad. Recently, as a de Mol sales lady had emerged from a Spanish programme director's office she had passed a van den Ende salesman on the way in. They both had organisations in Germany. A merger seemed to both of them to make good sense. They admired each other and their mutual reservations could be overcome. De Mol thought van den Ende too extravagant; van den Ende felt de Mol's outfit was too mean and miserable. A colleague characterised their sentiments in this way: van den Ende would say, 'People should feel at home and they work better.' To which de Mol's riposte would be: 'Bullshit, just give them a chair and a table to work on.'

De Mol walked into Jef Nassenstein's office the following week. He finally revealed to him that he had been talking to Joop van den Ende. Nassenstein was immediately suspicious: 'My first reaction was complete hostility. Van den Ende Productions were the enemy. They were fancy, we were down-to-earth. Joop had a driver, John drove himself. They had luxurious offices, we were lean and mean. There was a complete culture clash.' Herman van der Zwan had recently rejoined as the company's chief operating officer. He remembered van den Ende threatening them with hell, damnation and a writ back in the eighties when he had pulled a band out of a van den Ende production for a more lucrative gig in Britain. Van der Zwan could not believe it. But when they heard that the initial idea was only to merge their foreign sales operations they began to see the logic of it. Nassenstein was asked to join a small team to discuss with van den Ende's colleagues how the merger might be achieved. Van den Ende's negotiating team was led by his chief financial officer, Aat Schouwenaar.

The first thing they discovered was that merely combining their two sales operations would not work. It had to be all or nothing. Then they opened their company books for each other to look at and started work on the respective valuations. This provided the first shock, a pleasant one for de Mol but less palatable for van den Ende. Van den Ende's company was bigger than de Mol's. He had extensive interests in theatre as well as television. He was thirteen years older than de Mol and exuded success and experience. But de Mol's profits were four times his. This was chiefly because his theatre division was a far riskier business than television production. Their aim was to leave each of the two entrepreneurs with 45 per cent of the new company. The respective margins made that very difficult. In the end, after six months of secret negotiations, they had a solution. De Mol would draw considerable dividends out of his company prior to the merger in compensation for his only taking a half-share of the new company. Willem van Kooten, de Mol's original saviour ten years earlier, also presciently decided to convert the majority of his shareholding into an investment in the new entity. He kept 5 per cent. And the deal also enabled van den Ende to buy out most of a venture capitalist's holding, leaving it with the remaining 5 per cent. They still did not have a name for the new vehicle. They looked at a list of fifty suggestions. None seemed right.

The discussions about a name continued into November, long after all the other financial engineering had been completed. On 21 November van den Ende invited de Mol to New York for the

Broadway opening of his musical, *Cyrano de Bergerac*. The proposed merger was still a closely guarded secret. There were many Dutch guests at the opening night but none seemed curious as to why de Mol, no theatre buff, was there. At a meeting earlier in the day, at their New York hotel, they had found the solution to the company name: simply combine their surnames to form Endemol. Some have since unkindly remarked that it sounds like a manufacturer of suppositories. But they were all delighted with the idea and set off for the theatre in high spirits.

Cyrano had been no more than a qualified success for van den Ende in Holland. It was very risky to take it to New York. Despite this, the first performance appeared to go well. There was the obligatory standing ovation. But Broadway opening nights are brutal. Veterans of the ritual know that, at the aftershow party, you watch the production team closely. The newspapers come in just before midnight. If the reviews are bad they will quickly and quietly leave the party. That is what happened on this occasion: 'A mishmash of unspectacular spectacle, non-musical music and anti-romantic romance.' 'The lyrics are wooden.' 'Not a single memorable melody and comes in wave after wave of atonal, Eurowash sound.' 'It makes you want to run home and rip your ears off.' This was de Mol's introduction to van den Ende's business affairs. *Cyrano* was to provide the source of the first real friction between these two new business partners as it staggered on through the New Year of 1994 with growing losses. To make matters worse, an unprecedented fifteen snowstorms swept New York in three months, persuading even the most hardened theatregoers to stay at home.

But for now their new venture had a name and they were able to announce the merger and the creation of Endemol in December 1993. It was to be completed on 1 February 1994. They combined their foreign operations but, within the new group, decided to keep their Dutch production companies separate and competing. Together the new entity produced 2500 hours of programmes per year, generating a turnover of £150 million. This made them the largest independent producers in Europe. De Mol and van den Ende told the American trade magazine *Variety* that the number of television channels in Western Europe had expanded from 98 to 153 in just five years. They said this growth would continue and that all of them needed original, locally produced programmes of broad appeal. In other words, Endemol formats.

Aat Schouwenaar became company secretary for Endemol. He had personally been strongly in favour of the merger because he thought it would be healthy for his previous employer, van den Ende, to share management in future rather than be the sole, idiosyncratic, decision maker. The ailing *Cyrano* provided an opportunity for corporate decision making earlier than he had anticipated. From 1 February, the official day of the merger, de Mol started to scrutinise the losses. He didn't want to confront van den Ende so early in their new relationship so he came into Schouwenaar's office instead: 'What the heck is going on? We are losing a quarter of a million dollars a week. This can't go on. You need to close.' De Mol was famous for personally patrolling his offices in the evening to turn every light off before he went home. Now he had thrown his lot in with a man who appeared to be willing to lose a million dollars a month on a pet project. Finally, even the romantic van den Ende bowed to the inevitable and closed *Cyrano* down in March. It was said, in all, to have lost $10 million. This was the first, but by no means the last, crisis Endemol would have with its higher-risk, lower-margin theatre subsidiary.

Juan Villalonga, the man destined to make de Mol and van den Ende very rich one day, was leaving the huge American business consultancy McKinsey in the summer of 1993. He then re-entered the finance business with a number of short-lived appointments. Now he was offered the job of chief executive for

Credit Suisse First Boston's Spanish office. He was beginning to assemble around him a group of young, aggressive consultants and bankers who would assist him in some spectacular deal making at the end of the decade. He had not neglected his political contacts either. Wisely he remained close to his schoolboy friend José Maria Aznar, now a powerful politician. And Villalonga's wife, Concha Talleda, was also close friends with Aznar's wife, Ana Botella. Villalonga was thought of as a coming man with solid deal-making experience, strong contacts and a positively bumptious optimism. The stage on which he would display all these qualities was rapidly being constructed.

On 25 July 1994 *Time* magazine gave the newly fashionable internet its own front cover: 'The strange world of the Internet . . . battles on the frontiers of cyberspace.' The award of a cover in itself meant that the net and the web were entering the mainstream. As the synopsis of the feature put it: 'The world's largest computer network, once the playground of scientists, hackers and gearheads, is being overrun by lawyers, merchants and millions of new users. Is there room for everyone?' At this point there was indeed room for everyone to get on board, which investors were doing with an increasing appetite. A milestone was reached in December 1994. An internet service provider wanted to raise some capital by selling a minority of its shares and achieving a quote on the NASDAQ. Netcom was based in San José, California. How could you put a value on the shares of a company that, like all the internet start-ups, had no profits and paid no dividends? In conventional terms this company and all the others had virtually no value at all. The investment bank handling the IPO (initial public offering) borrowed an idea from the cable TV industry. Netcom had 42,000 subscribers and they based the whole offering on a value per subscriber. Astonishingly they put this at $2100. Based on that figure the company, which had never made a profit, was worth $85 million and the shares were offered at $13 each. They were lapped up on Wall Street. Could Netcom really be worth that amount? Nobody really knew but optimism, or, more precisely, greed, was starting to drive this market. Share offerings, mergers and acquisitions began to come thick and fast. In early 1995 there were only 27,000 web sites in total. The world wide web was still in its infancy. But in August a company with an internet navigator, Netscape, launched an IPO which shook the market. Again the company was making no profits but its shares, offered at $28 each, closed on their opening day at an astonishing $71 – two and a half times higher in no more than seven hours. This made one of the company's founders, Marc Andreessen (of Mosaic fame), worth $70 million. Netscape's adviser, from the bank Morgan Stanley, was Frank Quattrone. By 1999 he would be earning more than $100 million a year. In 2004 he would receive a prison sentence following a conviction for obstruction of justice and tampering with witnesses as his business affairs unwound.

Many conventional media companies, taking their own bankers' advice, had bought shares in the conviction that they had to join the bandwagon. A pattern was emerging. Conventional telephony and television companies were being drawn into a high-technology obsession. They could not afford to ignore the stampede towards convergence of media. If everything was going to be available from everywhere they felt they had to be there. And this was only the beginning.

CHAPTER FOUR

Unpopular Ideas

The only possible effect one can have on the world is through unpopular ideas. They are the only subversion.

VIVIENNE WESTWOOD

In 1973, in Britain, two individuals – who were each to compete with John de Mol to create the most successful television format of the twentieth century – were taking their first steps towards a media career. The first, Paul Smith, later the producer of *Who Wants to Be a Millionaire?*, was leaving the BBC. Smith is an Ulsterman whose obvious geniality hides a core of steel. Close colleagues praise his lifelong attention to detail which amounts, they say, to benign control freakery. In his twenties Smith had produced films for children's shows and made some of the early pop videos for the BBC chart show *Top of the Pops*. He even directed a documentary about make-up girls, largely in order to get them into bed, so he claims. But when his employers wouldn't promote him he decided to leave.

By 1977 Paul Smith was established as a freelance director, but he had an idea for a television format – collecting mistakes, 'outtakes', from programmes for an entertainment show. This is now a commonplace idea in TV schedules all over the world but Smith had it first. He was inspired by the celebrated incident on the BBC's live children's series *Blue Peter*. They had an elephant in the studio and it defecated in front of the cameras. With an elephant this function is performed on an almost industrial scale. It became a classic clip – shown over and over again to a nation which had always enjoyed a bit of scatology. But it took Smith time to get his show commissioned. New ideas are rarely welcomed at their first airing. The man he had to persuade was director of programmes at London Weekend Television, the company which supplied many of the Saturday night shows to Britain's only commercial network, ITV. Michael Grade is now the ultra-respectable Chairman of the BBC but back then he was Mr Show Business. Grade was not convinced at all. It took a full year to persuade him. Smith went into production and then had the difficult job of getting television and film producers to part with their most embarrassing moments: 'People were saying, hang on a minute, you want to air mistakes? Us doing things wrong? This is television, for God's sake. Piss off.' Smith flew to Los Angeles and accosted Blake Edwards on the set of a movie he was shooting. He wanted the outtakes from Edwards's Pink Panther films, rumoured to show Peter Sellers at his funniest and most surreal. He went to see Quinn Martin, who produced several of the US's most successful police series (*The Fugitive, Cannon, The Streets of San Francisco*). It turned out their 'bloopers' were already edited together because they were shown at the 'wrap' parties at the end of each series. Displaying the tenacity that would later help him create the world's most successful television format, Smith finally acquired all the clips he wanted. And in most cases he managed to get them free. *It'll Be Alright on the Night* was first broadcast on 18 September 1977. It was watched by twenty-two million people becoming the number one programme that week. John de Mol was learning that if you believe in an idea enough you cannot let it drop, however many times you are knocked back. After a while most normal people give up. Only a select few persist. They tend to become very rich.

In 1981 Smith sold his first format to network television in the United States. He had realised John de Mol's most cherished goal a full decade and a half before the Dutchman. NBC took *It'll Be Alright on the Night* and turned it into *TV Censored Bloopers*. The television industry then was insular and sleepy by comparison with today's. It took four years for American TV executives to cotton on to this British hit. Even then, there was no format fee paid to Smith or London Weekend Television. But they did receive a consultancy fee and Smith got to produce it, via Dick Clarke Productions. It proved very popular and 'blooper' shows have been a staple of the television schedules ever since. Paul Smith had not only invented a format, he had sold it to the United States. His pedigree was beginning to show.

In the early eighties Smith ceased being a freelance and set up his own production company to make programmes for the newly founded Channel 4. This was the second commercial channel in Britain and it was charged to commission its pro-grammes entirely from independent producers. They turned to Smith for large entertainment events. He was able to edit the programmes in the video facilities house he had also set up as a business, using funds from a venture capitalist. At this point the Prime Minister, Margaret Thatcher, decided to break up the cosy world of the main broadcasters, ITV and BBC. A law was passed that imposed a quota on them to commission some programmes from outside, independent producers. It was an attack on the vertical integration in their organisations. They made nearly all their programmes in house and this was judged to be inefficient, if not mildly corrupt. Now Smith could start making shows for the two entertainment channels, BBC1 and ITV. Their main-stream programmes were much closer to his roots than the more 'alternative' fare at Channel 4. He had soon established a comedy show called *Commercial Breakdown* with BBC1, star-ring his long-term collaborator, the comedian Jasper Carrot.

Now Smith had a small but healthy production company,

named Celador. Endemol wanted to expand the number of countries it operated in. Britain was a priority because the company needed to break into an English-speaking market. Aat Schouwenaar was given the job of looking at a variety of independent producers in London and decided to make contact with Celador. As well as his BBC shows Smith also had two successful hits on the main commercial network, ITV. One was a game show, *Talking Telephone Numbers*, and the other a vehicle for the stage hypnotist Paul McKenna. Smith hated having venture capitalists as investors in his business: 'I loathed them. I wanted them out. They were not interested in the company at all. They were only interested in getting money out.' When Schouwenaar approached him in 1995 about Endemol buying a share he saw it as an opportunity to be rid of his unwelcome investors. Smith went to Holland to meet John de Mol and Joop van den Ende. They got on very well. He then looked at Endemol's existing formats, which caused him some disquiet. He was uncomfortable with *All You Need Is Love*, which he found unpleasantly exploitative. He was appalled by a more recent Endemol format, *Now or Never*, in which contestants had to confront their worst fears – eating worms, handling spiders, jumping from heights. It reminded him of the legendarily extreme Japanese game show of the eighties, *Endurance*. And he hated the junior version of *The Soundmixshow*, *The Mini Playback Show*, in which sequined children aped the acts of well-known singers. Smith referred to it as child pornography. This did not immediately endear him to Joop van den Ende as a potential partner, nor was it necessarily an entirely sound basis for an enduring deal. But Schouwenaar persevered and Smith figured that if he was left to run his own business in London what the Dutch got up to elsewhere was not his concern. Smith and Schouwenaar even agreed the terms on which Endemol would buy the 49 per cent stake in his company from the venture capitalists. Then Ruud Hendriks intervened.

Hendriks had left RTL4 to run one of NBC's European channels from London, but van den Ende had persuaded him to return to Holland to help Endemol with its international expansion. So in 1995 Hendriks joined Schouwenaar on a visit to Celador in London. They climbed up the narrow stairs to Smith's comfortable office in a former eighteenth-century town house in Covent Garden's Long Acre. Hendriks was very clear about what he expected from the deal: 'I want Celador to be a clearing house for our Dutch formats. We want you to establish them in this market by selling them to your broadcasters.' Smith's jaw dropped. He said: 'We've seen your formats and we're not terribly impressed by them. We've told your people that we don't really think many of them will work on British television.' Hendriks then said, 'I believe they will sell over here and our Endemol employees will come in with you to pitch them to your broadcasters.' 'No, no, of course not,' countered Smith. 'I've built up relations with these people. I don't want someone from another country sitting beside me. I don't want anybody inhibiting that. No, categorically not, we've never ever discussed this. You're wanting to buy into us so you can have a production entity in the UK. We produce similar programmes. We don't want to be forced to take your programmes.'

As Hendriks remembers it Endemol, at this late stage, declined the deal. Smith says that, having heard all this, he told Endemol to go away. In any event, the deal was off. A few months later, in November 1995, someone else contacted Paul Smith with a business proposition. His name was David Briggs and he had an idea for a television game show in which the top prize would be more than a million pounds. They agreed a deal. The show eventually became *Who Wants to Be a Millionaire?*: the most successful format in television history. Agonisingly, Endemol had just turned down the chance to own 49 per cent of it.

Smith's one major international hit, *It'll Be Alright on the Night*, continued to be produced in Britain and America, but he had no financial stake in it. Now David Briggs offered him an opportunity to fill the gap in his business model. He would need the stamina of a long-distance runner to do so. New ideas are usually unpopular ones.

David Briggs had worked at Capital Radio, the commercial radio group in London. He had seen how on-air competitions drove listeners to the phones and enhanced income. Capital made an arrangement with the telephone companies to share the revenues. This worked particularly well on their popular morning show, hosted by Chris Tarrant. Briggs worked out a complex TV format in which a contestant would have to answer twenty-one questions of increasing difficulty. If they got them all right they could win a prize of up to £5 million. No television station anywhere in the world had ever offered such a large prize. The cleverness of Briggs's mechanics was that the prizes could be paid for out of the revenue from the 'premium' phone lines – the idea was to invite the public to call in and answer questions in order to get on the show. He wrote the format up and sent it to Steve Knight and Mike Whitehill who were collaborating with Paul Smith at Celador, developing ideas. Briggs, Knight and Whitehill had all worked together at Capital Radio. The beauty of the proposition was that it took a very traditional American format idea and propelled it boldly into new territory. One of the biggest game shows of the 1950s in the US was *The $64,000 Question* where competitors doubled their money with each question correctly answered. Another was *Double Your Money*, hosted in the UK by the ever-so-sincere Canadian and former RAF pilot Hughie Green.

Smith agreed that Celador would work with Briggs to develop the show. Agreements were drawn up and they set to work to refine Briggs's idea, elements of which seemed overcomplicated. This took three months. Early in 1996 the show, by this time called *Cash Mountain*, was ready to pitch to a broadcaster. Smith went to see Claudia Rosencrantz who commissioned entertainment for ITV, Britain's most popular network. Rosencrantz had recently arrived back in Britain after a disenchanting spell in Los Angeles. She had left after two years, having failed to win a regular network slot for Barry Humphries' creation, the fragrant Dame Edna Everage. She had heard the same old mantra – entertainment shows don't belong in prime time.

Smith sat in reception in the London Network Centre building on the Gray's Inn Road, dwarfed by the huge reception desk that dominated the entrance. A few other glum, nervous producers sat silently on the sofas, like petitioners at a medieval court, mentally rehearsing their humble submissions. Across the open-plan well in the modern building he could see the sub-editors of ITV's news service, ITN, scurrying around to prepare the next bulletin. By contrast it was deathly quiet in the reception area, leaving him to speculate how *Cash Mountain* would be received. They had simplified the format and made the top prize a million pounds. It remained, though, a daringly dramatic proposition. He was excited and apprehensive in equal measure. He need not have worried.

'I remember it very clearly. Claudia was very excited. I mean she was jumping up and down.' Her only reservations were that she did not like the title and was against the rather old-fashioned musical interlude that Smith was proposing halfway through the show. The meeting only lasted half an hour and the result was an invitation to return and pitch *Cash Mountain* to her boss, Marcus Plantin, the network controller. This happened only a few days later. This time Rosencrantz and Smith pitched it together to the man whose channel commanded more than 40 per cent of British viewing. At the time ITV was dominated by sitcoms, soaps and dramas. There were some game shows in the prime-time schedule but they were imported American formats with relatively modest prizes. The boldness of this idea, by comparison, should have been compelling. But it wasn't. Plantin turned it down, decisively, at their meeting. As recently as 1990 the highest prize permitted on British television had been a meagre £3500. He said he believed the general public were still not interested in seeing others winning large amounts of money. It was too downmarket. He told Rosencrantz that, like the Americans, he also believed entertainment was on its last legs in the prime-time schedule. Both Smith and Rosencrantz felt completely deflated but Plantin was adamant. The show that was to become *Who Wants to Be a Millionaire?* appeared to be stillborn. Smith returned to Celador and told his team. Rather than give up, they resolved to continue refining it and work out where else they might sell it. Smith believed in the idea so strongly he could not contemplate abandoning it.

While Smith was trying, unsuccessfully, to sell his format to television, there were plenty of internet pioneers in America who were suggesting that, in the future, they would be the first port of call for entertainment. In April 1996 the national magazine *Business Week* featured the chairman of America Online, Steve Case, on its cover. Steve Case was the internet messiah, destined in 2000 to make a deal with Jerry Levin of Time Warner that came to be regarded as the most disastrous in corporate history. His company, AOL, was an internet service provider that asked its customers to pay a subscription in return for being connected to the web. It was famous for its automaton voice that announced 'You've Got Mail' whenever a new email arrived. It had done an IPO four years earlier. In that time the market value of the company had grown from $70 million to $6.5 billion. By 1996 it had five million customers – impressive, but, as ever, in the Klondike economy that was developing, AOL was being valued on crazy assumptions of future growth. The article trumpeted: 'It is Case's America Online that has shown how to turn a community of cybernauts into a mass market and how to successfully turn a computer network into a new medium for entertainment and news.' AOL had decided to offer its subscribers what was becoming known as 'content' – news, personal finance, travel, entertainment and so on. The popularity of these services, however, was eclipsed by an option called 'Personal Connection'. This was the gateway to a host of some of the earliest chat rooms. With titles such as 'Married but Flirting', 'Submissive Men' and 'Crossdressers' these were well used. In October 1996 *Rolling Stone* magazine reported that around half the chat on AOL was sex-related. A system of online computer networking, invented for the exchange of academic information, was now in the hands of the public. It was developing as the public wished, reflecting their tastes. Video frames of a coffee pot put up had proved weirdly appealing. But the next images to capture internet surfers' imagination would amaze everyone. In the same month that Steve Case appeared in *Business Week* Jennifer Kaye Ringley started what became known as Jennicam.

Ringley was a twenty-year-old student at Dickinson College in Carlisle, Pennsylvania. She was intrigued by the net and borrowed a small video camera from the college library. She set it up in her apartment. With some simple software she connected the camera feed to the net and went online. With her life. Anyone who accessed the images could see her eating, sleeping, showering and working. She had a steady boyfriend who did not appear to mind having sex with her on camera either. The early images were mute, video stills updated every few minutes. To begin with hardly anyone noticed. Then news of Jennicam began to spread through the community of internet users like a virus. There were so many hits on her site that they could not be serviced properly. So Ringley introduced a $15 subscription and greatly increased the capacity of the servers she was using. Users would now get an updated image every two minutes. In time they also received audio. She installed more cameras and offered additional features, such as re-edited packages of the images revisiting and narrating recent incidents in Ringley's domestic life. At the height of the site's popularity she was receiving between three and four million hits a day (a hit is a discrete visit – the number of actual visitors would have been much lower since some heavy users would go to visit the site several times each).

Before long Ringley was receiving hundreds of emails a day from fans. Some would say, sympathetically: 'You're fat and ugly. Get off the camera.' Others became involved with her daily routine and would offer advice: 'If you sleep that way you're going to have back problems', and 'That toothpaste you use doesn't work'. One visitor, Justin Hall, said he had various motives for visiting the site: 'As a young man, you went there thinking she's exploiting all the boundaries and potentials. But in the back of your head you're thinking – gee, I hope she shows her breasts. It was the pornography of potential. It was a tease.' Katharine Kearney, another fan, worked in a six-person, all-woman company. They decided to have Jennicam displayed in the corner of their computer screens all day just to monitor what she was doing: 'It provided a diversion and all the girls would "check in" periodically to see what Jenni was up to. Nothing particularly exciting usually happened during our workday. Until she got the streaming audio and proceeded to have screaming anal sex. It was off camera but with live audio. Now that's something you don't usually hear in the workplace.' Bill, another frequent user of the site, now says: 'I followed Jennicam religiously, around the time of her on-cam (or just off-cam) loud sexcapades. My opinion of her changed from "interesting social experiment with a camera of girl who takes her clothes off occasionally" to "wonder how low she'll sink to get viewers next".' Others were more charitable: 'Putting your entire life on the internet will leave the door wide open to people calling you a whore and a liar, making fun of the size of your ass and second guessing the decisions you make. However, Jennifer Ringley can say something few can say – she changed the net as we know it today. I know that a lot of people think of Jennicam as no more than a sex/nudity lottery. But ... you'll note the sex was only ever a tiny fraction of what went on. Most of the time she simply lived a life ... and a life which is actually not that different from yours and mine.'

Sociologists dubbed the phenomenon 'vanity cam'. What were Ringley's real motives? She said her first idea was to rig up the camera so her mother could see how she was getting on at college. She insisted it just grew from there. Ringley made some money but not, it would seem, a huge amount after she had paid for the necessary server capacity. Later, she espoused higher motives than money or pure exhibitionism: 'On TV, you see all these people with perfect hair and perfect friends and people start to feel really inadequate. I walk round all the time with bad hair or stuff in my teeth. And I really think it makes people feel better to know they're not the only ones not leading glamorous lives ... I'm trying to prove the point that no matter what you look like, you're still just as interesting as people on the TV or in the magazines.' She pointed to a lonely student doing his laundry one evening who emailed in to thank her. When he accessed her site and saw her, alone, doing her washing too he felt less alone. 'I think it's human not to want to be alone. And with Jennicam it's like having someone in the next room. People are always waiting for their real life to start. We always feel like we have to measure up to something. Real life is right now. This is what it's all about.' In 1996 the world discovered that, with the aid of new technology, there was a group of people who wanted to be watched and a much larger number who wanted to watch them. These instincts would slowly feed into the culture of entertainment in a quest for the perfect application.

This was the point at which Ruud Hendriks joined Endemol. On his first day Hendriks was asked to travel to a remote hotel and join de Mol and van den Ende for a brainstorming session about the future of the company. One of the internet visionaries had been invited to address them in the afternoon. By this time there were a growing number of dotcom gurus who made a decent living out of predicting the cybernet future for bewildered managers of traditional companies. Hendriks was alive to the exciting potential of new media. Van den Ende was more sceptical. After the speaker had left he said: 'Listen, I don't understand anything of the internet. I don't know how to use a computer. But I tell you, if you want to make money, the money's in the telephone. Everyone thinks that I am the most expensive producer in the country ...' 'But you are the most expensive producer in the country,' interrupted de Mol to laughter. 'But I'm also going to produce the cheapest programmes too,' continued van den Ende. He proposed making super-cheap quizzes for TV, which would be funded by revenue from calls by members of the public competing to win prizes. They went on to establish such programmes in most Endemol territories and telephony revenue became a substantial part of the group's profit. It also lay at the heart of the funding mechanism for Paul Smith's *Cash Mountain*. All media companies were struggling to work out the real business potential of new technologies. And in that debate Hendriks turned out to be right as well. Not because the internet ever delivered huge revenues. It was a more calculating alchemy altogether. As the decade wore on, being able to say your company had some internet involvement, however tenuous, would drive up your value far more than real cash flow or solid profits.

In a rising market almost anyone can make money. It is a hallmark of the optimism that drives markets up that the bulls believe it will go on forever. This time it's different, they say. Tulips in the seventeenth century, South Sea stock in the eighteenth, railways in the nineteenth, radio and aircraft shares in the 1920s – among their enthusiasts you would always find theorists to tell you, with wild-eyed zeal, how the sky was no longer the limit. What a full-throttled boom needs is a group of evangelists in the market (mostly men) who are young enough not to have experienced a previous downturn but old enough to drive up prices. In other words, they know no fear and they are influential. As excitement at the potential of the internet took hold and Negroponte's convergent circles became common currency, this particular boom developed its own necessary myths. The dominant one was soon known as 'the new paradigm'. This was the idea that the net would completely transform Western economies by the turn of the century. Consumers would order virtually all goods online, doing away with the need for shops or the expensive holding of inventories at factories. The value of such efficiencies, impressive enough, paled by comparison with the next alleged benefit. Consumers networking with businesses and other consumers, buying and selling information and goods, would drive a period of unprecedented economic growth. For the entertainment industry everything could be enjoyed via every connection, and there would be lots more of it too. Between January 1995 and May 1996, as these ideas took hold, the NASDAQ rose from 750 to 1240, a 65 per cent increase. The seductive notion that the dotcom phenomenon could abolish the economic cycle of boom and bust was, in fact, characteristic of any boom. Economic cycles are merely expressions of human sentiment – classically, greed in a rising market and fear in a falling one. For this new paradigm to work nearly everyone needed to have erased their sense of fear. At this point they had. But it would return. It always does. The new paradigm could not alter human nature.

Owners of traditional media companies were desperately trying to converge their businesses so that they weren't left behind. More importantly, they could not afford to be perceived by the markets as having been left behind. In July 1996 Bill Gates of Microsoft and Jack Welch of General Electric (owners of the TV channel NBC) announced MSNBC. This was a twenty-four hour, interactive news service. In Spain, the telecoms giant Telefonica also pulled off two such deals in quick succession. The company was now led by an expansionist who had been converted to the great god convergence.

In June 1996 it was Juan Villalonga who had been made chairman of the part-privatised telephone company Telefonica. His boyhood friend José Maria Aznar had just, in the meantime, become Prime Minister of a right-of-centre, business-friendly government. Major shareholders in Telefonica nominated Villalonga for the job because they wanted good relations with the government which still owned 20 per cent of the shares. Villalonga was privately warned off the job by Aznar who feared it would look too incestuous. But, characteristically, Villalonga had already publicly accepted the post. Aznar took a further week to contemplate it but in the end he concluded he would have to approve the appointment. Within days Villalonga had bought a half-share in Antenna 3, a major commercial TV channel in Spain. This put Telefonica in the vanguard of convergence. Many other telecommunications companies in the world had considered a move into TV; few had actually done it. Within weeks Villalonga also announced a deal with the German Leo Kirch to set up a $1.2 billion digital television venture in Spain, later known as Via Digital. The plan was to offer digital satellite TV with home shopping and other interactive services, all through a set-top box. Via Digital never made a profit and was later abandoned, but at this juncture journalists and financial analysts alike looked favourably on these flamboyant deals. No one questioned in detail precisely how a telephone company would benefit from an association with a television company. Most observers expected and hoped Villalonga would set up further such alliances.

As yet Villalonga had not heard of Endemol, although by now it was producing formats in Spain. De Mol and van den Ende had bought a share in a production company in Barcelona to add to the companies they had set up in Germany and Portugal. But it was only piecemeal expansion. This odd couple, predicted to fall out personally within months of their merger, had now developed a mutual ambition to dominate European programming.

They worked out a strategy with Hendriks and Schouwenaar to establish strong production businesses in Europe's six main territories: Britain, Italy, France, Spain, Germany and Benelux. Their sense of purpose was endorsed by two Dutch companies, which were now interested in buying into Endemol. VNU was a newspaper and magazine publisher seeking a cheap thrill via a bit of convergence. If VNU injected their cash then Endemol would have the war chest necessary for their campaign of foreign acquisition. But the talks fell through. Hendriks also spoke to his old employer, RTL, which had folded their Dutch channels into a company called the Holland Media Group. Endemol already had a highly rewarding output deal with HMG – on paper it was worth £500 million over ten years. De Mol's competitors were astonished at how rich the deal was. Now the idea was that HMG and Endemol would buy 25 per cent of each other's shares. But their foreplay was interrupted by the European Commission, which judged the liaison to be anti-competitive. Where could they get the cash they needed to break out internationally?

With the advice of some willing bankers, de Mol and van den Ende concluded they would launch their own IPO. They decided to sell one third of Endemol to the market, issue new shares to raise extra capital and get themselves a share quote. They recruited Ben Verwaayen as chairman of the new supervisory board. He was at the time running a division of KPN, Holland's main telephone company. Sylvia Toth, who had recently sold her own employment agency business, also joined. Both would play roles in future dramas at Endemol, some welcome, others less welcome. The company prepared a detailed presentation of its plans for expansion and unveiled its vision for a dominant European content vehicle to potential investors and journalists. The performance was repeated to different groups for ten days. Then came the day of the flotation, with the shares available for the first time. They gathered nervously with their bankers at noon on 1 November 1996. If not all the shares are subscribed for in an

IPO it can be a disaster – bad for the company's reputation and worse for the banks who underwrite the offering and have to buy any unsold shares. They need not have worried. This was 1996. Media companies were sexy. At five minutes past noon the bankers' market makers rushed in to say that all the shares had been subscribed for. In the end the issue was eighteen times over subscribed. Investors scrambled for a slice of *The Soundmixshow* and *All You Need Is Love*, prior to their promised international roll-out. The shares were offered at forty-eight guilders and opened at fifty-five, a healthy 15 per cent premium. More to the point, de Mol and van den Ende each netted £40 million in cash. For the first time in their lives they were both independently wealthy. And they controlled a company now valued at £240 million. They did not have long to enjoy their newfound riches, though. Within weeks they would have to pay a hefty slug of the money back in order to save the reputation of the company.

For a few days the share price hovered agreeably above fifty guilders. At a modern office in Gutter Lane at the heart of the City of London some investors were feeling pleased with themselves. A Schroder Investment Management team, led by a Dutchman, Ton Tjia, had subscribed for the maximum number of shares they were allowed. They watched their screens and cheered at the premium achieved on the launch day. From their open-plan dealing room they started to buy additional Endemol shares as they became available. Eventually they built up a holding of 15 per cent of the available shares. Within a month, though, they were to have the opportunity to buy them at a much lower price.

Willem van Kooten was also pleased. The shares he held from bailing out John de Mol, bought for £300,000, were now worth £12 million. He had held on to them when the two production companies merged and he chose to hang on to them now the business had a share quote. But van Kooten was also embroiled with Endemol in a money-making scheme that quickly came back to haunt everyone involved in the IPO. Hendriks and de Mol had spotted an opportunity to seize the television rights to Dutch professional football and broadcast them on a new dedicated sports channel they wanted to set up: Sport7. In the general hype and hysteria of the time sports rights were spiralling up in value, like everything else. They had seen how Rupert Murdoch had cornered the rights to live football in the UK in order to sell satellite dishes for his BSkyB television venture. It had worked. So de Mol, Hendriks and van Kooten put a consortium of investors together. They cleverly and secretly concluded a deal with the Dutch Football League.

When this coup was revealed there was outrage. Outrage from the public broadcasters who were going to lose their football coverage, outrage from football fans who were going to be forced to pay for a new channel in order to see their favourite teams and outrage from politicians who knew which side their bread was buttered. Newspapers, television and radio poured abuse on the heads of de Mol, Hendriks and Endemol, even though they only owned a minority of the new channel. Hendriks also received death threats: 'We totally underestimated the emotions that come with something like football. We were some business guys who were basically commercialising the national heritage. We didn't have a proper communications strategy because we had been working in total secrecy.' Hendriks was jostled in public, even when with his children at a Michael Jackson concert. He hired personal bodyguards. (In 2004, renovating a property in Amsterdam, Hendriks ordered bullet-proof glass for the entire house, so scarred was he by the events eight years before.)

But the public outcry was, in a sense, the least of Hendriks's problems. The Dutch Cabinet met and the Prime Minister, Wim Kok, said publicly that his government would not allow football to be completely removed from the free, public channels. So much for buying the football rights for seven years. A further problem was the revelation that the Dutch Football League did not, technically, have the rights to sell. Even though they had done so for thirty years the rights were, in law, owned by the individual clubs. To make matters worse Sport7's business plan was to offer a low subscription (the equivalent of about £1.50 a month) and go for a big audience, which would make advertising spots valuable too. But it turned out that whereas the minority of hardened football fans might have paid twenty times as much for their beautiful game, the majority of the population (as they featured in the business plan) were not very interested. And that was in areas where the channel was available. Dutch television is largely delivered via cable systems. The channels that are available on it are governed by the local town councils. It now emerged that these only met to decide television issues once every six or nine months. Until they met and approved it Sport7 could not be offered. This meant that, in the first year, Ajax Amsterdam's matches would not be available to viewers in Amsterdam. Try telling that to home-town fans of Manchester United or the New York Yankees. In short, Sport7's revenues were tumbling, it no longer had exclusivity on the football, it was way behind on its business plan and it was reviled by the very football fans it had hoped to recruit. To keep Sport7 going the shareholders would have to put in substantial amounts of extra capital. This they refused to do. Sport7 duly closed down and handed the football rights back.

The cost of this debacle to Sport7's shareholders, Philips, KPN, ING (the Dutch bank) and Endemol, was £60 million. Two hundred and fifty people were made redundant and several studios were closed. Just four weeks after its confident launch Endemol's share price was sinking rapidly. John de Mol and Joop van den Ende took decisive action to protect their now fragile quote. They paid off Endemol's losses personally. It cost them approximately £6 million. In addition they had, personally, to guarantee debts of £12 million. This impressed their investors, but the whole episode was an embarrassment for the company and its advisers who had floated Endemol's shares just a month before without anticipating any clouds on the horizon. A European banker who witnessed these events felt it showed up a hole at the centre of Endemol: 'There wasn't any real sense of corporate management – the normal levels of supervision and finance you'd expect in a public company. It was driven along by John de Mol as a locomotive churning out creative ideas. It was obviously going to work with his unifying vision. But I don't think John realised, at the time of the IPO, how uncomfortable he was going to be as the leader of a publicly quoted company. He just hated everything to do with it.'

The Sport7 disaster revealed that, like many driven, self-willed entrepreneurs, de Mol resented the disciplines of the public market. He despised financial analysts, often 'teenage scribblers' just out of university. But – via their circulars – they had the power to influence share prices. He didn't like talking to investors and would sit at meetings with Hendriks and Schouwenaar cursing everything he had to do as head of a public company. Van den Ende, while publicly more genial, felt the same way. Particularly as his theatre dealings came under closer and closer scrutiny.

In reality, Sport7 represented only a small part of Endemol's business. Their core activity, television, was growing rapidly. In 1997 they bought into production companies in Italy, South Africa, Poland and a second one in Spain. And the entertainment formats kept on rolling off the production line. Despite all this, in November 1997, a whole year after Sport7's closure, Endemol's share price was languishing at twenty-seven guilders. This was half the level it had reached on its opening day. As a circular from Goldman Sachs, the investment bank, pointed out, the company had underperformed compared to the rising Dutch stock market by more than 50 per cent. This represented a sort of daily torture for both de Mol and van den Ende. By that time there was one remaining reason for investors' doubts about Endemol: van den Ende's theatrical division. As ever, the market did not like its lower margins and higher risks. Something would have to be done about it if the share price was to start performing again.

In Britain Paul Smith also had unwelcome investors in his production company. For that brief moment in 1995 it had looked as though Endemol might buy these venture capitalists out. But the deal had foundered. In 1996 a company called Avesco expressed an interest in buying 49 per cent of Smith's company. Avesco owned the TV studios in which Celador recorded many of their shows. Their chairman, Richard Murray, understood the entertainment business personally, to the extent that he was also chairman of the then First Division football club, Charlton Athletic. For just £713,000 Avesco bought a half-share in the team which would create *Who Wants to Be a Millionaire?*. Eventually the show was to deliver revenues a thousand times bigger than Avesco's original investment. But at this point, *Cash Mountain* was still getting nowhere.

After being rebuffed by ITV Paul Smith had approached the two other, free-to-air commercial networks, Channel 4 and Channel Five. Both turned it down. Early in 1997 Smith returned to see the head of ITV's programming, Marcus Plantin, once more. At this meeting Smith made a final attempt to change his mind: 'Marcus, I don't understand why you won't take this show, because as far as I'm concerned, this is a massive, great big hit.' Smith added, trying desperately to find a way through, 'Look, I have a feeling that maybe you think an independent shouldn't be producing a show like this and it should really be one of the network companies.' By this, Smith meant Carlton or Granada, two of the larger regional companies, which owned ITV and supplied most of its programmes. He remembers Plantin replying: 'Yes, you're right. You see, you haven't been listening to me.' Smith replied: 'OK, I'm

hearing you now. You want us to partner? Do you have a view
as to which partner?' Plantin replied, 'Go and see Simon Shaps
at the fun factory. They're not doing terribly well at the
moment.' This was a reference to Granada. So Smith made an
appointment with Simon Shaps. He offered to co-produce *Cash
Mountain* with Granada if they would pitch the show to
Plantin. Shaps was perplexed as to why Smith needed his help.
He said that Granada did not do co-productions. Smith
implored him to make an exception in this case. ' Well, I'm
seeing Marcus next week,' said Shaps. 'I'll let you know.' Smith
returned to Briggs, Knight and Whitehill at Celador and told
them he had finally, apparently, made some progress. They
waited a week. Then Smith recalls receiving a letter from
Shaps: 'I've discussed it with Marcus and Marcus said he's not
interested.' After one of the wilder goose chases of his career
Smith had still made no progress. The list of people who had
turned down a chance to be involved with *Millionaire* was
growing. And Smith had to take the decision to cut the staff in
his production company. 1997 saw the end of two of his more
successful shows, *Talking Telephone Numbers* and Paul
McKenna's hypnotism specials. Celador's production slate was
shrinking. He badly needed to sell some new projects. The sensible decision would have been to give up on *Cash Mountain*
and swiftly move on to some fresh ideas. But he couldn't. He
still passionately believed in it even though, in British television, the real action seemed to be elsewhere for the moment.

In June 1997 BBC1 had an unexpected hit that took the docu-
soap principle of the Australian family from hell in Sylvania
Waters one step further. *Driving School* became the third most
popular programme in Britain that summer with audiences
approaching twelve million. It simply followed the disasters of a
group of learner drivers whose road sense was non-existent and
whose temperaments were wildly mismatched to the Highway
Code. Maureen Rees, who had failed her test six times, became

a star. Her struggles with her husband and instructor, Dave, as he tried to stay alive became addictive. Here members of the public, carefully cast, had entered into a pact with the producers – to act up like hell in front of the cameras for maximum entertainment. And yet the situations remained real enough to strike a resounding chord. At those festivals of insincerity, the various television awards, it was the likes of Maureen who were now going up on stage to receive awards rather than the producers or directors who had made the programmes. They were being rewarded for having been on television, for simply being themselves. Television had crossed a Rubicon.

That autumn in Holland one of the many successful entertainment formats that Endemol had running was a show which concentrated on a particular year and reminded viewers of the events of the time blended with reprises of the hit songs of the day. The vogue for nostalgic television was at its height. People were particularly entertained by the reappearance of ageing rockers, a decade or two after their original hits, to perform once more. The potbellies, the receding hairlines, the drug-ravaged features – all these delivered the pleasure of nostalgia and the comfort that even pop idols decay, like everyone else. Endemol produced the show for the public broadcaster KRO. KRO decided to move its slot to another night of the week and asked John de Mol to come up with a second programme to fill the gap. Had the broadcaster not made this request *Big Brother* might never have come into existence.

De Mol called three of his closest colleagues together one Thursday evening in late September. It was raining and decidedly gloomy by the time they assembled in his office at the end of the day. They were there to brainstorm this new idea for KRO. There was a ritual to such meetings. De Mol would sit behind his desk. His employees sat around a rocket-shaped extension that protruded from the front of his desk. It put him in a physical position of power. Most meeting tables have two ends. This only had one and de Mol occupied it. On the desk in front of him were a notebook of yellow paper and a pen. Beside it an ashtray which, as the meeting progressed, would resemble an art installation. De Mol only ever smokes the first half of a cigarette; then he stubs it out, leaving a succession of rigid stumps sticking up awkwardly at all angles. Also on the desk was a large supply of chewing gum and, in his drawer, bottles of the vitamin pills that he liked to take regularly throughout the day.

Grouped around the de Mol console were two brothers, Paul and Bart Romer, and a third entertainment executive named Patrick Scholtze. The conversation was somewhat desultory. Like many brainstorms that don't catch fire they ranged over a series of half-ideas without hearing anything that excited them. Paul Romer recalls mentioning Jennicam, which he had read about. He was intrigued by the way in which she had made her everyday life an attraction on the web. One of them talked about sabbaticals – whether you could take people out of their every-day lives. Someone else mentioned the growing proliferation of security cameras, even now being built into domestic entry phones. After several hours they felt they had got nowhere and resolved to call it a day. They chatted casually before leaving the office. Bart Romer mentioned an article he had read about Biosphere II, the environmental living experiment in the US. Here a small group had been isolated and asked to live in a self-sufficient plastic dome for a year. This caught the group's imagination. Suddenly – and no one can remember quite how – they found themselves speculating what it would be like to lock a small group of people up and video them. Paul Romer remembers one thing clearly: 'John was absolutely triggered. He started "broadcasting". He talked a lot. He tossed up ideas. It seemed like he wasn't listening to what we were saying, but he was. Just processing it all in his head, spitting out ideas.' One over-riding thought dominated de Mol's imagination. This is how he put it to the others: 'What would happen if you brought people together in a closed environment? Tape it for twenty-four hours. Every month they do an assignment. If you do that right you're allowed one phone call to your wife.'

They talked on late into the night without noticing the time. Paul Romer saw de Mol doodling on his yellow notepaper, as he always did, but somehow more insistently. When he glanced at the doodles later he didn't see the triangles and faces that he was used to de Mol idly sketching. Instead there were random lines of numbers set out across the page. As yet, though, there were no dollar signs. They would come later. But de Mol was definitely excited and on edge. So was Bart Romer. Paul Romer was more sceptical, tending by nature to see pitfalls in any new idea. Scholtze was impossible to read. But the Captain Kirk of this meeting now knew where he was steering the ship: 'The first half-hour I started, sort of, to get nervous, to feel butterflies. I said to myself – Jesus Christ, this is special. It's different.'

It was late. The others all wanted to go home. For a while de Mol drove them on, imagining all the different things they could do in their own version of the Biosphere. Finally, he said he too was ready to go to bed (he puts the time at 4.30 a.m., the others feel it was a bit earlier). Before they went de Mol gave them a clear instruction: 'I really believe we have something special. I don't want you to talk to anyone about this. We'll get together again on Monday. The meeting will be diaried as 'Project X'. No one is to know about it yet.' De Mol drove home through the empty outskirts of Hilversum in the early hours of the morning. A depressing drizzle was falling steadily, but he was elated. He went to bed, expecting to be unconscious within seconds but he couldn't sleep. He was physically exhausted but he had a feeling in the pit of his stomach, like the nerves you experience before a visit to the dentist. In the space of a few hours Project X had become a personal obsession.

They met twice the following week. The proposal, as it stood, was six people in a luxury house for a year. They would be tested, almost beyond endurance, to induce them to leave. But if they made it through the twelve months they would win a million guilders. By this time de Mol had filled two yellow notebooks with a range of possible format elements. But they realised that inventing an ever-longer list of the challenges and stunts they could set the guinea pigs in the Project X house was getting them nowhere. They now had to test the logistics of the idea. They had to figure out whether it was ethically acceptable and psychologically possible. In short, would it work? Paul Romer was given that task. As the basic premise of Project X leaked out to their closest colleagues they were frequently told that the idea was outrageous. It might even finish the company off.

Jef Nassenstein found out first. The former bass guitarist was extremely exercised. He rushed into the international sales office: 'We can't do this. We can't lock people up. I don't want to cooperate in something where we buy the life of someone for a year. It's not done.' Nassenstein felt Endemol itself was threatened by de Mol's idea. That autumn he attended a private dinner with John de Mol, Linda de Mol and their partners. It was a reunion for the group – they had all been skiing together the previous winter. Late at night, after drinks, Nassenstein challenged de Mol about the project. This time he found that Linda agreed with him too – it was risky and it was wrong.

Ruud Hendriks also heard about Project X early on. He thought it was insane but he was also rather excited by it. He was with de Mol when he confidentially explained the idea to the manager of a video facilities house. 'Yes, yes, great idea,' said the man who depended on Endemol's business. But Hendriks could see him thinking: 'This is disgusting.' Aat Schouwenaar's reaction to de Mol after hearing the idea was equally to the point: 'You can't do that. You can't do it, no you can't. This is awful.' De Mol replied: 'Wait and see, Aat', and carried on with the development. It was clear that Joop van den Ende was also doubtful. His formats tended to be sunnier than de Mol's. Project X seemed more sinister than anything he had ever come across before. In fact, there was only one person in Endemol who wanted to pursue the idea – John de Mol. But then, he was the only person that mattered. Project X was isolated but not dead.

CHAPTER FIVE

Ideas Won't Keep

Ideas won't keep. Something must be done about them.

ALFRED NORTH WHITEHEAD

Charlie Parsons was the third man to vie with de Mol to create the biggest worldwide television hit at the turn of the century. He eventually became the producer of *Survivor*. In the early 1970s he was still at school. But he had already launched a journal in his home village at the age of eleven. At fifteen, he started his own school magazine and was dreaming of a life in newspapers or television. He was a quick-thinking but short-tempered, charming but mercurial, individual.

Five years later Charlie Parsons started his media career as a junior reporter on a local newspaper in west London, the *Ealing Gazette*. He had already learnt the essential skills of journalism – in particular, the 'Death Knock'. This stratagem involved going to the house of someone who had been killed in an accident, posing to their family as a best friend and gathering all the personal photographs the paper might need for their memorial spread. Parsons' two greatest scoops thus far were 'Jilted at the Altar', which he unearthed by following up a small ad selling a wedding dress, and 'Secrets of a 100-Year-Old', which turned out to be the daily consumption of lemon juice. Parsons was just about ready for television.

By the age of twenty-nine, Charlie Parsons had worked his way out of newspapers and up the television ladder. He had done his time as a researcher and producer, notably under Greg Dyke at London Weekend Television on *The Six o'Clock Show*, a topical entertainment show about the more ludicrous aspects of London. Now he was to become boss of his own series, a wild entertainment show aimed at the youth market (or 'yoof', as it was known by its detractors). *Network 7* was broadcast at Sunday lunchtime on ITV. It was now in its second series and was already famous for wacky camera angles, using its trendy office as a presentation studio and a series of outrageous stunts, calculated to create weekly talking points. John de Mol was not the only one testing the boundaries of what was acceptable on television. Parsons commissioned a live relay from an inmate's cell on death row in an American prison. His plan was to use it to launch a telephone vote with his viewers: should this man live or die? The idea was leaked to the British tabloids which, in time-honoured fashion, fed greedily off the story while affecting moral outrage. The senior executives at ITV capitulated to what they perceived to be public outrage and ordered Parsons to change the question to a blander: 'Are you in favour of capital punishment?'.

Another stunt thought up by a member of Parsons' team was seized upon by him and commissioned immediately. It was an idea that would obsess Parsons for the best part of the next decade and, in the end, make him very wealthy. One morning the production team were assembled in their office-cum-studio to think up new items for *Network 7*. It was a huge vaulted room that dwarfed the team, huddled together in a small semi-circle. The building itself, a disused warehouse in London's docklands, was scheduled to be pulled down shortly afterwards as part of the construction of the Canary Wharf tower on exactly the same spot. 'Why not,' asked Murray Boland, a researcher, 'isolate a handful of celebrities on an island and film them?' But could they afford to do it? With Parsons' guidance

the team persuaded the Sri Lankan Tourist Authority to help
them fly a small group to a classic desert island in the south
Indian Ocean. The group included Pete Gillette, a former convict
and associate of the London gangsters the Krays, along with
Annabel Croft, an ex-tennis player, Simon O'Brien, a soap star,
and a stockbroker. Not exactly a typical dinner party selection.

The idea became so elaborate that Parsons decided he had to
run it over several weeks rather than as a single item. Murray
Boland reported it, shot it and sent edited packages back by
satellite. The relationship of the castaways was followed by the
camera. They had hoped for an element of sexual intrigue under
canvas but what they got, instead, was a rather good-humoured
scout camp. Without knowing it Parsons and his colleagues had
invented the modern celebrity reality show. The biggest controversy arose when a chicken, taken by one of the participants as
a luxury, was slaughtered and eaten. To make matters worse for
a nation of animal lovers, the doomed fowl had been named
Janet (after Janet Street-Porter, who founded *Network* 7) and
therefore been given some sort of personality. Despite this, the
feature was only seen by a very small television audience for four
weeks in 1988 and then forgotten. But not forgotten by Parsons.
He continued to be obsessed by the potential of this idea for a
series. And like John de Mol and Paul Smith, when Parsons
believes in an idea he never lets go of it.

Next Charlie Parsons set up his own company, 24
Productions, to make a new show for Channel 4. This publicly
owned, commercially funded station had a specific remit to
make innovative programmes that were socially and ethnically
diverse. Parsons interpreted this as an invitation to shock and
came up with *The Word*. It ran late on Friday nights and was an
anarchic, teenage melange of music, interviews and entertaining
obscenity. Parsons ran his company with his male partner in
life, Waheed Alli. So, unlike de Mol, he was not going to be
remotely squeamish when a regular strand, called 'Secret Love',

threw up an eighteen-year-old boy with a passion he wanted to declare on television. It was for his sixty-year-old male land-lord. It worked as a wind-up for the audience who had no idea that this would be a gay secret. And since the landlord in question turned out to be gay as well the item worked as planned.

Parsons is described by a colleague at the time as 'passionate, at times even demonic'. He hid cameras in the dressing rooms of his two male presenters and sent a Liverpudlian actress in, unannounced, to seduce them. His relationship with the talent fronting his shows could be tempestuous. It certainly was on this occasion.

The Word set out to shock in an endearingly adolescent way. There were reports about sex addiction and penile extensions, performers who could thread condoms through their nasal passages and who invited the audience to drink their vomit. The senior producer said: '*The Word* is produced by geniuses for losers.' Parsons added: 'I'd really rather TV was appallingly bad than mediocre'. Distressingly for 24 Productions they only managed to fall foul of the British television regulator once. *The Word* was held to have breached standards of taste and decency with a seasonal item. An intrepid man dressed as Santa Claus was pulled along on his sleigh by a rope attached to his genitals. Why did he want to do that? Because he, like many others, was responding to a challenge *The Word* had set its viewers. They called them 'The Hopefuls' and the item became known as 'I'd Do Anything to Get on TV'. This idea was, in retrospect, Parsons' first really significant contribution to television culture. With a deliberately absurd reduction of Andy Warhol's 1968 dictum he was giving people fifteen seconds of fame in a piece of entertainment poised provocatively between satire and farce. People queued up with bizarre petitions for their moment under the studio lights (I'll sit in a bath of pig's urine, or I'll cover myself in leeches). They really would do anything to get on TV.

In 1992 Channel 4 asked independent producers to bid for a fat contract to make a new, all-year-round breakfast show. It was

based on the apparently suicidal idea of being entirely for
teenagers. Since adolescents never get out of bed until they are
forced to go to school, how could they be persuaded to watch
television at that time? As maker of *The Word*, Parsons was
encouraged to have a go. But he needed to present 24
Productions as a more substantial company, capable of delivering a vast commission. So, in 1992, he and Waheed Alli merged
their company with that of Bob Geldof's to form Planet 24. Bob
Geldof's first incarnation was as the front man of the seventies
band the Boomtown Rats. His second was as the inspirational
instigator of the Live Aid charity that raised £100 million for
famine relief in Ethiopia in 1985. And now his third was as an
independent television producer. Planet 24 duly won the contract from Channel 4 to make the daily morning show. They
called it *The Big Breakfast*. Through 1993 it buried the conventional wisdom. Teenagers rolled out of bed early to watch a
mad rolling format held together by a shrewd and wildly entertaining radio presenter called Chris Evans. There was more than
a flavour of *The Word*'s anarchy but sanitised to go out in the
morning without regulatory intervention. The whole confection
looked and felt like a children's programme on acid. Parsons
watched the ratings climb until it became the most popular
breakfast show on British television: 'It was ridiculously successful and made us ridiculously wealthy. We thought – right,
now we're a big company we ought to be coming up with formats.' This was the time to open his bottom drawer and see
what undeveloped ideas were lurking there.

In 1994 Parsons spent twelve weeks in the United States with
Disney's distribution arm, Buena Vista. On the strength of *The
Big Breakfast* he had signed a development deal with them. He
disinterred the desert island idea from *Network 7* and asked his
creative team to take it further. First it was called *Lord of the
Flies* and then *Survive*. The gentle scout camp had become a
much tougher competition. The format had been optioned by

Granada, the Manchester company which made a large slice of ITV's programming. They wanted to call it *Island of Dreams* and it was almost commissioned. But then the head of entertainment at the network left and everything was back in limbo. In the US Parsons developed it further with Michael Davies at Buena Vista, the man who was later to introduce *Who Wants to Be a Millionaire?* to America. Davies was British by birth and had actually watched the original *Network 7* stunt as a schoolboy. They got the ABC network interested and agreed a development deal. This money allowed Parsons to flesh out the idea of marooning sixteen competitors on a desert island in more detail. He also went to visit Bunim–Murray to discover how they cast and organised *The Real World* participants. *The Real World* was now in its third series based in San Francisco. This was the year the series really took off. They invited an Asian medical student, an HIV-positive Cuban, a black rapper, a Jewish cartoonist, a self-confessed beach babe, a Republican Latina and a bike messenger to live together for six months. The audiences trebled as the rows, rapprochements and relationships unfolded. Now Parsons was offering ABC a similar idea with the added attraction of a desert island and an eventual winner. But the usual institutional lethargy and referrals upwards between timid executives occurred and there was no commission.

Parsons returned home to Britain undaunted. He recruited a tall, shaven-headed South African called Gary Carter to help him sell the show in Europe instead. His team had by now added perhaps the most crucial element of all to the format: the idea of a popularity contest in which the participants would vote each other off the island one by one. This 'balloon debate' mechanism was to dominate most successful reality shows for the next decade. Carter was a former actor and agent who enjoyed taking part in exotic fringe theatre in his spare time. He understood and liked the format and was adept at deal making. Planet 24 went to Canvey Island – bleak, downmarket and on the dank Thames

Estuary, as far from the South Seas as could be imagined – and shot a short demonstration tape. Gary Carter provided the voice-over, something that would come back to haunt him. Armed with the new format and the tape Carter set off for Cannes where a television market takes place twice a year.

Mipcom is officially a market place in which television companies can buy and sell programmes and formats. In practice it is a Chablisfest in which no crustacean is safe. Every autumn Cannes' beach-front restaurants echo to the sound of silky sales pitches and dark glasses are required to protect the eyes from a thousand Amex cards glinting in the October sun. Carter succeeded in selling two options for *Survive*, one to a Swedish production company called Strix and the other to a newly formed Dutch producer, Endemol. The deal with Endemol was later to form the basis of a bitter legal dispute between John de Mol and Charlie Parsons. But at this stage both parties were happy to do business. Endemol did separate deals for Holland, Belgium, Germany and their two latest territories, Portugal and Spain, where they now had production outfits.

Like de Mol with Project X and Paul Smith with *Cash Mountain*, Charlie Parsons was truly obsessed by *Survive*. He had failed to sell the idea to the BBC, and also to Marcus Plantin at ITV. But he continued to pitch it to broadcasters. Three years later, in 1997, Strix finally persuaded a new programme director, Pia Marquard, at the Swedish state broadcaster SVT to make the show. They called it *Expedition Robinson*, after the popular book about a shipwrecked family, *The Swiss Family Robinson*. At £2 million it was the largest, most expensive entertainment commission in the history of Swedish television. And one of the participants died.

When Gary Carter got the news that, finally, *Survive* was to be produced he immediately trumpeted the breakthrough to Parsons. He found Parsons strangely cool about it. This was because Parsons had worked for three years to sell the show in the US and the UK. This was his obsession. A commission in Scandinavia, in a country with a population of eight million, did not seem like hitting the big time. But Carter knew if the format could actually be seen to work on television, worldwide sales would follow. Early in 1997 he flew Parsons to a weekend workshop with Strix's producers at a hotel north of Stockholm. There they refined all the rules of the format already sketched out in some detail for the pitches in the US some years before. This included the rule that a psychologist should be involved in selecting the sixteen men and women who would compete on the desert island for the cash prize of £33,000. Everyone realised that the rigours of the competition coupled with the experience of being voted off by your peers needed robust individuals to take part.

The Swedish production team and the sixteen competitors then flew off to a remote Malaysian island. Parsons' company, Planet 24, sent two of their own executives to oversee the production. One was Mary Durkin. There were long, arduous hours of filming. Carter remembers her on a crackling telephone line from the Far East: 'All I could hear was this demented cockney voice going: "It's the fucking Vietnam War here, Gary. It's the fucking Vietnam War!"' But they completed the filming, the various contestants voted each other off the island and they had their winner, a policeman named Martin Melin. Now they had to fly back to Sweden and edit all the videotape into a compelling narrative while keeping the name of the winner secret. In the opening programme they had to assemble the footage of the very first eviction. After just four days the islanders had voted off a thirty-four-year-old Bosnian, Sinisa Savija. When the verdict is announced Savija looks momentarily startled, gives a resigned smile and shrugs. He then shakes hands with his executioners, stands up and, by way of a farewell, says: 'Get on with supper.' He is then led away by the host. He left for his home in Sweden shortly afterwards.

Savija lived with his wife, Nermina, in Norrkoping in central

Sweden. They were refugees from Bosnia. 'He was half-Croatian and half-Serbian. I'm a Muslim. We didn't belong anywhere,' said Nermina. Savija had managed to win himself a place at a Swedish law school, enabling them to leave the Balkans. On his application form for *Expedition Robinson* he described himself as 'peaceful, not subject to moods and very active'. A journalist who interviewed the contestants beforehand found him shy but positive. He interviewed him again, three days into the competition, and got the impression Savija was finding it difficult. The eventual winner, Martin Melin, said: 'Sinisa was a bit of loner. It works the same way as it does in the country as a whole; if you are a refugee and you don't know the language and the culture – well, you're not in the group. You're different.'

On 11 July 1997 Savija walked to a level crossing near his home and stepped into the path of an express commuter train. He was killed outright. His apparent suicide came as a shock to everyone. But his wife Nermina blamed *Expedition Robinson*: 'He became deeply depressed and agonised. He felt degraded as a person and didn't see any meaning in life. He was a happy and stable person before he went away and when he came back he told me: "They are going to cut away the good things I did and make me look a fool, to show that I was the worst and that I was the one that had to go." It is not a game when you choose ordinary people and put them under great pressure, constantly in front of the camera.' The Swedish newspapers had already attacked *Expedition Robinson* as 'fascist television'. Now a storm broke around the heads of Strix and SVT. Questions were asked in the Swedish parliament. Despite this SVT broadcast the first edition on 13 September. They had edited Savija's contribution to the barest minimum. But then they could withstand the pressure no longer and took the series off air. Pia Marquard, who had commissioned it, resigned. And they set up an enquiry. The fate of the format would rest on the verdict.

When there's something in the water, everyone is influenced by it. Jennicam, *The Real World*, *Love Letters*, *Expedition*

Robinson ... by 1998 creative minds were routinely witnessing ordinary people exposing their lives for mass consumption, often at the behest of powerful TV executives. In the US, *The Jerry Springer Show* scheduled an edition entitled 'I Married a Horse'. The news organisations now had helicopters to cover crimes as they happened. A local Los Angeles station broadcast live pictures of a man, naked from the waist down, committing suicide on the freeway. He shot himself having first burnt his truck with his dog inside. In Japan Nippon Television shut a comedian called Nasubi in a tiny apartment. He could only eat if he won money or goods from magazine competitions. He was ordered to remain naked and stayed in there for a year. Nasubi had no idea his ordeal was being shown on both television and the web.

Was all this real life or was it a performance? What had really happened to Sinisa Savija? Where was the line between television capturing it and actually *making* it happen? This was the moment that *The Truman Show* was launched. The movie script had been written by Andrew Niccol in 1995 but the film was released three years later.

Truman Burbank is a clerk for an insurance company in a town in middle America. He leads a normal life, except that everyone around him – his wife, his best buddy, his work colleagues – is an actor. The town is a massive TV set with artificial weather and a special-effects sun. Poor Truman is unwittingly the star of his own top-rated, TV soap. The irony is that the viewing public's obsession with the minutiae of Truman's life is the very thing that keeps him imprisoned. Had the ratings waned he would have been set free years ago. Eventually Truman rumbles the trick that has been played on him since birth and attempts to escape, first down a film-set road and then across an ersatz lake. The all-powerful producer breaks in, as a voice from above, to persuade him that a fake life inside his personal biosphere is better than the real world outside. But Truman chooses freedom, to the cheers of his fans watching live.

The Truman Show's director was the Australian Peter Weir, the man behind the cult films *Picnic at Hanging Rock* and *The Year of Living Dangerously*. He also directed the more mainstream *Dead Poets Society* and *Green Card*. In his round of publicity interviews for the film's launch Weir said, 'People are losing a sense of reality, blurring reality and unreality.' In a reference to the influence of *Candid Camera* he described his movie as 'the ultimate hidden camera show' and, drawing on the death of Princess Diana only months before he added: 'Was society morally capable of something like this? It really became clear to me that it could be, during the cutting process, when the Lady Diana tragedy unfolded . . . You noticed, with Lady Di, the audience turned on the paparazzi. Yet the paparazzi were working for them. They hadn't put the connection together. And I thought, that's very good, because I'm writing the reaction of my audience in the movie – where they had forgotten that this person was being exploited on their behalf. Their sense of reality was gone . . . and that's really the heart of the film.'

There really was something in the water. Because also ready for release in 1998 was *Edtv*. In this film a TV producer tries to save an ailing channel by following the life of a normal person, live and round the clock. Ed, a video store assistant, agrees to this and his life begins to unravel as the network takes off. Ed reveals that his brother is cheating on his girlfriend, becomes entangled with the same girl, is targeted by a model on the make and exposes his parents' marriage problems. Like *The Truman Show*, *Edtv* had been born some years before. Two French Canadians were lunching in Quebec in 1990, some time before *The Real World* or Jennicam were conceived. Sylvie Bouchard pitched her friend, comedienne and writer Emile Gaudreault, with the idea of a movie about someone being filmed by TV twenty-four hours a day, seven days a week. Gaudreault loved the idea and they wrote a screenplay together. It was released as a French language movie in 1994, under the title *Louis 19, King of the Airwaves*. In France it was called *Reality Show*. Universal then bought the rights and rewrote it as *Edtv*. Television and movies were chasing each other's tails. But, unlike de Mol's Project X and Parsons' *Survive*, the movies were taking off. Even a third film was underway featuring the ultimate TV reality show in which the contestants had to kill each other or be killed. *Series 7* was written in 1995 by Daniel Minahan. It was eventually shot in 1999 and released in 2000. Here was a fictional idea closer to *Survive*, although much more extreme. At this point Minahan was unaware of Parsons' idea.

Edtv was lighter in tone than *The Truman Show* or *Series 7*. When it finally went on release in 1999 a reviewer in Chicago, a long way from Hilversum in Holland, asked how long it would be before TV actually tried out the idea of a man living twenty-four hours a day on television. The answer was, as soon as John de Mol could find the right way to do it and a television company willing to broadcast it. The same reviewer queried whether we would rather be true voyeurs – that is, watch people without their knowledge or consent (Truman) or merely be viewers of self-promoting exhibitionists (Ed). On the world wide web it was definitely the latter as more individuals followed Jennicam to offer their lives, voluntarily, to net surfers.

In March 1998 Sean Patrick Williams, a computer programmer, switched on a web cam in his Washington, DC, apartment. Sean Patrick Live! offered an updated video still every thirty seconds. The images were mostly of him watching television, working at his desk or emailing. But Williams was gay, he slept in the nude and occasionally had his boyfriend over. The site was soon attracting seventy thousand visitors a day. Williams's own description of his installation was as insouciant as Jennifer Ringley's: 'What I'm trying to show is that what goes on in somebody else's life always seems bigger and different and fabulous than what's going on in our lives. But that's not true. We all stay home sometimes on Saturday nights and watch TV.' The message board of his site, though, was full of entries from site users offering to trade nude images of him. Williams asked them to stop and by early July he posted this message of his own: 'For all of you who think it is unrealistic for me to make these requests, I have one thing to say (well, actually a few): 1. Fuck off 2. Do not return to the site 3. Don't let the doorknob hit you on the ass on the way out.' But like many such sites, launched innocently enough when the technology became affordable, Sean Patrick Alive! is now a fully fledged porn site. Williams long ago tired of his personal exposure and gave way to others only too willing to exploit the brand he had created. Some were intent on dollars right from the start. VoyeursDorm.com paid six female college students to allow their sorority room to be webcast. It cost fans of these girls $30 a month to watch. Another, Isabella@home, laid on lap-dancing displays from her own apartment at $21 a time. She was reported to have made $2 million in 1998, her first year of operation. And the hazards of self-exposure became apparent when Elizabeth Ann Oliver allowed the birth of her baby to be broadcast live. She was recognised by the Florida police and arrested for cheque fraud.

Peeping Moe.com was a site which regularly updated its community on who was exhibiting on the net and what excitements they were offering. In its chat rooms aficionados could chew over their common experiences. In a question and answer session a communicant defended this apparent voyeurism, arguing there was nothing derogatory about it. For some it was entertainment – no more corrupting than TV or the movies. For others it was a method of observing human nature as if through a microscope. Crucially, they could now participate in the web cam operator's life via email, chat rooms and message boards. Interacting with the exhibitor and other fans was proving far more satisfying than traditional forms of entertainment. These observations are typical of web users who love being unmediated. A great prize awaited anyone who could replicate this experience as part of an entertainment format. John de Mol was working on it and one hurdle had been removed from his path.

SVT, the Swedish broadcaster of *Expedition Robinson*, had completed their enquiry. They concluded that there was no proof that Savija's death was as a result of his taking part in the programme. The rest of the series was transmitted and, by its final, became the most popular show in Sweden in 1997. Now SVT was planning a second series for 1998 and other countries in Scandinavia were gearing up to launch their own versions. Charlie Parsons' idea had, itself, survived and was now beginning to prosper. Parsons was in the United States producing a daily, late-night talk show for the Fox channel, *The Keenen Ivory Wayans Show*. Keenen Wayans later became very wealthy by directing *Scary Movie*, but he had started as a comedian from a family of black entertainers. Parsons hated working with him: 'They'd given him too good a deal. So much money and total creative control.' Now that *Survive*'s name had been cleared, and believing, hoping even, that *The Keenen Ivory Wayans Show* would soon come to an end, Parsons decided to make another attempt to sell his pet project. He went to see the Fox Network. The programme chiefs he spoke to there were enthusiastic but noncommittal. They recommended that Parsons team up with a producer called Mark Burnett, who had been producing a successful series for USA Network called *Eco-Challenge*.

Burnett was a former British army paratrooper who had fought in the Falklands and served in Northern Ireland. He landed in Hollywood as a children's nanny, a job he won by pointing out to the family that he could double as a security guard. He began working in television by accident. Competing for an American team in a bizarre French race, he needed to find a sponsor: ten days in the Middle East with camels and horses was expensive. He managed to borrow television footage of the contest and have the programme aired on a Disney-owned channel. Burnett was, first and foremost, an adventurer and he made things happen.

Unfortunately, after his experience with Keenen Wayans, Parsons did not feel like collaborating with anyone. He wanted to control his next project so he dismissed the idea. But shortly afterwards he met Burnett by chance, at a party: 'What are you doing?' asked Burnett. Taking a deep breath and stepping over his most recent experience, Parsons replied: 'I'm developing a format called *Survive* – a challenge on a desert island.' 'That sounds good,' said Burnett. In fact it was perfect for this rugged soldier of fortune. The dialogue that started that evening led to Burnett being earmarked as the executive producer of the first US series of *Survive* if it was ever to happen. In the meantime Parsons returned to Britain and, with renewed energy, went back to the ITV network. The previous network director, Marcus Plantin, had left. His successor, David Liddiment, presented a new target for Parsons. He went to see him and offered *Survive*. He remained passionate about the idea but he blew the pitch. Once he had described the games, the challenges and the desert island it sounded very complicated. Liddiment was unimpressed: 'All great shows in the end are very, very simple ideas. The cleverness of *Survive* was the balloon debate – the voting out of the people one by one. Parsons overcomplicated it.' Nor did he show any of the Swedish programmes on tape. Parsons knew the meeting had not gone well: 'I never even got a letter saying "thanks for coming"'. Liddiment turned it down flat. In his country of birth Parsons was still getting nowhere. He would now have to concentrate all his efforts on the US.

John de Mol had given Paul Romer the task of working out how to make Project X. Was it possible to produce? How much would it cost? He had no idea where to start. But Romer is very calm and methodical – balding, softly spoken, bespectacled – he looks more like an insurance salesman than a producer of high-octane television. He started to compile a list of the logistics required for a programme the like of which had not been seen before. An enclosed, film-set house ... fixed cameras shooting twenty-four hours a day ... the generation of vast quantities of videotape rushes . . . the need to turn round a skilfully edited programme every day for a year. Romer was drawing up budgets that, in their scope and ambition, resembled the preparations that a medium-sized country might make for war. He consulted the largest television facility company in Holland. They brought in Sony to advise on cameras and editing systems. He spoke to two psychiatrists from the University of Amsterdam. They said that if the idea of Project X was to make life as unpleasant as possible the participants would crack. So Romer dropped the idea of harassing the housemates – the confinement itself was pressuring enough. By this time they had found a name for it – *The Golden Cage* – emphasising both the sense of captivity and of being watched.

From January 1998 Romer had instituted a series of tests that convinced him this mad idea they had concocted in the early hours of the morning might actually work. First he had asked some colleagues to sit in a room and pretend they were cooped up in a house. They did this with such conviction that, in the space of an hour, they began to get irritated with each other. Then he asked a group of six strangers to congregate in a bare TV studio for a few hours while he played the cameras on them. Romer hired a voice-over artist to make God-like announcements to them over some loudspeakers: 'You have all been in the house for two weeks. Housemate A had a task – to clean the toilet. He has not done it. How do you all feel?' Romer watched from the control gallery as the six guinea pigs began to argue. They became angry and highly emotional. He videotaped it and showed it to John de Mol. They both felt they had to take the project further.

By May 1998 Romer had finally decided upon a production approach. He had finished costing it and established that *The Golden Cage* would cost thirty-five million guilders – eleven and a half million pounds. That was half the entire programme budget of some Dutch channels. The project was unfeasibly expensive. At this point Romer readily admits he would have given up. It just wasn't practical. But de Mol challenged him to keep working on the idea. He said they should turn the luxury house into a simple cabin. Now that they were no longer trying to coerce the competitors out of the house he introduced the idea of a nomination vote among the housemates. This would ensure they would be able to evict them and narrow down the Golden Cagers to a single winner of the million-guilder prize. De Mol added a dynamic new element. Once the participants had nominated two of their number for eviction the viewing public would make the final decision via a telephone vote. This innovation would eventually prove to be the single most popular and remunerative element of *Big Brother*.

In London Paul Smith saw a new opportunity for *Cash Mountain*. ITV had announced their target of growing ITV's audience by a percentage point in prime time for each of the next three years. In an era of declining channel share this seemed ambitious to the point of recklessness. To achieve it they needed some big hits and a new approach. Just as Charlie Parsons had done with *Survive*, Smith had to have another go at Britain's premier entertainment network. If he had known of Parsons' failure with the new man, David Liddiment, would he have bothered? Yes, because he believed in his show so much. He immediately contacted his great ally, Claudia Rosencrantz, and said that they had to repitch to her new boss: 'I know it's the right time to do it.' 'No, it isn't, it's too early,' replied Rosencrantz. She preferred a softly-softly approach to getting Liddiment interested. 'Will you allow me to go to David direct?' asked an impatient Smith. 'I can't stop you,' she responded. Smith wrote her a letter to confirm that that was what he was going to do. He then sent the *Cash Mountain* idea to Liddiment. He got a call a few days later: 'Come in and see me.'

So in April 1998 Smith once more found himself in reception at ITV's Network Centre. He was sitting beside a massive, tropical tank. Big, predatory-looking fish were chasing nervous minnows across its wide expanse. He identified instinctively with the minnows. But that was about to change. He took the lift up to the fourth floor. The small reception area looked straight across the open well of the modern building to the director of programmes' glass-walled office. Liddiment was issuing instructions to his secretary. Then she walked round to usher Smith in. Claudia Rosencrantz joined them. Smith was psyched up to pitch *Cash Mountain* as passionately this hundredth time as he had at the beginning. What Smith did not know was that Rosencrantz had prepared the ground well. Liddiment had some research his predecessor, Plantin, had already commissioned. It showed that British viewers would be quite happy to see £1 million given away on television.

Liddiment had different reservations. For the first time in a television quiz Smith and his team intended to give the competitors four multiple-choice answers to choose from. Surely giving the answer away like this would make it too easy and destroy all the tension. Smith was prepared for this. He put his briefcase on Liddiment's desk and took a list of questions out of it. He asked Liddiment to empty his wallet on to the desk. It contained £100. Smith matched it with £100 from his own pocket and invited Liddiment to play *Cash Mountain*. The prize money was £200 and he could, of course, go 50/50 or phone a friend, in this case Rosencrantz, poised on the sofa. As Liddiment answered the questions and built up his prize pot he began to realise that the four multiple-choice answers were, in fact, a brilliant device. They empowered the participant and every viewer, however ignorant. But as the money at stake rose and the possible answers drew closer together the dilemmas and uncertainties grew dramatically. He cashed in once he had won the £200 rather than risk it further. This answered his second big question – whether competitors would win the top prize too often and bankrupt them all.

Liddiment was now completely hooked. But he had a third problem. What if not enough viewers phoned up to take part? Then the prize money could not be raised and, once again, the network could rack up unaffordable losses. At this point Smith

took the single biggest risk of his career. He promised to underwrite any prize money unsecured by call revenue. It could have
turned out to be millions and millions of pounds, it could have
ruined him. But he believed in the mechanics of his show and its
appeal to the public. Privately, though, even Smith took precautions, checking that his co-shareholder, Avesco, had the
back-up cash and pledging his own shares to cover the cost if
things went badly wrong. ITV indicated they would help by
covering half of any deficit. This was beginning to sound more
like financial risk management than television production.

Liddiment finally announced he would commission *Cash
Mountain*. After two and a half years someone wanted it. For
Smith it was like being told you were sane after an enforced
period in an asylum. Liddiment asked Smith if he could get it on
air by the summer. He wanted a new show to combat the BBC's
coverage of the football World Cup. Smith declined. He knew
from experience how much work they still had to do piloting the
show to get it right. Then Liddiment and his scheduler, David
Bergg, made a much more extraordinary suggestion – that they
should 'strip' the show every day. At the time the only stripped
programmes ran in the daytime schedule. It was universally
acknowledged that stripping in prime time would be a disaster.
Audiences liked variety. Liddiment had made this bold, almost
reckless, suggestion because of how Smith had explained the
format to him: 'Look, David, the great thing about this show is
that it isn't conclusive. There isn't one beginning, middle or end
in each show. There are lots of beginnings, middles and ends.
You can stop it wherever you want. But ideally you stop it when
someone's sitting there, saying, "I don't know if I want to go for
the half-million-pound question or not." You have someone on
a knife edge, a cliff edge, at the end of a half-hour and therefore
you get a hold over the audience. They will come back the next
day to see what's going to happen. This is genuinely rare for a
game show.' How many blank looks had Smith received when

delivering this speech in the previous two years? This time Liddiment simply got it. He had already decided on the need for 'stunts' in his schedule and this was perfect.

But Liddiment was so worried about the prize money he made one more suggestion. How about limiting the top pay-out to a single million per series? Smith argued strongly this would water down the proposition – there should be the possibility of a millionaire every night. Liddiment relented and, with a deep breath, confirmed the commission. Smith finally had *Cash Mountain* up and running, and with a revolutionary, stripped scheduling pattern. He staggered back to see his partners in the quest – Briggs, Knight and Whitehill. It was game on.

The programme deals with ITV were more advantageous to the producer than those with any other British broadcaster. ITV would simply take a licence to transmit the programme three times over a period of five years. Everything else – ownership of the format, the finished programmes and the merchandising revenue – stayed with the producer. But there was a drawback. Because they were not sharing in the booty ITV paid producers little or nothing to make pilots and did not cash-flow the production. Paul Smith was now betting all his company's resources, a good deal of his own savings and, ultimately, his home, on the belief that *Cash Mountain* would succeed. If it were to be cancelled prematurely he would be financially ruined. If it were a huge hit but with a million pound winner a week he would be equally ruined. Without hesitation he took the bet.

At his spacious house in Surrey he set up all the computers and graphics generators that were to drive the show. For days on end throughout a humid summer he and his colleagues rehearsed. They had agreed on Chris Tarrant as presenter – David Briggs had worked with him at Capital Radio when they had concocted cash-prize competitions to drive the ratings of Tarrant's highly successful breakfast show. Tarrant joined them as they painstakingly worked out the catchphrases that were to become world famous within a few months: 'Is that your final answer?'; 'Fastest Finger First'; and, of course, 'Phone a friend'. Once a format has entered the popular imagination its plot and rules seem perfectly clear and almost part of the natural order of things. But that's not how it is at the development phase. Then nothing is obvious and there's little more guidance than personal hunch as to whether each element will gel. Smith's team were working towards a week of pilots in August and transmission in September. That's when they would find out if they had been wasting their time during the previous three years. And when Smith would discover whether this idea was to bankrupt him.

Meanwhile, someone else was also working on creating a game-show millionaire. But it was rather a different game show. De Mol decided it was time to pitch *The Golden Cage*, however unethical, impractical or unaffordable it might be. He started with RTL4, the channel for which he now produced *All You Need Is Love*. 'The reaction was very disappointing. I was prepared for an extreme reaction like – hey, idiot, go home and don't talk to me about it any more . . . this is too far out . . . this is impossible. Or even an extremely positive reaction. But I got – yeah, um, yeah, I don't know. Could be interesting. Maybe. Yeah. Blah blah.' It took them two weeks to come back to de Mol with the message that the only thing they knew was that they didn't know. Then de Mol moved on to the other commercial broadcaster, SBS. There the chief executive was Fons van Westerloo. De Mol invited him over to his house one Saturday morning for a personal pitch over coffee: 'De Mol's a great salesman. He never believes it can be anything than a big success. He tells you it will cost thirty-five mil-lion guilders. Then, later, when he offers it for less it sounds cheap. He reaches for the stars and lands on the moon.' Van Westerloo was excited but aghast at the same time. He had never heard such an original but dangerous idea. They had a number of subse-quent meetings as they explored the idea together. Eventually he had to decide whether to commission *The Golden Cage*. The thirty-five-million-guilder price was as much as a fifth of his entire programme budget for a year. But he still felt there might be an imaginative solution to the cost. He called twelve of his closest colleagues together in a Chinese restaurant in Amsterdam. He described *The Golden Cage* to them. They were all very scared by it. Fortified by egg fried rice and spring rolls they decided to reject *The Golden Cage*. He called de Mol with the decision. In frustration de Mol then ordered Paul Romer to make a tape to explain *The Golden Cage* in a more positive way.

One copy of this original videotape still exists. Against a soundtrack of *Carmina Burana*, the dramatic, profane oratorio composed by Carl Orff, a bold title emerges: *The Golden Cage*. And it is swept by a red stripe of radar, just to establish the theme of surveillance. Then, with shots of a NASA space launch, a dramatic voice-over announces: 'Total isolation! Lonely but not alone! No normal life, no normal time, no newspaper, no telephone, no TV. Compared to this new television project space travel is like a Sunday School picnic!' The tape goes on to deliver the hardest sell that de Mol had ever concocted: '*The Golden Cage* throws the ultimate challenge to a group of volunteers. A long year together in an isolated building somewhere remote. Dependent on each other without contact with the outside world. Can anyone stand this? Nobody's tried it. But whoever pulls it off becomes a millionaire. Six people trying. Why? People who've never met. Why are they doing this? Is it adventure? Pushing their limits? Money? Whatever their reasons, they'll do it. But what does this kind of thing do to you? Can anyone stand this?' Next a bearded German professor speculates threateningly about the dissolution of an individual's personality. And two members of the American Biosphere project talk about how incarceration for two years led to breakdown of trust between those taking part. The voice-over drives on: 'Totally isolated. Constantly observed. Life in a glasshouse ... watched by mission control and the TV audience. Scary?'

Then the tape begins to sound eerily as though it is, in fact, a promotion for *The Truman Show*: 'They'll be stars of a series written by life itself. Wherever they are, whatever they do, whatever they go through ... Every breath will be recorded and broadcast.' It then cuts to an interview Endemol had done with Jennifer Ringley about Jennicam, now two years into her triumph of self-exposure. It is followed by footage of one of Romer's experiments. Six people who had met each other just an hour before are shown to be only too happy to vote one of their number out of the studio. He departs with a surprised, rueful expression on his face. The voice-over continues over security camera footage: 'Big Brother is watching you is never truer than in *The Golden Cage*. What does being constantly observed do to you? There's never been a TV project with so unpredictable an outcome and so glorious a victory. *The Golden Cage* week in, week out. It can't be done but it will be. Observation. Manipulation. Hope. The naked truth of *The Golden Cage*!' This tape was destined to be shown widely to companies within the Endemol group. *The Golden Cage*'s detractors were even more appalled than before. And at that moment the detractors were in a clear majority.

In 1998 Endemol had bought stakes in production companies in France, Sweden and, finally, Britain. Broadcast Communications was a television producer owned by The Guardian Media Group. It specialised in leisure entertainment formats which it had sold around the world, shows such as *Ready Steady Cook* and *Changing Rooms*, the latter known as *Trading Spaces* in the US. I was one of its principals, Tom Barnicoat was the other. We had decided that our company would be better off allied to a television company than a newspaper group. As the deal was being negotiated Endemol began to reveal some of the formats it felt had the most potential for English-speaking territories. *The Golden Cage* was top of the list. We Brits were as nervous of the idea as everyone else. On 11 May I sent Barnicoat a memo: 'This is far too cruel, and wilfully so, for the UK market. The only way this would work would be if some organisation needed to carry out such exercises with people so they could be assessed for team working and leadership. Say, to judge suitability for a polar trek. But which organisation?' On 10 July I faxed a more diplomatic memo to John de Mol:

> We have now had the chance to consider *The Golden Cage* more fully in our creative meetings. Our views are as follows. It is a bold innovative concept. It takes the relatively well-known 'desert-island' concepts and catapults them on to an altogether more dangerous level while, at the same time, making the action much closer to home. If I may make an absurd reduction: the rats-in-a-cage-who'll-do-anything-for-money is something that I doubt we could sell on to terrestrial television. These somewhat conservative chaps would need to inject a socially positive agenda such as some sort of ecology angle (i.e. biosphere) or problem-solving exercise (i.e. to make the participants better people). They'd be particularly nervous of the way in which the producer plays God for the entertainment of viewers. The one network, which might have the money and might like the outrageousness of the idea is Sky One. So we could pitch it to Liz Murdoch. But as currently constituted, we feel the show has a narrow market in the UK.

The doubters of *The Golden Cage* were lining up in a queue that was becoming longer and longer.

In August 1998 Paul Smith finally began piloting *Cash Mountain*, or *Who Wants to Be a Millionaire?* as ITV had now pressed for it to be called. It was a matter of days before this show had to appear on ITV prime time. The launch date was set – Friday 4 September. Smith had put a production team together and told them to design a set in the round. He wanted a highly pressured, almost gladiatorial atmosphere. Then he let the team get on with it. When he saw the set and the lighting for the first time he was desperately disappointed. It was brightly lit and full of chrome – much like any other game show set. The music was oppressively jolly too – a jingly pop song from Pete Waterman's hit factory called 'Cloud Nine'. Claudia Rosencrantz called it laughable. Smith resolved to change everything. They hated the design of the television screen as well. To accommodate the multiple-choice questions the competitors were shrunk down into a tiny box. Smith burst out: 'Someone is deliberating whether they're going for a half a million pounds. You want to see the sweat on their brow. You want to see their nostrils dilating. You want to see all the signs of panic, nervously biting their lips.' In truth, he was worried sick. There was no atmosphere in the studio. It all seemed so flat. On the way home Smith sat in his car hyperventilating. The man dubbed by his peers as one of the most tense, anxious people in television now had plenty to be anxious about.

Smith told them to redesign the set, reconfigure the graphics and come up with new music. He demanded two cameras on the contestant at all times to deliver intimate close-ups. This meant thousands and thousands more pounds of expenditure by Celador even before they were on air. The already huge financial risk was growing greater by the day, as were all the other risks. The abyss that habitually opens before you launch a brand-new, prime-time show seemed wider and deeper than ever. David Liddiment was less downcast when he saw the pilot. He wrote a letter confirming all the changes needed, adding, 'There's still a great idea there trying to get out.'

Smith's team had to revamp the entire look and feel of the show in two weeks flat. They then all reassembled in the studio in the first week of September 1998. They were to record the first programme on Thursday 3 September, video-edit it overnight and then transmit it the day after. The dramatic, dark lighting and the driving music were revealed for the first time. The trademarks of *Who Wants to Be a Millionaire?* are now known the world over. Here they were at the prototype stage. Would they work? It was the beginning of September, the most competitive point in television's calendar. Would Britain watch, particularly ten nights in a row? Most critically of all, would viewers phone in to get on the show? Only if they did in their millions would Smith be able to pay for the prizes. This was agonising.

Claudia Rosencrantz's darkest moment came the night before the first transmission. She rang David Liddiment. 'Am I mad?' she asked him. 'I'm so depressed. I don't know why we're doing this.' 'You're wrong,' comforted Liddiment. 'This is just first-night nerves. We'll be fine.'

At eight o'clock on Friday 4 September a sponsorship message pops up on to the ITV network. A bored looking family bursts into life as *Who Wants to Be a Millionaire?* is announced on their television set. The bringer of this joy into their lives is revealed as the *Sun*, Britain's biggest tabloid newspaper and the show's marketing partner. At one minute past eight the ITV network cuts to a very sombre Chris Tarrant, standing against a plain, black backdrop: 'Tonight and for the next ten nights you'll be watching British quiz show history. For the first time on UK TV we have a top prize available of one million pounds and it could be won here tonight. No tricks, no traps. Contestants will leave here tonight with big cash prizes and if they have the skill and nerve someone could leave here a millionaire. To find out how you could take part or just share the tension, the tears and triumphs at home join us for *Who Wants to Be a Millionaire?*' The new programme titles follow. They have a nakedly religious theme and the god in question is Mammon: rays of light fall on fervently happy members of the British public. Then the source of the light is revealed – a sun composed entirely of pound signs.

Chris Tarrant welcomes viewers from the dramatic amphitheatre set. He looks and sounds nervous, cracking a scripted gag about Monica Lewinsky that isn't necessary – this new show doesn't need padding out with comedy. The very first winner of 'Fastest Finger First' is a Graham Elwell. It takes him 0.69 seconds to answer correctly that a bit is the smallest unit in a computer's memory. He joins Tarrant in the centre, the lighting plunges to a cold blue and *Millionaire* has finally started. Elwell's initial question, for £100 is, 'Which part of its body does a woodpecker use for pecking?' The now classic musical underlay – a heavenly choir with an insistent heartbeat, drives on as Elwell gets the first ever answer on *Millionaire* right. A brief break in the tension with applause, the lights go up and then back to the pressure of question two for £200. Questions about wordplay, Wellington boots, darts and the Oscars get Elwell to £1000. All with the trademark four options on the screen. The genius of this multiple choice is that viewers across Britain, whether polymaths or ignoramuses, are now all having a go at the correct answer.

At this point Tarrant issues his second invitation to viewers at home to call in and book a place on the show so they too can be just fifteen questions away from a million pounds. Up to the launch Paul Smith knows that they have received around four hundred thousand advance calls – a promising start but not nearly enough to fund the prizes. Further questions on lexicons, biathlons, car manufacturers and Houdini take Elwell to £16,000. Celador are blessed with an opening contestant who is going to win some serious money. The next question is for £32,000. 'Which religious group shelters Harrison Ford in the film *Witness*?' Before he can answer they go to the commercial break. This is followed by another promotion of the telephone numbers to call. By correctly choosing the Amish, Elwell then chalks up his £32,000, a point at which he is offered a cheque for that amount. It is guaranteed whatever happens. He chooses to go on and try for £64,000. The studio audience is genuinely hushed and tense. For £64,000 Tarrant asks him which stately home was the first to open its doors to the public. He decides to go on but relies on the first of his lifelines – '50/50' – to remove two of the incorrect answers. He now has to choose between Wilton House or Blenheim Palace. He chooses Wilton House. Tarrant teases him: . . . 'Is that your final answer?' He sticks to it. He has won £64,000 and the audience goes wild. He then decides to look at the question for £125,000: 'Which country is sandwiched between Ghana and Benin?' Before he commits to answering he takes his second lifeline and calls his grandfather, John Williams. Tarrant tells him: 'Graham has just won £64,000.' 'That's nice,' responds Grandad to audience laughter. He's then given thirty seconds to come up with the answer for his grandson. But he can't. Elwell decides to take the £64,000. The audience screams as Tarrant announces: 'How about sixty-four thousand smackeroos?'

True to Smith's promise that *Millionaire* is the show that rolls on from progamme to programme, they have time to select another player, Rachel Da Costa. This is the contestant that Smith will always remember more than any other, even those who actually won a million pounds. Da Costa reaches £500 before the end of the show. There is yet another call for viewers to phone in and Tarrant invites everyone to watch the next day, Saturday, to see how Da Costa does. And then the half-hour is up.

Smith was not going to receive any ratings for the Friday night show until the following Monday. The only barometer he had was the number of phone calls received. This was promising – two hundred thousand in one evening. But a relatively small number of people can generate a large number of calls by multiple dialling. No one at Celador could know how many were watching for another two and a half days. They were recording each show the day before it was broadcast. At the end of the second show's taping Smith called Rosencrantz excitedly: 'It was incredible tonight. It was all about emotions and life-changing decisions!'

At 8.01 the next evening, Saturday 5 September, the second edition of *Millionaire* opens with a potted version of the night before. Elwell wins his £64,000 all over again just to whet the appetite of viewers. Among these is the Network Centre director of programmes, David Liddiment, sitting with his mother Bessie at her home in Huddersfield. The show opens with Tarrant reintroducing Rachel Da Costa, who remains on £500. Tarrant asks her what she would do with a million pounds if she won it. 'Clear my debts, clear my fiancé's debts, sort out our business . . . and get married.' There is a cutaway to her fiancé in the audience and an audible 'ah' from the studio. 'When are you planning to get married?' asks Tarrant. 'May 2000,' she replies. 'Because our business is not in a situation to do it.' 'Well,' says Tarrant to her fiancé, 'it might be May 2000 but it might be tomorrow!'

Da Costa hears her first question of the night for £1000. It is based on wordplay and she gets it right. Tarrant leans towards her fiancé and says that brings the wedding forward at least to January 2000. Another question requiring Da Costa to identify the function of an abacus takes her to £2000. Now, for £4000, she has to name the café owner played by Humphrey Bogart in *Casablanca*. Was it Sam, Kyle, Jack or Rick? She doesn't know. She chooses the 50/50 lifeline. Two wrong answers are removed and she is left with a choice between Sam and Rick. 'Play it again, Sam' is the line going through her head but she doesn't dare choose Sam. She can't decide. She puts her head in her hands. The studio audience, to a man and woman, is willing her on. She decides to use a second lifeline and ask them. They press their keypads – 31 per cent think the answer is Sam, 69 per cent say it is Rick. Now she is really nervous. She puts her head in her hands again. Her fiancé looks on, unable to help her. Tarrant presses her for her final answer. 'Rick.' He pauses. Then, 'You've won £4000.' The cheers in the studio sound as though she has won a million pounds, so emotional is the atmosphere. Everyone wants her to win the money she needs to marry her fiancé. Da Costa is now visibly panting and has to gulp down a glass of water. But she decides to press on and try for £8000.

'What is the most common bird of prey found in the United Kingdom – a kestrel, a red kite, the golden eagle or a barn owl?' She pauses. 'A kestrel,' she says. 'You've won £8000,' she is told. There are more screams from the audience. She looks at her fiancé. He laughs with relief. She says to Tarrant, 'I'm going to be sick.' 'You can't be sick in front of your fiancé,' he replies. He goes on to warn her that if she goes for £16,000 and gets the question wrong she will fall back to £1000. Da Costa asks to hear the question. 'Which English county has only one border with another county – Devon, Norfolk, Cornwall or Kent?' She doesn't know the answer. 'I'm going to phone my dad,' she says. Jack Mendez Da Costa is staying in a hotel in Scotland. Tarrant gets him on the phone and explains his daughter is trying for £16,000. 'I understand,' he replies solemnly. The clock ticks down from thirty seconds as Rachel reads the question to her dad. He says immediately: 'I've no idea. I'm sorry, Rachel, I can't help you on geography.' He pauses. There's twenty seconds remaining. 'Give it to me again.' She reads it again. There are fifteen seconds left. 'Dad, help me,' implores Rachel. And in reply he begs her, 'Take the eight grand, Rach.' Rachel is in tears, her father Jack is in tears and, in the control gallery, Paul Smith is also in tears. Rachel wipes her eyes. 'I'll take the money,' she tells Tarrant. 'Sure?' 'Yes,' says Rachel. 'Is Jack sure?' 'Yes, I'm afraid so,' says Jack down the telephone line from Scotland. Tarrant checks one more time that Rachel does not want to play on. She confirms her decision and wipes her eyes again. The lights go up, the audience screams and claps and Tarrant shouts above the clamour, 'She's been extraordinary! She's won £8000!' When the applause subsides Tarrant says, 'Just before you go – which county *would* you have said had only one border?' 'Cornwall,' she replies. 'That would've been your answer?' 'Yes.' 'You would've won £16,000.'

Rachel Da Costa had only won £8000 – just one eighth of what Graham Elwell had won the night before. But for Paul Smith this had been the defining moment for *Who Wants to Be a Millionaire?*. At the commercial break he had rushed down the corridor to the control room, still in tears, and embraced the director, Martin Scott: 'Martin,' he gasped. 'You're directing the best drama on television. It's incredible!' After the transmission on Saturday night they learnt that the calls had shot up to 339,000. That couldn't be bad news. The next day, 6 September, a Sunday morning, Smith was driving down the A40 to the studio to record Monday night's show. He got a call on his mobile from Liddiment: 'Brilliant, Paul! My mum loves it. This show is incredible. Anyone can get on, anyone can take part. Everything you've promised happened last night.' Neither of them yet knew the ratings but both were ecstatic. They had reason to be. In just three days they had received almost one million phone calls. This would pay for all the prizes and deliver a substantial surplus. Then, on Monday at 10 a.m., they learnt that the first three shows had won audiences of 9.5 million, 7.8 million and, following the Da Costa episode, 12.4 million. The third show had gained a share of 55 per cent. More than half of British viewers that evening had been watching. By this time Britain had five terrestrial channels and hundreds of satellite channels. This was a sensational result. *Millionaire* was actively reversing ITV's decline, as Liddiment had promised to do a year before. And after three, long years of being rebuffed and ignored Smith and his colleagues had a hit on their hands.

By Monday evening news of the extraordinary twelve-million audience had spread. The bush telegraph was rather more alert than in the 1970s, when it took four years for Smith to sell *It'll*

Be Alright on the Night. On the Tuesday morning faxes and phone calls were streaming into Smith's Covent Garden office: 'Everyone that pertained to be a friend of mine, or that I had met briefly or had a cup of coffee with once, was suddenly my new best friend. Calling from everywhere around the world, saying they want to licence this format.' But Smith was still totally focused on the daily recordings of *Millionaire* for the first run of ten shows. They were still refining the format as they went along. Displaying an extraordinary single-mindedness Smith said to his PA, 'I can't deal with this. I'm producing a TV show at the moment.' Smith was actually sitting in the studio doing the job of monitoring every question that the computer randomly selected to ensure there were no repetitions. He did not have a minute to spare. And he cannot have realised, despite the early ratings, quite how much of a hit he now owned. It was to be a monster. Arguably, measured in viewers and territories, *Millionaire* turned into the most successful TV format ever. Even by the end of the first run of ten days they had chalked up another pair of twelve-million audiences, one of which rated as a 59 per cent share. And just as importantly for Celador's bank balance, they had stimulated more than three million phone calls from fans desperate to come on the show, as Graham Elwell and Rachel Da Costa had.

Between Smith, Parsons and de Mol, Smith had been the first to invent a format and the first to sell one abroad. Now he had a property that the entire television world was trying to buy. Parsons had a property too but no deals in the important territories such as the UK or US. That left de Mol bringing up the rear. It was far from clear that he had a property at all, merely an idea that only he believed in.

Despite de Mol's failure to make any progress with *The Golden Cage*, Endemol remained a far bigger production company than Celador or Planet 24. Towards the end of 1998 the media market was heating up even more rapidly. De Mol looked

at some of the valuations put on other companies and wondered whether there might not be an opportunity for him. In
September Juan Villalonga extended Telefonica's media empire
by buying Spain's third biggest radio network to add to his
existing asset, the TV network Antenna 3. In the US, on 13
November, a company called The Globe.com launched an IPO.
Globe offered a homepage net service and hoped to sell advertisements around it. Up to September that year they had lost
$11.5 million on revenues of $2.7 million. Their shares were
offered at $9 and ended the day trading at a mere $87. On 28
November the NASDAQ passed 2000 for the first time. At that
point AOL bought Netscape, the web browser, for $4.2 billion –
all paid for with rapidly inflating AOL shares, of course. Real
cash did not come into it. The market had truly gone mad.
Could Endemol benefit and find a buyer to remove the company
from the Dutch stock market that de Mol so detested? There
was one possible drawback – Endemol was a company with real
cash flow and real profits. At the time the market demonstrably
preferred companies with little cash flow and no profits. Yes,
read that again – little cash flow and no profits. However, it was
worth a try, so de Mol and van den Ende appointed the London
bank Rothschilds and the Amsterdam bank ABN AMRO to
work together on a sale. They started preparing a slick presentation with the most positive figures possible.

In October de Mol had called all the Endemol group's operating companies together for a conference in Cologne. It was an
abnormally close evening as the managing directors from Europe
and South Africa arrived at a modern, concrete palace of a hotel.
They were greeted by a bizarre and dishevelled town-crier figure
in a tricorn hat. Endemol Germany, the hosts, were trying to
lend some gravitas to the occasion but succeeded only in impart-
ing the proceedings with an air of surreality. This atmosphere
was compounded when de Mol sat his colleagues down to watch
the completed *Golden Cage* tape. At the end there was total

silence. No one spoke. Finally de Mol intervened: 'Come on, gentlemen, say something.' There were a few coughs followed by some noncommittal remarks. But the truth was that everyone was petrified by the idea. Only one person spoke up for *The Golden Cage* – Carl Fischer from South Africa. He believed in it and was enthusiastic. But he was the only one.

Not long afterwards de Mol decided to shorten the show from a year to one hundred days. He cut the prize money from a million guilders to two hundred thousand. And he resolved to try to sell the idea on the back of the forthcoming millennium. The winner would emerge from the house at midnight on 31 December 1999. The title *The Golden Cage* was dropped in favour of *Big Brother*, although de Mol had never properly read George Orwell's novel *Nineteen Eighty-Four* (nor would he ever). So, at the end of 1998, de Mol had set himself two big challenges for the year ahead. Sell *Big Brother* by September or miss the millennium. Sell Endemol or remain subject to the tyranny of the stock market. The more pressing of the two was *Big Brother*. There had already been two movies – *Ed TV* and *The Truman Show*. On 8 October 1998, unbeknown to de Mol, a stunt was launched on Australian radio. A maverick disc jockey called Andrew Denton had come up with *House From Hell*. He locked a handful of volunteers in a televised house for three months. He then gave them challenges and played tricks on them. The results were broadcast daily on his radio show and, later, once a week in a TV show on Channel 10. Ideas do not keep. Who else would have this one before de Mol could get *Big Brother* on air?

CHAPTER SIX

The Worth of a Man

You can calculate the worth of a man by the number of his enemies, and the importance of a work of art by the harm that is spoken of it.

GUSTAVE FLAUBERT

De Mol remained obsessed by *Big Brother* – ten people, one house, one hundred days and no buyers. He tried to stoke up interest in Germany, Endemol's other main market. He made evangelical calls to the heads of its main television stations. Among these was Georg Kofler, the boss at ProSieben, the network in which Leo Kirch owned the majority of the shares. It remained predominantly a film channel, its character still defined by the movie deals Kirch had done years before. Kofler's job was to try to increase its share of the television market from 13.5 to a target of 15 per cent. To achieve this he had appointed a new director of programmes, Borris Brandt, with the brief to inject entertainment shows into the programme mix. Brandt had worked in advertising, then for both Twentieth Century Fox and Disney importing American shows into Germany and finally as a writer of movie thrillers. Kofler hired him to improve the quality of ProSieben's TV films and within six months had made him director of programmes. He was told that if he could deliver that 15 per cent share he would be paid a million Deutschmark bonus, approximately £400,000.

Borris Brandt is short with curly blond hair and piercing blue eyes. He positively overflows with cherubic enthusiasm. He had commissioned an early success – a comedy show based around a German comedian, Stefan Raab. He also bought in a format from Belgium which, like *Big Brother*, was an early example of reality television. *The Mole* sets a team of competitors various physical challenges. Their ability to complete them is hampered by one participant who is in league with the producers and whose job is to sabotage the efforts of the rest. They, in turn, have to unmask the saboteur. *The Mole* was hard evidence that the television market was rapidly catching on to the possibility of 'real' people shows and that *Big Brother* was facing growing competition. Neither of these formats was going to be powerful enough on its own to propel ProSieben to the magic 15 per cent. Brandt needed more. He thought up the germ of an idea, *Roses From Your Ex*, in which divorced couples might be encouraged to get back together again. He admired Endemol's existing hits in Germany, *All You Need Is Love* and *Love Letters*. Brandt suggested to Kofler that de Mol should produce *Roses From Your Ex* for ProSieben. Kofler owed de Mol a call anyway, having been contacted about *Big Brother*, so he agreed and Brandt called de Mol in Hilversum. 'No problem,' purred de Mol down the telephone, his charm enveloping anyone who presented the prospect of a sale. 'Come here and we'll discuss it. We'll do it for you.'

Brandt was genuinely flattered because de Mol was, of course, now a big figure in European entertainment. He took a taxi from Schiphol Airport outside Amsterdam to the new Endemol headquarters at Hilversum, a modernist building of white stone and clean, geometric lines designed by Richard Meier. It nestled in woods surrounded, by contrast, with gabled, comfortably bourgeois Dutch houses. Its car park had concrete cubes poking out of the grass verge containing television screens. These outdoor monitors pumped out Endemol programmes, twenty-four hours a day, lest any visitors should be in any doubt about the entertainment factory they were about to enter. De Mol personally came down to greet Brandt in reception and escort him to his office: 'I felt very cosy. He was really taking me seriously, not like the boring, cautious executives at ProSieben. I called my wife, Dani, and I told her that de Mol was a great guy, so friendly and so open.'

The moment they reached de Mol's office, however, the small talk came to an end. *Roses From Your Ex* was touched upon but only briefly. Once Brandt had said he was willing to take risks de Mol saw his chance: 'There is something. But till now everybody has been afraid of doing it. Perhaps you're the one.' De Mol then described *Big Brother* to him. Brandt's eyes widened and there was a churning sensation of nervous excitement in his stomach. He was immediately sold on the idea. It was true that Big Brother had a particularly unsettling, totalitarian significance for Germany. His colleagues might take some persuading. But he knew he had to sell it to them and be the first channel in the world to make this shockingly avant-garde programme.

Back at ProSieben's offices, on an industrial estate on the outskirts of Munich, Brandt assembled a handful of key executives. He wanted to seduce a majority of them and then seek Kofler's blessing. He had prepared carefully: 'Big Brother in Germany had the feeling coming from the fascist kind of thing – hidden cameras, looking at what people do – it's a strange feeling.' So he decided to concentrate on how modern and exciting the idea was. As members of ProSieben's executive board sat in silence he explained the concept of *Big Brother*. Rainer Laux, the head of magazine programmes, loved the idea. (So much so that he later produced *Big Brother* – but not for ProSieben and not in 1999.) Other departmental chiefs were also intrigued. But then it came to the head of press and public relations, Thorsten Rossmann:

'No way. This will lead to appalling press coverage. Nobody is interested is this sort of stuff. Forget it.' Rossmann's objections were to be taken seriously. He was known to be close to Kirch. Rossmann was strongly supported by another colleague, but they were in a minority. Next Brandt lobbied Kofler himself, pointing out that a majority of the executives were in favour. Kofler could also see the dramatic benefits if the show became a hit. He needed to reach a 15 per cent share just as much as Brandt. But he wanted wholehearted support from his management. Kofler suggested renaming the show *The Experiment* to remove the fascist stigma (no one seemed to realise that *The Experiment* could be seen as an altogether more sinister title). It was then agreed to invite de Mol to come to try to win over the doubters personally.

Shortly afterwards de Mol travelled to ProSieben's offices at Unterfoehring. Well briefed, he pitched *The Experiment* with absolute conviction. He did not mention *Big Brother* or show the original tape that Paul Romer had made for *The Golden Cage*. A new, heavily edited, version had been produced. The entire performance was designed to excite them without alarming them.

John de Mol remembers very clearly walking into the ProSieben boardroom: 'There were twenty people, sat there looking at me, like – who the hell are you that we have to sit here altogether and listen to you. I showed them the reworked tape. I explained, for the first time, how the twenty-four-hour pictures could be put out on the internet. To the internet guys from ProSieben this was all new – they were crazy about it. After two hours twenty stubborn Germans were jumping on the table. We flew back to Holland really excited. If we'd had a bottle of champagne onboard we would have opened it. We were a hundred per cent sure we had a deal.' But to be more precise, eighteen Germans were jumping on the table. Two remained not just unconvinced but hostile.

After de Mol left the room Thorsten Rossmann returned to the attack, saying the idea of ten imprisoned housemates meant they would be seen as '*Untermenschen*'. This was a shocking word for everyone in the room to hear. *Untermenschen* means underclass and it was the term the Nazis employed for the Jews and other races they despised. Brandt and de Mol had unwittingly torched a deep scar on the German psyche. Rossmann's belief that *Big Brother* involved inhuman, degrading treatment was then supported by another colleague: 'Nobody will watch it. This is not premium TV. This is dirty TV. You would be treating people like animals.' Despite these emotional outbursts a majority were still in favour. So was Kofler. Before de Mol's departure Brandt had assured him that the project would go ahead. He even went home that evening and told his wife: 'We will be doing the most thrilling thing ever in the world of TV and I will be leading it.' But he had underestimated his opponents. Whether they formally enlisted the support of Kirch and other shareholders or not, within forty-eight hours Kofler felt unable to proceed. Brandt was deputed to call de Mol: 'John, I told you two days ago we will do it. But we can't. I have been defeated by the programme's enemies.' De Mol replied, forcefully: 'Are you crazy? This is shit. How can this happen? You told me it was a "yes".' 'I'm so sorry,' replied Brandt.

Not long afterwards Kofler left ProSieben and was replaced by Ludwig Bauer, the former head of the cable division and a man with his own doubts about *Big Brother*. To quell Brandt's continuing obsession with the format he rang his fellow programme directors at rival German broadcasters such as RTL. They assured him they would never commission such a disreputable programme either. Brandt's days were numbered. Like many other former de Mol clients, he would eventually end up working for Endemol. But in the meantime he needed a new job. His departure was somewhat softened by a £160,000 payoff with which he bought himself a compensatory toy – a limited edition Jaguar sports car. By now de Mol was wealthy enough to buy several fleets of Jaguars, but that did not interest him. He wanted to sell *Big Brother*. He would have to return to doing the rounds once more in Holland. But it was the spring of 1999 and he only had six months to get the show commissioned and on air if he was to complete it by the eve of the millennium.

In contrast, *Who Wants to Be a Millionaire?* was winning every available award in the twelve months following its launch. It was also spreading across the world, territory by territory. Eventually the show would air in 106 countries and earn Celador and their partners revenues of more than $750 million. One early deal was with Endemol. John de Mol found himself back in the familiar position of having to buy in a successful format from elsewhere. This could have been a double source of resentment. Endemol had also turned down the opportunity to own half of *Millionaire* back in 1995, but de Mol did not tend to dwell on such regrets and irritations. He instructed Gary Carter, who had left Planet 24 and Charlie Parsons to work for Endemol, to acquire the rights to *Millionaire*, whatever it took. Carter persuaded Paul Smith to fly to Schiphol Airport. In the coffee shop in Terminal A Gary Carter and he worked out deals for eight Endemol territories. It took just two hours and then Smith returned to London. Acquiring the format for so many territories was, in reality, a coup for Endemol. John de Mol had some genuine frustrations to deal with elsewhere. *Big Brother*'s failure to sell was only one of them.

The other concerned Endemol's share price. It had fallen as low as €20, below its launch price in 1996. It began 1999 at €32, an improvement but still a long way below the level at which it had been offered to the market in the original IPO. The reason for its poor performance was simple: investors still did not like Joop van den Ende's unfathomable theatre division, 'Live Entertainment'. It continued to under perform Endemol's television business. At Schroder Investment Management in

London, which still owned 15 per cent of the available shares, they had seen the price bump along in the mid-twenties (or worse) for three years. Unlike Joop van den Ende, investors cared nothing for the smell of greasepaint. They wanted profits. Van den Ende agreed to buy out 'Live Entertainment' from Endemol into his private ownership. To pay for it he sold one and a half million shares. Endemol's share price rose at the news, which, in turn, enhanced the value of van den Ende's remaining holding. The increase more than compensated for the cost of the theatre division's purchase. In a piece of serendipity the entire transaction paid for itself. John de Mol took the opportunity to sell enough shares to keep his holding and van den Ende's approximately equal. Together they now owned 54 per cent of the company. They had kept control. De Mol still wanted to escape the tyranny of shareholders altogether if he could. And the media markets of the US and Europe were now awash with mergers and acquisitions. It was a time of opportunity for deal makers.

The previous year de Mol and van den Ende had instructed two merchant banks to work together to find a buyer for Endemol. Rothschilds was one of London's oldest merchant banks, having lent the Victorian Prime Minister Benjamin Disraeli the money he needed to buy control of the Suez Canal. The official price of gold was still agreed in a room of the bank, as it had been for two hundred years. ABN AMRO was Holland's largest merchant bank. Together they developed a prospectus and presentation on the company's glowing future. First they had to present this to Endemol's supervisory board. The chairman, Ben Verwaayen, questioned them closely on their tactics. Was this in the interests of all shareholders or merely something to suit John de Mol? Verwaayen was sceptical, despite being on a roller coaster of his own at the time. He had left the Dutch telecoms company KPN. His day job was now vice-president of Lucent Technologies. A fully paid-up member of the US new media boom with the requisite soaring share price. Lucent designed and built networks. Any corporation with any connection to the internet was, for the moment, a glamour stock. Endemol was, by contrast, somewhat conventional. Based on its sluggish share quote Endemol was worth around $700 million. The board finally agreed that they should seek a buyer and the required price was set at $1 billion. On paper, this would make van den Ende's and de Mol's stakes worth approximately $250 million each. These two former rivals had pooled their interests to make each other rich. But such valuations would, within a year, turn out to be hopelessly modest.

Ruud Hendriks was still in charge of Endemol's international expansion. He was now despatched to America and Britain in the role of door-to-door salesman. The product was Endemol, the doors those of the major entertainment corporations. Accompanied by Endemol's bankers he painted a picture of five years of uninterrupted growth to come. It involved taking full control of their international subsidiaries and developing a range of blockbuster formats. Several were named, among them *Big Brother*. But it was given no particular importance or prominence at this point. They were received politely by the heads of each corporation's international division. In Los Angeles Hendriks led the assault on Sony, Universal and Paramount. In London they presented to News Corporation, Disney and Time Warner. The companies heard about an impressive Dutch company that dominated the market for television entertainment in Holland and Germany. It had also built an international network. This did not include the US. But it was an expansive era when deals were presented daily, like so many betting tips. In this case, only the asking price was a problem. $1 billion, despite the blind optimism of the times, was seen as over the odds. Just one company kept the conversation going through the spring and early summer of 1999. Significantly, it was Time Warner, some eight months away from its nemesis deal with AOL in

January 2000. De Mol and Jeffrey Schlesinger, Time Warner's International TV president, dined together in Amsterdam. There were further meetings in Los Angeles with Time Warner's mergers and acquisitions advisers. But Endemol's asking price remained a sticking point. As spring turned into summer, Time Warner's interest also seemed to wane.

Back in Britain, in March 1999, Charlie Parsons and his two business partners received an offer for Planet 24. Carlton was one of the franchise holders making up the commercial network ITV. Led by the mercurial entrepreneur Michael Green, it had won the franchise seven years earlier, but in the intervening period it had failed to produce many successful programmes for the network, unlike its far more successful rival Granada. One solution was to buy more production expertise. Planet 24, with its hit show *The Big Breakfast*, seemed a good target. Another attraction was the idea of placing Parsons' partner, Waheed Alli, in a senior position to see if his infectious energy could galvanise their underwhelming company. By now Alli was a man of substance. The new government of Tony Blair had made him a member of the House of Lords. Lord Alli, gay, in his thirties and of Asian descent, made a statement that appealed to New Labour. Not long afterwards the third partner in Planet 24, Bob Geldof, had also been given an honour by the trendy Blairistas – an honorary knighthood. So Lord Alli, Sir Bob Geldof and plain Charlie Parsons contemplated an offer of £15 million from Carlton for their business. Not quite in the de Mol class but an attractive proposition nevertheless. They decided to accept but shrewdly made the rights to *Survive* a separate matter. Parsons had been trying to sell the show to Britain and America for seven years but he still believed in its potential. *Survive* was wrapped up into a separate company, Castaway, from which Carlton would derive a small share if the show ever became a hit. But the bulk of the equity in *Survive* remained with Parsons, Alli and Geldof. More than ever, Parsons had an incentive to get the show off the ground.

Since his chance meeting with Mark Burnett the year before Parsons had kept in touch with him. They now determined to sell *Survive* together. Parsons travelled to Los Angeles, the city in which he had had his distressing experience with Keenen Wayans. But he had recharged his batteries. Burnett and Parsons pitched the show to each of the main networks – ABC, NBC, Fox and CBS. This time there was interest from all four of them. The wind had changed in Hollywood, and it was chillier altogether. Cable stations were eating into the networks' hitherto dominant audience share. It was now a time to take risks, even with the unmentionable – European formats. Parsons did not make the mistake he had made with David Liddiment at ITV. This time he came armed with a videotape containing edited highlights of the high-rating Scandinavian shows. Remote though these foreign-language versions seemed to network bosses, they could discern how compelling the narrative of the desert island competition was. The best deal they were offered came from CBS, the channel that needed to take the biggest risks. By late 1999 it had slipped to third in the rankings and had the most elderly audience. CBS was characterised by cheesy old series like *Murder She Wrote* – murder to watch and murderous for the ratings. Leslie Moonves, a former actor, had been made the network boss. His task was to halt this decline into senility. Parsons accepted CBS's offer – he now had a broadcaster and a producer. He had finally sold *Survive* into the biggest television market in the world. And he had arranged his deal back home so that most of the proceeds would flow to him and his two partners. As for *Big Brother*, Parsons had no idea it was in development. There would be an explosion when he found out.

ABC had passed up the chance to produce *Survive* in the midnineties and, by allowing CBS to win the auction, had now passed a second time. But the network was not concerned. It already had a breakthrough hit of its own – another British format which had enabled them to overtake CBS in the ratings: *Who Wants to Be a Millionaire?* That a game show had appeared in a US prime-time schedule was extraordinary. That it came from Britain was simply incredible. It had happened as a result of the efforts of Michael Davies. Like Mark Burnett, he was an Englishman who had fallen into American television production by accident.

Davies's elder brother, William, was a movie scriptwriter with the Danny de Vito/Arnold Schwarzenegger vehicle *Twins* to his credit. Michael left Edinburgh University and flew to Los Angeles with the same ambition – to become a Hollywood writer. To make ends meet he gave tennis lessons. To win his Writers' Guild card (a union ticket) he finally managed to get a job scripting the veteran Merv Griffin game show, *Let's Make a Deal*. In 1992 Davies became a producer at Buena Vista, Disney's production arm. There he made a friend of someone who had started out working in daytime TV himself and loved game shows: Disney's chairman, Michael Eisner. In the mid-nineties Davies created and produced new game shows for various cable stations. One day Eisner called Davies aside: 'Michael, I really believe the next big show that will work in prime time will be a big-money game show.' Eisner encouraged Davies to acquire the rights to one of the old 1950s hits, *The 64,000 Dollar Question*. This and other big-money quizzes had fallen out of the prime-time schedules in 1958 as a result of a major scandal. The shows thrived on contestants taking apparently massive risks to win huge sums. CBS's *The 64,000 Dollar Question* had featured a New York policeman who chose Shakespeare as his special subject and won a pot of $16,000, a big payout for the time. There was also a shoemaker who answered questions on opera and a housewife who knew her Bible backwards. Both won $32,000 and became celebrities. The most startling winner, though, was an eleven-year-old called Robert Strom who walked away with a pot of $192,000. The rising thresholds of prize monies were evidence of the tough competition for ratings between rival formats. In 1956 *TV Guide* questioned the producers of *The 64,000 Dollar Question* as to whether it was all on the level. They strenuously denied the contestants were rehearsed. But in 1958 NBC's rival format *Twenty-One* was finally exposed as completely rigged. Robert Redford's 1994 movie *Quiz Show* chronicled the whole sordid episode. The show's most celebrated winner, a college professor, lost a newly acquired role on NBC's *Today* show and, more humiliatingly, his academic position too. By November 1958 all the shows had been taken off air.

Encouraged by Eisner, Davies had piloted *The 64,000 Dollar Question* several times. But each time he met an insurmountable problem. In reality contestants would never take a risk and try to double their money to high levels. Davies couldn't prove why they had forty years before, but he was not surprised.

Within two years Disney bought the ABC network and Davies went to work for them. His job was to find 'alternative' series – ideas which did not cost much and would act as fillers in the schedule. He bought in the improvisational comedy *Whose Line Is It Anyway?* from Hat Trick in the UK and made it a success. When Davies heard, in 1998, that ITV were going to put a big-money quiz back into prime time he was intrigued. His mother, watching at home in south-east London, videotaped Paul Smith's first two episodes that September weekend and posted them to him. The moment Davies saw them he was open-mouthed. The guys at Celador had solved all his fundamental problems. The multiple-choice answers and the various lifelines enabled anyone, however ill-educated, genuinely to take risks and try to go all the way. There was no longer any need to fake the big-money moments. With the tapes came the spectacular early ratings from the UK. Davies was sold on the format and became obsessed with getting it on to ABC prime time. He called Smith immediately, before the end of *Millionaire*'s first run. Smith told him what he told all the other callers: 'Put a bid in a letter and I'll look at it when I've got time.' Davies showed the tape to his network bosses. They airily dismissed it as 'Interesting – it might work on cable'. He told them he had to fly to London to secure a deal with the elusive Smith. They knew he was wrong. US prime time was a scripted medium – sitcoms and dramas. Davies must be mad. They expressly forbade him from flying to London.

Davies no longer cared about his relationships at ABC or his job. He just wanted to produce *Millionaire* for America. He asked Ben Silverman, the London representative for the world-wide agency William Morris, to do a deal for him with Celador. He had no authority from his employers for this, nor any prospect of being able to place the show on ABC. But he did manage to persuade his old colleagues at Buena Vista to put up half a million dollars for an option. Silverman went into action. Now Davies needed to subvert his bosses at ABC. They knew he saw Eisner every few weeks at a regular management meeting. To ensure he had no chance of furthering his crazy scheme they specifically warned him against mentioning *Millionaire* to Eisner. Davies was prepared to obey them . . . up to a point. But he kept a copy of the *Millionaire* tape in his briefcase. If Eisner happened to ask him anything about quiz shows he would be obliged to show it to him, wouldn't he? It would be wrong to hold out on the chairman of Disney, the most powerful man in US enter-tainment, surely? In November 1998 Davies sat at a table in ABC's office in New York. Opposite sat Eisner. Davies was will-ing him to return to his pet theme – putting quiz shows back in prime time. Eisner looked at him: 'Michael, how's that *64,000 Dollar Question* project of yours going?' Bull's-eye. 'I've found something a hundred per cent better. I'd like you to look at it.' Davies slid the tape across the table. Within forty-eight hours he received an email back, copied to all Davies's superiors. Eisner was prepared to stick his neck out: 'I am not embarrassed to say this. This show is going to be a hit.' From this moment Davies knew two things were true. First, he would finally succeed in getting *Millionaire* on to ABC prime time. Second, he would have to leave ABC. His bosses were furious that he had gone behind their backs. In April 1999 Davies managed to patch up a deal whereby he would produce *Millionaire*, via Buena Vista, for ABC. Paul Smith, under bombardment from Silverman, finally agreed to grant Davies the rights for the US. In the end the decision was made for him because the other networks – NBC, CBS, Fox – would still not touch a prime-time quiz. They knew it would never work. Equally convinced of the lunacy of the commission, but powerless to stop it, the ABC chiefs scheduled the debut of *Millionaire* for the dead month of August. Nevertheless Smith had gone one better than selling sand to Arabs or ice to Eskimos. He had sold a TV game show to the Americans.

By late April 1999, John de Mol had only four months left to get *Big Brother* on the air, allowing for one hundred days of transmission before a millennium finale. He put the debacle with ProSieben behind him and decided to go back to the Dutch broadcasters with a bold, new tactic. Endemol would partner with a broadcaster and share the risk if *Big Brother* flopped. No programme producer had ever proposed this before, and certainly not one with the additional burden of a public share quote. But de Mol thrived when taking huge risks and he just had to pull off this deal. One night he exploded to Paul Romer: 'I tell you, Paul, I am going to get this show on television even if I have to pay for it myself.' His latest scheme meant that that was exactly what might happen. If *Big Brother* failed to find an audience the losses incurred would seriously depress Endemol's share price and, with it, de Mol's wealth.

First de Mol went back to Fons van Westerloo at SBS. Instead of thirty-five million guilders for a year he was now offering sixteen million for one hundred days. On top of that he was prepared to share the losses if ratings were poor and advertising around *Big Brother* remained unsold. But van Westerloo had two problems, one old and one new. The main reason he had not taken their conversations further last time was that the majority of his senior management, gathered in a Chinese restaurant, had spoken against the show. In addition van Westerloo, along with his lieutenant and son-in-law Ronald Goes, was bidding for the television rights to some of Holland's international football matches. This was going to cost them twelve million guilders. It was one or the other. They chose the football. At this point *Big Brother* was in real danger of disappearing altogether – a minor footnote in television history about something that might have been.

Refusing to accept defeat de Mol returned to the Holland Media Group – HMG – majority owned by RTL and proprietors of the commercial channels RTL4 and Veronica. RTL had bought the name Veronica from the public broadcaster that had used it before. Now it was branding a minority-interest channel of theirs. The new Veronica was aimed at younger viewers and had a market share of around 8 per cent. Its programming boss was the devotionally named Unico Glorie. Glorie, in fact, was a thoughtful man with an appetite for the internet. He already knew about *Big Brother* and was intrigued by the way in which the idea could link to the internet. He had wanted to buy *Big Brother* before but its cost dwarfed his entire programming budget. Glorie and de Mol met at the HMG offices. De Mol knew he was desperate to commission *Big Brother* but simply didn't have the money. De Mol smiled at Glorie as if to say: 'I have the solution – I'll look after you.' De Mol then said: 'Unico, why don't we do it together? We'll create a joint venture where every cent spent on the production goes on the cost side. All the income – merchandising, telephone calls, internet, advertising, music rights, sponsoring . . . you name it – is on the other side. If we have a deficit we share the deficit. If we have a positive result we share the upside.' It sounded very rational. But de Mol's suggestion had a bomb buried in it. No broadcaster had ever shared their advertising revenue with a producer. This commercial income was their lifeblood and considered sacrosanct. Glorie was unperturbed by that. It seemed he had found a way to do *Big Brother*. He went off to discuss this controversial but seductive proposal with his fellow members of the HMG board. He came back to de Mol with good news. They would do it. Contracts were being drawn up for them to sign. Endemol and HMG had an agreement.

Or had they? Glorie's boss was Pieter Porsius. The more he thought about the deal, the more he thought about *Big Brother*, the more nervous he became. He heard that Paul Romer had several test tapes of *Big Brother*. He wanted to see one of them, and right away. De Mol and Romer were reluctant. This was work in progress and not the real thing, not what they eventually intended *Big Brother* to be. Romer's latest experiment had been to put six students in a hut on a Center Parcs holiday campus at De Eemhof in northern Holland. For three days their every move and conversation was recorded by twenty cameras. Watching were the technical experts from Sony, anxious that their proposed rig for *Big Brother* would actually work. And psychologists were monitoring the events to ensure Endemol did not endanger the health of the participants. They knew about the death of Sinisa Savija in Sweden and were being ultracautious. At Center Parcs they asked the six guinea pigs merely to live together and vote one person out every day. They watched spellbound as the students bonded, fell out, elected individuals to go and, in some cases, bared their souls. Once again Romer could see how compelling *Big Brother* would be. Everyone involved in this test remembers, in particular, a cadet policeman who broke down as he described how he had once attempted suicide. So powerful was the intimacy in that holiday hut that it had turned into a confessional. This was the tape that, eventually, de Mol let Porsius have on 1 May. They waited for a reaction as they continued finalising the paperwork of the deal.

What was it about the tape that appalled Porsius? Being confronted with the reality of reality television, perhaps? Or was it that nothing so intimate, so exploitative, had ever been deliberately set up by a television company before? Some of his colleagues speculated that he was particularly alienated by the police cadet's confession. But an excitable leak about Veronica's interest in *Big Brother* to the Dutch newspaper *Trouw* on 5 May may have been equally disquieting for him: 'Absolutely everything will be shown ... arguments, lovemaking, going to the loo ...' Whatever the reason, he contacted Glorie and told him that the deal was off. Veronica was not going to host *Big Brother*. He demanded they go together to de Mol to cancel the project. They set off for Endemol's headquarters in Porsius's car. Glorie tried to reason with him. He pointed out that they already had a deal with Endemol that was, in all probability, binding. He reminded Porsius that, as a board director, he had the power to make such deals on behalf of HMG. As they drove into the Endemol car park, with its monolithic concrete televisions pumping out Endemol shows, Porsius exploded: 'I've got to fire you. Unico, you are fired.' These two HMG employees, at war with each other, then marched into de Mol's office. Porsius announced that they had to unstitch the deal. De Mol was very cool, convinced that they would have difficulty cancelling and that the HMG board would probably back Glorie not Porsius. This was high brinkmanship but no one was better at it than de Mol.

After the unhappy pair left, de Mol attempted to put an insurance scheme in place. He called Fons van Westerloo at SBS and told him that another broadcaster was about to buy *Big Brother*. Well, it was sort of true. He gave him two days to reconsider and commission the show on the same joint-venture terms. Van Westerloo declined. So it really was HMG or bust. De Mol waited for forty-eight hours. The HMG board met and were decisive. Porsius was overruled and Glorie was reinstated. De Mol had a deal. After twenty months of proselytising *Big Brother* finally had a buyer. The contract was formally signed on 8 May 1999.

Ruud Hendriks was also looking for a buyer – someone who would pay a billion dollars for Endemol. As the summer wore on the interest of the entertainment giants had melted away. There was one other company in the hunt: Pearson. Pearson was essentially a publishing company. It owned the *Financial Times*, part of *The Economist* and Penguin Books. Although it had a share quotation in London the most significant part of its business was a range of educational publishers in the US. Pearson also had a television division. Earlier in the nineties it had hired Greg Dyke to go on a spending spree. The former chief executive of London Weekend Television and future Director-General of the BBC had been given the money to build a television business. He bought three primary assets: in the US he acquired All American Fremantle, a format distributor and producer of the scantily clad *Baywatch*. In Australia he bought Grundy Television, whose biggest asset was the suburban soap *Neighbours*. And he rounded off his new division with Thames Television in the UK, producers of *The Bill* and *Wish You Were Here* for ITV. The chief executive, Marjorie Scardino, did not believe television production and distribution fitted with Pearson's core publishing business. She was irritated by the financial press referring to her company as 'the *Financial Times*-to-*Baywatch* conglomerate'. She wanted to get rid of the television division, but her problem was finding a buyer to pay a top-dollar price to match the sums Dyke had spent a few years before. At the time Pearson was seen as a glamorous, quasi-internet stock with online plans for its education business. Scardino herself was a member of the internet elite, having a place on the board of AOL. Pearson's share price had recently shot up to £20 and more. Scardino did not want to dispose of the television division at any price and damage the positive view of Pearson in the City. Rather than look for buyers, both Endemol and Pearson became attracted to the notion of a merger.

Hendriks set up a series of meetings. De Mol visited Scardino at Pearson's headquarters in central London, behind the Royal Academy of Arts. Pearson's finance director, John Makinson, attended negotiations with Hendriks and Aat Schouwenaar in a claustrophobic suite at the top of the Airport Hilton at Schiphol. Bankers, hungry for fees and willing participants in the late-nineties deal mania, attempted to sort out the planning for a merger. The major issue that emerged was what the respective valuations of the two companies should be. This would dictate how much of the new entity each side would own. Seventy/thirty in our favour, said Pearson. We're more profitable than Endemol and we have Fremantle's valuable format catalogue. Fifty/fifty, said Endemol. We're more creative than Pearson Television and our affiliated entrepreneurs around the world will create more value in the future. This dialogue had some way to go. It is never easy merging two companies with different cultures. But the prize, if they could agree, was the world's largest production house of television entertainment and tradeable formats.

In Holland, the leak to the newspaper *Trouw* set off a bout of hostile press speculation. *Trouw*'s headline was 'Big Brother: a hundred days with cameras everywhere'. The journalist Ton Lankreijer claimed he had plied someone from Veronica with drink and that she had given him a flavour of this extraordinary new show. Loneliness, doubts, fear of abandonment and perhaps even escapes were promised: 'The idea is not completely new but it is still bizarre.' This article was followed up by *De Volksrant*, Holland's leading heavyweight broadsheet, three days later, the day the deal was formally signed with Veronica. It was headlined 'Voyeurism?' and was a compendium of reactions, from the positive to the very negative. It quoted Nermina, Sinisa Savija's widow: 'The producers of the series [*Expedition Robinson*] have to accept their responsibility and make sure nothing like this happens again.' It quoted an *Expedition Robinson* producer: 'We do not film people going to the toilet, in the bath or going to bed with each other. That is really going too far.' Sean Patrick Williams was mentioned as an internet exhibitionist. A web designer, Eelco Anneveldt, drew a distinction between Williams's activities and *Big Brother*: 'With webcams on the internet you decide for yourself how much privacy you have, but these volunteers cannot switch the cameras on and off themselves. I think it will make them paranoid. No romances are going to develop, as the producers hope, because all spontaneity will be lost as people show off in front of the camera.' And an MTV producer in London drew a distinction between *The Real World* and *Big Brother*: 'In *The Real World* the aim is to expose social conflicts, sexuality or class differences. But what Veronica is planning, just to let viewers watch people in their living room, is an improper kind of voyeurism. That's not a nice way to make television.' De Mol's television peers were reacting with characteristic generosity.

These were the very first stirrings of a media circus that was to occur each time *Big Brother* was produced, anywhere in the world. Once the news got out and the shock value of a camera trained on a toilet had worn off the professional community of psychologists and psychiatrists would be enlisted. A week later *De Volksrant* had found a social psychologist at the Free University of Amsterdam, Paul van Lange. With the voting out of unpopular housemates and competition for a prize fund of £80,000 he said some of the volunteers would not be able to stick it out: 'It will definitely go off the rails ... these people could be troubled for the rest of their lives.' Next in the queue of opponents came a local politician from the area where *Big Brother* would be filmed, Alderman for Cultural Affairs, Arie-Willem Bijl. He had ethical reservations. As did Harry de Winter, an entertainment producer and long-time rival of John de Mol:

'Programmes like this are made by trampling over these people, like shutting people up in a house like that. It will lead to disaster. People could be driven crazy. What is the next step? Letting someone commit suicide on camera?' De Winter was followed by fourteen doctors in Almere, where the *Big Brother* house was being constructed. They were quoted in another paper, *Gooi & Eemlander*: '[*Big Brother*] creates a climate in which it pays to amuse yourself at the distress of fellow citizens. The more arguments and conflicts, the higher the viewing figures ... purely in the interests of the commercial broadcasting company'. Thomas Notermans, head of press and publicity for Endemol, was used to handling controversy for de Mol, but he had never experienced this sort of hostility before. And all before anyone had seen even a frame of the new show: 'Opposition in Holland was huge – enormous. That summer I thought the show might not even make it through to the end. It could get taken off mid-series.'

On 1 June, in *Haagsche Courant*, the Netherlands Institute of Psychologists joined in the attack, warning people not to take part. Their spokesman said: 'I don't know how big the risk is but I would not rule out suicide ... Suppose one person becomes the laughing stock. The damage could be really serious.' But it was too late. The house was already being constructed. Veronica and Endemol had appealed for participants. And they were keeping their nerve. Notermans retaliated by issuing a press release with the barest details about the format but admitting the popularity contest and the eviction would increase tension: 'The question is whether they will become each other's friends or enemies in this abnormal situation, whether solidarity will win out over selfishness, and whether they will be able to cope with homesickness and loneliness.' Paul Romer finally gave an interview to *NRC Handersblad* on 19 June. When asked where he would ever draw the line, he made the distinction between voyeurism, where people are spied on without their consent, and *Big Brother*: 'In our programme the people choose to take part themselves.' And he attempted to explain the, by now, celebrated toilet cam: 'Suppose we didn't do that and three of the group go and sit on the toilet whispering to each other. Then the viewer would not be able to follow what is going on any more. Then there is the safety aspect. Suppose someone had a heart attack on the toilet, and then after an hour you think – where's Peter got to? But we will never show pictures of participants peeing, having a shit or having their period.'

To begin with nearly everyone in Endemol had been horrified by the idea of *Big Brother*. Now the sentiment had gone public. But what was it, precisely, about this format that was so shocking? Traditionally television had been a smiley place. In entertainment shows presenters beamed, participants grinned and everything was perfect. In factual programmes when the bleaker sides of life were exposed it was always said to be for a higher social purpose. When an entertainment producer like John de Mol came along, whose ambition was to provide a spectacle and earn a buck, there was a feeling that this couldn't be right. Television had always been heavily regulated, partly because, to begin with, there were only one or two channels, usually under government control. And partly it was because television was so much more pervasive than print media, always on in the corner of the room. So the broadcast services carried a burden – social, political, cultural – that was never placed on other media in such a formal way. For some there was outrage that de Mol should ask members of the public to perform, just by being themselves. It couldn't be right that this new sort of television had no script and no actors. The housemates were going to be talentless exhibitionists. What right did they have to bypass the blood and sweat of a professional training? They were all cheats. Finally, there was the prospect of nudity. Older couples in their sixties and seventies were sometimes the first generation to have seen each other naked. The apparent openness of those applying to take part in

Big Brother, unfazed by each other's nudity or the performance of bodily functions on television, seemed like a descent into barbarism. The battle lines were drawn. If *Big Brother* was to succeed there would have to be a younger generation of viewers who were uncensorious about consensual nudity, sex and self-promotion. They would have actively to enjoy participating in a popularity contest with real-life heroes and villains. *Who Wants To Be A Millionaire?* had garnered massive audiences but was hardly provocative. *Survive* began controversially but, as *Survivor*, was to be regarded in the US as a novel and exotic game show – no more, no less. Neither caused the hostility that *Big Brother* was already provoking. Neither had the same potential to change the ethics of television. Let the outrage begin.

CHAPTER SEVEN

Put Me on Television

Have I given you enough? Reward me. Put me on television.
Let me share this with millions. I will do it slowly, subtly,
tastefully. Everyone must know. I deserve this. I have this
coming. Am I on? Have I broken your heart? Was my story sad
enough?

DAVE EGGERS

Over the summer of 1999, in the grounds of a studio complex
near Almere in Holland, a very strange construction began to
appear. Was it the beginnings of an ultracheap holiday camp? Or
the foundations of a detention centre for delinquents? Barbed
wire fences, arc lights, interlinked Portacabins – was it for keeping people in or out? The local residents were in no doubt. Only
a hermit could have missed the publicity. This was the world's
first *Big Brother* house. Paul Romer had to deliver *Big Brother*
to Veronica for an opening night on 17 September. At its core
was a 'camera cross' which enabled cameramen to patrol a darkened camera run and film the inside of the house through
two-way mirrors. Attached to the huts was a larger complex
containing forty screens. This was to be the control gallery in
which the producers and directors could monitor all the cameras, remote-controlled and manned, mounted in the house. In
all, Romer needed to recruit a team of more than a hundred

people to manage this monster. None of them would know what they were doing because no one had made a programme like this before.

Romer also had to begin the task of deciding who would go into the house. Over the summer three thousand people applied to take part. They had to be sifted, short-listed, interviewed and screened by a psychologist. This 'casting' process was seen as being just as crucial as that for any movie or soap opera. Romer realised that he needed a number of young, good-looking house-mates to appeal to Veronica's target audience of twenty- to thirty-four-year-olds. But his initial idea was also to build a diverse 'family', including a father figure, a matriarch, a rebel boy and a girl-next-door type. De Mol concluded that the person to do this job should be nakedly populist with a feral appetite for human stories. Someone from outside television, not hide-bound by the stuffy conventions of the industry. He had a candidate in mind. Hummie van der Tonnekreek was known in Holland as 'The Queen of Gossip'. She had edited a number of sensationalist, human-interest magazines. This fiery blonde had, at the age of forty-five, fallen out with her employers and was pursuing a very public legal row with them. Romer had his doubts about van der Tonnekreek. But she wanted to do the job: 'Not many people liked me in the Endemol building. They believed I was a nasty woman with no ethics. And I was blonde, so maybe they thought I was stupid too. Even Paul Romer was privately against hiring me.'

Hummie became the first editor-in-chief of *Big Brother*. It was she who, with Paul Romer, chose the housemates. One was Bart Spring in't Veld, blond, muscular and newly discharged from the army. He was in his early twenties and intended to fill the role defined by Paul Romer as rebel. Hummie spotted him early in the interviews: 'With Bart it was love at first sight. My intuition told me, that's one of them. I couldn't help looking at him. He was naughty, witty and single. He seemed to understand

the *Big Brother* idea even though it had never been done.'
Hairdresser Sabine Wendel had also applied. To Romer she was
the attractive girl next door. Not to Hummie: 'She seemed like a
blonde bimbo. I didn't like her but I had to look at her. It was a
good sign if I felt jealous. She had a beautiful, big smile. She was
a femme fatale, in a girlish way. We had two people for definite –
we were sure from when we first met them.' Bart and Sabine and
the others short-listed still had to be screened by psychologists.
Endemol was taking enormous care to ensure that all those
selected would be robust enough for the experience. In a process
that was later to be repeated all over the world, anyone with a
history of drug abuse, depression or childhood trauma was quietly dropped. This was obviously for their own good. But *Big
Brother* also needed healthy extroverts – quiet or depressed
people who said nothing would not make good television. Bart
and Sabine came through with ease. They were joined by others
including the masseur of a women's cycling team, a shoeshop
assistant, a car salesman, a housewife recovering from cancer
and a probation officer.

At Veronica, one of the reasons that Unico Glorie had been so
excited by *Big Brother* from the start was his understanding
that this could be a first for television entertainment. It would
have a daily, documentary-style report from the house. But
because the cameras were to be on twenty-four hours a day
there was the possibility of streaming those pictures via a web
site. *Big Brother* on Veronica could become the first programme
in the history of television to offer its rushes live to the audience,
an entirely revolutionary concept. John de Mol's commercial
director, Gerard Antvelink, was equally excited. But de Mol and
Romer were sceptical. Where was the money to come from to
pay for this service? How would it raise any revenues? The web
at that time carried precious little advertising and the predominantly young users of the internet had come to expect everything
on it for free. Undeterred, Antvelink borrowed an element of his

marketing budget to pay for the design of a *Big Brother* web site. The first version was too ambitious and proved indigestible to the average home PC. It was rebuilt more simply. But it was going to need massive server capacity in order to cope with the anticipated demand from *Big Brother* fans. This, Antvelink discovered, was very expensive. The solution was provided by the internet boom which, by August 1999, was reaching Klondike proportions in Europe as well as the US. Enter Nina Brink, Dutch dotcom entrepreneur and, for the moment, mistress of the universe.

Nina Brink was a hard-grafting, sharp-dealing, fast-talking businesswoman. The late nineties internet boom seemed to have been designed with her in mind. They were made for each other. She had become wealthy as the head of an electronics components firm. In 1996, witnessing the new media 'tulip fever' in the US, she had become one of Europe's earliest dotcom entrepreneurs. She set up World Online, which, like AOL and Yahoo, was an internet service provider. Unlike rivals such as Freeserve in the UK and Wanadoo in France, she was determined to compete with AOL across Europe. There was a World Online company in fourteen European countries. Her expansion was funded via a Swiss private investment vehicle, the Sandoz Family Foundation. Its managing director described Brink as 'a war machine' and took just under half the company for £100 million. Like all the ISPs in the US, World Online's losses dwarfed their revenues. But the financial markets lapped up World Online's success in attracting around a million subscribers by the autumn of 1999. Even when the competing ISPs in Europe started abolishing subscription fees and Brink was forced to follow suit, everyone remained bullish. She knew how to hype an idea. She paid Sarah Ferguson, 'Fergie', the Duchess of York, almost £700,000 for promoting World Online. It was well known that Brink lived in a sumptuous villa in Antwerp, its walls festooned with Dutch Old Masters. She was internet royalty. She and her business were sexy.

As in the US, in the absence of profits internet companies such as World Online were being valued by the number of subscribers they had. The seductive idea was that each of these would be worth a fortune over the long term – a captive audience viewing online advertising, ordering goods and services and using lots of chargeable telephone minutes along the way. Brink wanted to stage an IPO in early 2000. With the market heating up nicely it was speculated that World Online might achieve a valuation of £3.5 billion, making her personally worth £350 million. To satisfy these febrile ambitions Brink needed subscriber growth. When she was contacted by Endemol she leapt at the chance of involvement. She wanted to make all those potential *Big Brother* fans World Online clients. She agreed to put up two million guilders to sponsor the *Big Brother* web site, approximately £700,000. Now the site could be properly planned by Endemol and Veronica, with the capacity for all the users they hoped would be attracted by twenty-four hour streaming of video pictures from the *Big Brother* house. The web site, like the house, had to be ready for the programme launch on Veronica, set for 17 September.

Millionaire's US premier was to be a month earlier than *Big Brother*'s in Holland. Michael Davies had the Sony TV studios in New York booked for the second half of August and the opening night was agreed as 16 August, largely so that the anticipated debacle could be dismissed as an unimportant glitch in the dog days of summer. The first suggestion for presenter from ABC's programming chiefs was the retiring President, Bill Clinton (yes, network bosses really do think like that). Once they had come down to earth Davies was able to hire Regis Philbin, an urbane daytime presenter of mature years – a man with a prominent ego and even more prominent toupee. Philbin had travelled to London to rehearse the format in the British set with some American students. He was sold on the format, completely understood its appeal and was one of the few who agreed with Davies that *Millionaire* could be a powerful success.

Next Davies had to line up sponsors. The business model for the American *Millionaire* had to differ from the British. In some states mass phone-ins from which producers derive a cut were illegal. So Davies persuaded AT&T to offer a free entry line for all viewers. McDonald's agreed to publicise this in all their burger bars. *People* magazine became the third partner, providing marketing support.

For the first recording, on 5 August 1999, Paul Smith flew over. Davies was so anxious to stick to the British production model that he actually played a tape of Celador's British programme into the studio control room in tandem with the recording of the ABC version. He could then spot any discrepancies immediately. This was a novel approach for the US market. Normally the few formats that had been brought across the Atlantic were so Americanised that they were lost in translation. The classic example was Jennifer Saunders's sitcom *Absolutely Fabulous*. The central joke was its politically incorrect script. The US pilot managed to generate a politically correct script. That had been the end of that.

ABC broadcast their first edition of *Who Wants to Be a Millionaire?* at 8.30 p.m. on 16 August. It was an immediate and emphatic hit. Within days (if not hours) Fox, CBS and NBC were dusting down rival quiz formats from the past. Television bosses that had been decrying ABC's folly one day had done a neat volte-face the next and were opining learnedly that the prime-time game show was (of course) ready for a revival. Failure, as television producers know, is an orphan. Success, as everyone in the media demonstrates daily, has many parents.

By Wednesday 18 August *Millionaire* was the most popular show on any network that evening with 12.5 million viewers and an 18 per cent share. Michael Eisner called Davies: 'Congratulations, Michael. You have a hit.' 'Thank you,

Michael, for believing in it,' replied Davies. Programme Four, the day after, had to survive two mistakes in the questions and answers. A contestant was facing a $64,000 question about the Great Lakes. He answered it correctly but was told he was wrong. In the same programme another contestant was penalised when his 'wrong' answer also turned out to be correct. But the publicity around this, and the admission of error (unlike the scandals of the 1950s) probably worked to the show's advantage. It certainly set the stage for Programme Five, when the US version had its Rachel Da Costa moment. Doug van Gundy from West Virginia was a poet, a fiddler and, he revealed to Philbin early on, he only earned $11,000 a year. He had just married his long-term girlfriend, a park ranger, and he said he wanted to win the money for her because she had always had to support him. By the time he had won $8000 he was in tears. But he went on and on.

His question for $250,000 is to name the location of the finishing line for the annual Alaskan dogsled race, the Iditarod. He doesn't have a clue. He phones a friend. His friend just happens to be a fan of the race – he always watches it on an obscure cable TV channel. From the four options he tells van Gundy the finishing line is definitely at Nome. Van Gundy then decides to go for $250,000. This is the highest sum of money at stake on a US game show since an edition of *The 64,000 Dollar Question* in 1958. It is higher than anything yet won in the first year of *Millionaire* in Britain. 'Nome,' says van Gundy to Philbin. 'Is that your final answer?' asks Philbin. 'Yes, it's my final answer,' replies van Gundy. He wins a quarter of a million dollars, he is given the cheque and he is once again in tears. The following day he appears on *Good Morning America* as the entire country celebrates his victory. *Millionaire* has truly arrived in the US.

In the succeeding three years Celador would derive a rich dividend from their hit with books, video games and many other spin-offs. But not everyone welcomes breakthrough entertainment on television. The *Guardian* had called the original British version of *Millionaire* 'the crassest, brassiest, bottom of the domestic television market'. Now Tony Kornheiser wrote in the *Washington Post*: '*Millionaire* is a quiz show for people ugly enough to put out a fire just by showing up. You rarely see people like this on network TV unless it's on *America's Most Wanted*.' The opportunity for the likes of van Gundy to get on television, a sort of emancipation, was obviously not universally welcomed. They did not believe just anyone deserved to be put on the screen. Frank Rush in the *New York Times* was also critical, but he linked this new hit to the madness of the financial markets in 1999, calling *Millionaire* 'the giddiest manifestation yet of a culture that offers a pornography of wealth almost everywhere you look'. As it happened, *Millionaire* would outlast the bull market by several years. This particular economic boom only had a few months to go. Time enough, though, for a final flurry of deal making.

John de Mol had a reputation in Endemol for working harder and for longer hours than anyone else in the company. His one concession to relaxation consisted of brief trips to his holiday home on the Algarve. There he played golf with his two or three close friends – all Dutch businessmen who owned adjacent properties. In the summer of 1999 this was where de Mol would receive daily reports from Paul Romer on how preparations were going for *Big Brother*'s launch on 17 September. Tapes of the final list of housemates and press reports arrived in an Endemol diplomatic bag. His colleagues remained doubtful. His rivals were rubbing their hands anticipating a festival of *schadenfreude*. He had taken a massive risk by agreeing to share any losses with Veronica. He had joined Unico Glorie to present the project to Dutch advertisers but, in the face of a hostile media, they had not yet booked many of the spots available during the transmission of *Big Brother*. This was the one moment when even de Mol himself had doubts: 'I realised that if this was not going to work we were in deep shit. Also for financial reasons. That was my nervous period, where I thought, Jesus Christ, what have I done?'

Paul Romer had no time for doubts. In early September he placed ten guinea pigs in the completed *Big Brother* house in Almere. He needed to test the cameras, the hidden microphones and the videotape systems. The production team had to be put through their paces: 'Of course, it did not work at all. We had to show John a tape and it was hell because it was no good, nothing, boring, terrible. We were afraid to death to go to John. I thought he would be outraged.' De Mol did not react as expected. He was calm. He got the team to discuss how to put it right. They needed a voice-over to provide a narrative. They needed to work out how to use the innovation of the diary room properly – the guinea pigs could not just sit in the chair staring vacantly at the camera. The editing was crude, the camera work was jerky. This material was simply not transmittable.

Despite these disasters behind the scenes, they were stuck with the launch date of Friday 17 September. In the final week de Mol addressed the team at his office in Hilversum with extraordinary chutzpah: 'Guys – *Big Brother* will be for Endemol what Mickey Mouse is for Disney. We are working on something that is going to be huge: twenty years from now, talking about television, they will talk about TV before *Big Brother* and TV after *Big Brother*.' He followed this St Crispin's Day address by giving an interview to national television news containing a confident, if not reckless, prediction: 'Within a year this show will run in ten countries.' The truth was that they were placing ten individuals in a televised house for one hundred days and they had no idea what, if anything, was going to happen. They had undertaken to provide Veronica with almost a hundred hours of television but, at this stage, they did not know what it would consist of.

The opening show was relatively easy by comparison. They had to introduce the ten housemates. They had to explain the format. They had to put them in the house. There they would discover the 'back-to-basics' regime, with chickens to look after and bread to bake. A crowd of thousands greeted Bart, Sabine and their fellow housemates as if they were major celebrities. The show was soon over, but the streaming continued on the web. De Mol sat in a viewing room watching the new house-mates gossiping and getting to know each other. Smoking and drinking cold coffee, he stayed up till 5 a.m., fascinated by the social trivia that was unfolding and the intimacy with which it was shot. These live pictures were available via the web site. It was even, everyone agreed, fascinating watching them tackle breadmaking for the first time. To those who already disap-proved of this immoral show, this added a sense of bafflement to their outrage.

The first night of *Big Brother*, capitalising on the unprece-dented publicity the show had attracted, opened with a share of 20 per cent of viewers. And their rating for the key demographic of twenty- to thirty-four-year-olds was double that, at 42 per cent. For Veronica this should have been seen as spectacular. The main opposition at eight o'clock every night was the national news on the public channel and the soap opera *Good Times Bad Times* on RTL4. Veronica's typical share in the slot was nearer 3 per cent or 4 per cent. Even the channel's average share was only 8 per cent. But there was no celebration. Advertisers were still not supporting the programme and at this stage it still looked as though Endemol and Veronica would lose money. They were committed to fourteen weeks. In the first week of transmission the ratings slipped back to 16 per cent, 14 per cent and then 13 per cent. *De Volksrant* took this as its cue to trumpet on the front page, 'Boring TV peepshow attracts fewer and fewer viewers'. Then, ten days in, one of the housemates, Tara, decided she missed her family and could no longer take the pressure of twenty-four-hour scrutiny. She determined to leave, which the rules clearly stated she was allowed to do. Romer was called away from his son's birthday party to arrange a special live show for Tara's unscheduled departure. Driving to the *Big Brother* house he thought that this could spell the end of it – if the housemates started leaving en masse that would be that. Privately, he had also concluded that the housemates were turning out to be pretty dull. Not enough was happening. The live show gave them a temporary ratings boost but Romer was praying for something to happen between the housemates. Perhaps a row, such as he had witnessed in the early studio test. Or personal revelations like the ones he had seen at the Center Parcs dummy run. Romer was under pressure from de Mol to intervene more in the house and pull off some controversial stunts. So far Romer had resisted him. But for how long could he carry on like this?

Throughout this nervous period the negotiations between Endemol and Pearson continued. The argument as to mutual valuations had narrowed, but only a little. From 70/30 in their favour Pearson had softened to 67.5/32.5. Endemol had acknowledged Pearson was worth more but had only moved to 60/40. Now de Mol conceded further, offering 62.5/37.5. So there was 5 per cent separating their respective valuations. On Saturday 2 October a conference call was organised to see if the gap could be narrowed enough for a deal to be possible. Pearson's finance director, John Makinson, was patched in from his half-timbered Tudor house in the Essex marshes. John de Mol was connected from his thatched mansion near Hilversum, with Aat Schouwenaar and Ruud Hendriks on the line too. The companies' respective bankers listened in. Marjorie Scardino was away for the weekend and was happy to leave negotiations to Makinson. But privately de Mol felt a little slighted that she was not taking part. From that unpromising start very little progress was made. Neither side was willing to alter their valuations materially. It was stalemate.

Later that weekend de Mol flew to Cannes for his annual trip to the Mipcom television market. Endemol traditionally took an expansive stand on the fourth floor of the Palais. It had an outside balcony from which Endemol's sales team and their clients could look down on the luxury boats moored on the quay, known as the Croisette. This was a useful vantage point since they could keep an eye on many of their rivals who rented the yachts for the week of the market. They were cheaper than the extortionate hotels and an agreeable location for sales pitches. Best of all, the humblest of television executives could pose as St Tropez gin swiggers for the week and all on expenses. On the morning of Monday 4 October de Mol arrived at the Endemol stand. Its three prominent liquid-crystal screens were all playing looped tapes of the Dutch *Big Brother* house. And at the counter were thirty buyers desperate to see de Mol and seal a *Big Brother* deal for their own territory. They had all seen Veronica's ratings. They knew nothing of its poor advertising sales.

De Mol was briefed by Gary Carter, the man who had sold *Survivor* to the Swedes and voiced its first demo tape. Now, having joined Endemol, he was responsible for foreign sales of *Big Brother*. Carter showed de Mol the long list of appointments he had made for key buyers, but before de Mol could see any of them he was told that Marjorie Scardino was on the line. He took the call in one of the sales booths. Scardino told him that Makinson had reported back to her about Saturday's unproductive conference. She assured him that Pearson still wanted the merger to go ahead. She offered to accept Endemol's position of 62.5/37.5 as the valuation. No one at Pearson now remembers this call having taken place. But senior executives at Endemol do, because of what happened next. De Mol looked up and eyed the queue of buyers for *Big Brother*. This turned out to be a pivotal moment in his business career. He had never accepted anyone's 'final' offer in any negotiation. But this time he backed his intuition much further. He now firmly believed *Big*

Brother was going to be an international hit. In an excitable market he saw it for what it was – a dotcommer's wet dream. It was too early to sell out. After a pause he told Scardino he was no longer interested in a merger on any terms. The deal was off.

Shortly afterwards Tom Barnicoat from Endemol UK and Ruud Hendriks were briefed by de Mol in his suite at the Majestic Hotel: 'Pearson have taken too long to come back to us. The time's not right. I'm going to pull out of the deal.' Hendriks was very depressed. He had been working on the merger for months. He had got to know all the senior Pearson executives and liked them. He really believed in the deal. At this point he thought de Mol had made a big mistake: 'These opportunities only come once in a blue moon,' he told Barnicoat. 'We've blown it.' Hendriks might have been even more alarmed had he known of some share sales ordered from London. The fund managers at Schroders had decided to start offloading some of their media stock. Their view was that with the NASDAQ already approaching 3000, the market was overheating. They began to reduce their 15 per cent holding of Endemol shares. By this time Willem van Kooten, the man who had acquired his stake in Endemol by bailing out de Mol's first company in the early eighties, had also decided he distrusted the market and sold his shares. Were things on the turn? Hendriks feared de Mol had missed his chance of a big deal. His views were soon to change.

Meanwhile, Gary Carter busied himself arranging the sales meetings for *Big Brother*, mediating between rival buyers who insisted they had to see de Mol immediately. He held a private viewing of the *Big Brother* tapes with Duncan Gray from Granada. Carter and Gray had worked together for Charlie Parsons in the US, when they were all trying to sell *Survivor* the first time, in 1995. Gray watched a sequence in which a dentist attended to a housemate to extract one of his teeth. This simple process had lasted ten minutes, unedited, on a single camera. Something as mundane as this had rated well on Veronica and was, by now, a big talking point in Holland. *Big Brother* was turning a corner and becoming positively avant garde. Gray sat there and said: 'Fuck, fuck, fuck. You've done it, haven't you? You've really done it.' Carter knew that Gray was thinking what he had already concluded: 'It was just going to kick shit out of the competition.'

Later that Monday Carter had agreed to address a Mipcom formats seminar. First he listened to a talk from the sales rep for the old US format *Jeopardy*. Then he got up to introduce *Big Brother*: 'Being an old theatre queen, I did a whole thing about, this is my problem – I've got something so revolutionary that people won't know what to do with it. I told them about the ratings. The audience was divided between those who thought they had seen the devil and those who thought they had seen the future. And from some of them irritation too at my chutzpah . . . saying, all you people, you're now history because – look at this.' He likes to point out that within six months the lady selling *Jeopardy* did not have a job. But Carter's elation was somewhat short-lived. The next day he and de Mol received a surprise.

Variety is the Los Angeles-based daily trade newspaper for the entertainment industry. In September 1999 they published their usual roundup of the latest formats for American TV executives who were travelling to Mipcom. The article led with the success of *Who Wants to Be a Millionaire?* around the world. It quoted John de Mol, praising the format which Endemol was now producing in Holland, Germany, Belgium and Poland. Towards the end of the article there was also this paragraph: 'Endemol has its own version of a reality game . . . called *Big Brother*. It sequesters eight people in an isolated house for 100 days, during which they are to perform certain tasks while sharing very close quarters. Their every action is recorded by way of 140 microphones and 45 cameras. The catch is that every few weeks people are voted out of the house until there's one left. The "survivor" takes home $125,000.' Reading *Variety* that day was Conrad Riggs, Mark Burnett's business partner and the man who was finalising the details of the deal with CBS for *Survivor*. He contacted Charlie Parsons in London immediately. Did he know about this Dutch format? Didn't its voting sound similar to *Survivor*? Riggs was particularly alarmed at the *Variety* journalist's inadvertent use of the word *survivor* in inverted commas.

Parsons was equally alarmed. It had taken him five years to sell *Survivor* into the US. He did not want to be frustrated when he had a deal within his grasp. What if CBS had read this too and started asking why they were paying millions of dollars for *Survivor* when it was already on air in Holland under another name? He ordered videos of *Big Brother* from Holland. He knew that Gary Carter now worked for Endemol. In addition, Parsons was aware that he had sold an option for *Survive* to Endemol some years before.

Parsons viewed the tapes when they arrived. He was not pleased with what he saw: 'I was really angry and upset. I felt that I had, with the help of my team, developed a groundbreaking programme which was literally a milestone in the history of television. I'd sold it to some people who had scraped off all the good bits and applied their own thing so that they could take the credit and the money from it. That's what I felt.' Parsons, Waheed Alli and Bob Geldof quickly got legal advice for their company, Castaway, in London and realised that any action would have to be taken in Holland. They hired Loeff Claeys Verbeke, a firm of Amsterdam lawyers. Their lawyer, Onno van Klinken, wrote to Endemol on 1 October. His letter pointed out that *Survive* (*Expedition Robinson*) had been produced in Scandinavia six times and was a format that Endemol should know about since it had taken out an option for it in 1997. It summed up the *Survive* format in this way: 'A group of people are confined in close proximity ... The group is shown on an uninhabited tropical island to add additional interest to the programme. There they are filmed over a two-month period. Regular votes are taken to remove one of the group from the number.' The letter went on to assert that *Big Brother* had taken the idea, 'be it in a cheaper and less challenging version by hosting the event in an apartment. This amounts to a clear adoption of our client's format.' Parsons's lawyer then demanded that Endemol cease selling *Big Brother* at Mipcom as well as pay Castaway a licence fee and damages.

This was the letter faxed to the Endemol stand for de Mol to read. It was very personal in that it also alleged that Carter had brought confidential information from his time with Charlie Parsons which had been used to help develop *Big Brother*. The only part of the hostile document that made them smile was the assertion that *Big Brother* was already a 'huge success' in Holland. Not quite, but they were working on it. De Mol walked up to Carter, sitting on the Endemol terrace, and dumped the letter in front of him. 'You're nothing but trouble, you are,' he said and walked off. Carter detected (or hoped he detected) a twinkle in de Mol's eye. Endemol certainly responded robustly. They believed the confined house, the fixed cameras, the public telephone vote and the live transmissions on the internet made *Big Brother* a very different show. They sent a letter denying all the allegations and making it clear that, as far as they were concerned, Carter's role was not relevant to the development of *Big Brother*. A further letter from Parsons' lawyers on 15 October said that Endemol's reply was not satisfactory and that they were now going to sue. For good measure they sent a threatening letter to us at Endemol UK as well: 'In a recent edition of *Heat* magazine it stated that Peter Bazalgette is about to sell the [*Big Brother*] format . . . we hereby put you on notice that our client objects . . .' Parsons knew that it was difficult to win a format dispute, but not impossible. Three months earlier Paul Smith had succeeded in persuading a Danish court to ban a copy of *Who Wants to Be a Millionaire?* on the state broadcaster DRTV.

Endemol had responded confidently to Parsons' accusation. But this could not disguise how much was at risk. If *Big Brother* was genuinely turning into a worldwide hit there could be billions of pounds in danger. As the events of the next six months unfolded it transpired that that was exactly the magnitude of what was at stake.

CHAPTER EIGHT

Deals Are My Art Form

Deals are my art form. Other people paint beautifully on canvas or write wonderful poetry. I like making deals, preferably big deals. That's how I get my kicks.

DONALD TRUMP

There are three crucial factors in the production of *Big Brother*: casting, casting and casting. While buyers queued up to buy the format in Cannes and lawyers' letters clogged up Endemol's fax machines, the very first *Big Brother* housemates were getting to know each other. Paul Romer and Hummie van der Tonnekreek had taken care to recruit several young, single participants. As well as Bart and Sabine there was Martin Jonkman, an air-conditioning salesman also in his early twenties. From the second week it became clear that both Martin and Bart were suitors of Sabine. They both took every opportunity to chat her up. She received the flattery of the two rivals with an amused tolerance. Bart was happy to take his time, but Martin went in for the kill. He led Sabine into the garden where he felt insulated from the cameras. In a whisper that he imagined the personal microphones would not pick up he told her a 'secret'. Sabine recalls it now with a smile: 'He said, I have to tell you something. I think Bart is gay because he touched my feet.' Sabine took this revelation with mock seriousness – there had never been anyone less gay than Bart.

The housemates soon became irritated by Martin's puppy love. They nominated him for eviction at the first opportunity. Now matters were in the hands of the viewers. They had seen Martin's perfidy. They had discussed it heatedly in the chat room of the *Big Brother* web site. Martin had been exposed as *Big Brother's* first villain. He was voted out. This was real-life soap, where the viewer could participate in and determine the unfolding drama. And the audience's compulsion to vote was developing a valuable new revenue stream – Endemol shared part of the revenue from each call. For Endemol and Veronica this was a virtuous circle.

With Martin out of the house, the field was clear for Bart: 'After two weeks we discovered each other. We figured you need someone you can do things with.' Sabine was agreeable: 'At first we were friendly. It grew to something like love. You have no idea what's going on outside. We said to ourselves – we think nobody's watching this.' But they were. As Bart and Sabine spent more and more time together their romance became a front-page story in the popular newspapers. The ratings, after three weeks, began to rise. In the two key age groups, – thirteen- to nineteen- and twenty- to thirty-four-year-olds – Veronica was often getting shares of between 30 per cent and 40 per cent. These were extraordinary figures. They were matched by an unprecedented seven million hits on the *Big Brother* web site thus far. Advertisers, seeing the growing interest, particularly among the viewers in their teens and twenties, started to book slots in the show. De Mol and Glorie, from this point, finally knew that they not only had a hit on their hands but also a profitable one. De Mol's intuition and capacity to take huge risks had once again paid off: 'When the romance between Bart and Sabine happened it really exploded. All of a sudden you saw interviews with people who said – this is brilliant. Professors were on TV praising it. And the most critical newspapers now changed their tune. Like with Elvis Presley in the 1950s, we were moving from being the devil himself to being establishment.' *De Telegraaf*, which had greedily followed the *Big Brother* controversy, now devoted eight breathless pages of its Saturday colour magazine to the phenomenon. Not long afterwards Holland's Minister for Culture declared that *Big Brother* was the best thing that had happened to Dutch TV in decades.

Once a relationship develops in the *Big Brother* house, whether driven by affection or hatred, there is a narrative. Viewers turn the programme on day after day to find out what will happen next. In Holland everyone was waiting for Bart and Sabine's first kiss. But the other housemates didn't share the viewers' addiction; they began to resent the intimacy of these two lovers. They felt excluded and, possibly, jealous. After five weeks they took their revenge, inadvertently setting up an extraordinary denouement. They each went into the isolated 'diary room' to make their confidential nominations for eviction. One by one they voted for Bart and Sabine. The couple had to face the public vote. Now Holland was to decide which of the two would be evicted. Bart and Sabine, Dutch television's Romeo and Juliet, would definitely be split up when the result was announced that Friday.

Bart or Sabine? All week Dutch viewers voted, on an unprecedented scale. More than a million phone calls were made. The choice they had to make was described, in retrospect, by Sabine with absolute frankness: 'People had to choose between a nice boy and a bitchy girl. It's not a difficult choice.' Maybe Sabine had a presentiment about the disposition of the *Big Brother* audience. More women than men were watching the show and voting in the evictions. For some reason women are particularly tough on women. This is why men usually win *Big Brother*.

As the week progressed Bart and Sabine had no idea how the vote was going. Bart was evidently upset by his predicament. He alarmed the producers by saying that if Sabine was voted out he would leave with her. On their final night together the other housemates, as much out of guilt as sympathy, offered them the chance to be alone. The house had two bedrooms. They transferred mattresses from one to the other and congregated there. Now Bart and Sabine had a room to themselves.

Late in the evening they were kissing on the sofa in the main room. Bart suggested they go to bed. Sabine hesitated. It looked as though she would decline. They seemed to be making their way to separate bedrooms. They embraced again. She then succumbed and followed Bart to the empty bedroom. They took off their clothes in the dark. The images were picked up clearly by *Big Brother*'s infrared cameras: two very attractive twenty somethings, each with good bodies. They climbed into bed. Their last night together was spontaneous and irresistible. More than three million people were watching – one in five of the population.

Dutch newspapers had been simultaneously condemning and encouraging the prospect of sex in the *Big Brother* house. Privately, they were now disappointed by how real the scene was. No Hollywood camera lingering lovingly in Technicolor on heaving thighs. Just two dimly perceived figures whispering and sighing under a duvet. Later Bart and Sabine did not reveal what actually happened. 'We spent the night together in the same bed. Everybody is suggesting things. But the camera didn't show. It's private and I don't have to tell,' said Sabine.

But the production team were in little doubt. When they edited the videotape for the next programme they let the camera show a certain amount of furtive fumbling. They cut to the others chatting in the second bedroom. Then they cut back to Bart and Sabine, now sitting up in bed enjoying a cigarette. Van der Tonnekreek is clear what she was after: 'I'm going for the erotic way, not the sexual way. They gave us the moment. It was a gift they did it that way. The symbolic cigarette.' Was there a moral backlash after the transmission of this? Not in down-to-earth Holland. Van der Tonnekreek recalls that most people were swept along by the story and charmed by tenderness between the couple. 'By this time even the serious newspapers had turned round because we made it in a delicate way. People were more worked up about the condition of the chickens we had put in the garden!'

The next day the housemates gathered to hear the result of the vote. Bart and Sabine sat together holding hands. The *Big Brother* presenter, from the programme's studio, greeted them over the public address system. 'The next person to leave the *Big Brother* house is . . . Sabine.' She smiled quickly, having predicted the result days earlier. Bart looked thunderstruck. A little later tears appeared and rolled down his cheeks. In the control room Hummie, the hard-bitten Queen of Gossip, was also in tears. By 85 per cent to 15 per cent the predominantly female audience had voted to keep eligible Bart in the house, in front of the cameras. And in a matter of five days a further four and a half million discrete hits were made on *Big Brother*'s web site, making it by far the most popular site in Holland. For the first time in television history viewers were being offered a truly interactive, multi-media piece of entertainment. The idea of convergence may have been a mirage in much of the media sector. Here it was a reality.

By this time the tiny fringe channel Veronica was rewriting Dutch television history. In the space of five weeks it had become a mainstream network. In the week of Bart and Sabine's romance and Sabine's eviction, *Big Brother* was winning half of the thirteen- to thirty-four-year-olds watching television, an extraordinary statistic. It had caused a dramatic fall in the ratings of the nightly news on the public channel and, far more damagingly, of the soap *Good Times Bad Times* on RTL4. Not only was this Veronica's sister channel but, worse, it was produced by Joop van den Ende Productions. One Endemol show was cannibalising another Endemol show. It was John de Mol versus Joop van den Ende – just like the old days. De Mol's son

Johnnie was by this time nineteen years old and working as a floor manager on *Good Times Bad Times*. He reported back to his father the consternation among the actors of Holland's most popular soap opera. They suddenly found their hit show in steep decline and their jobs in jeopardy.

Old rivalries took a more bitter turn when a topical programme, produced by van den Ende's company, decided to strike back. With van den Ende's knowledge, they hired a light aircraft and dropped their presenter and a cameraman by parachute over the *Big Brother* house. The presenter, Willibrord Frequin, missed the target, but the cameraman successfully steered himself into the garden, landing on the grass. He pulled open the house door, much to the shock of the housemates, who started screaming. This stunt was executed by Endemol colleagues without discussion or warning. Romer and van der Tonnekreek had to have the uninvited guest bundled out. They then turned off the cameras and spent an hour and a half personally pacifying the housemates. It was almost open warfare between two related channels and two sister production companies. Glorie and de Mol decided to sort it out. From Monday 1 November *Big Brother* was moved an hour earlier, to a 7 p.m. slot. The result of this was immediate. *Good Times Bad Times*' ratings recovered, *Big Brother*'s viewership leapt even higher and peace was restored within the Endemol family. From the beginning of November Veronica, the channel with an 8 per cent share, was achieving a regular 33 per cent every evening. This concealed an even more extraordinary statistic of huge commercial value – they were regularly capturing 60 per cent (and sometimes 70 per cent) of viewers in their teens and twenties. The only reason that the overall ratings remained obstinately at around 33 per cent was that very few of the Dutch population over the age of fifty, and hardly anyone over the age of sixty-five, could bring themselves to turn *Big Brother* on. To them it was unspeakable. This would be the generation that not only avoided *Big Brother* as it spread across Europe, but roundly condemned it. And it was a very influential age group, containing cultural commentators, politicians and regulators. For them the barbarians were not just at the gate, they had got into the citadel. Worse still, they were on television.

By the end of Mipcom week Endemol already had deals for *Big Brother* with RTL in Germany and Telecinco, a commercial channel in Spain. In each case it would be produced by Endemol's local production company. In Britain I opened *The Times* at breakfast one morning to find a full-page feature about Bart and Sabine. If I did not sell *Big Brother* now, and quickly, rival lookalike formats would get in first. I took *The Times* article into work and photocopied it four times. I sent it, with a covering letter, to four of the British commercial channels – Channel 4, Channel Five, ITV and Sky One. At Sky One, Liz Murdoch, Rupert Murdoch's daughter, never replied. The head of factual programming at ITV, Grant Mansfield, discussed *Big Brother* with his boss, David Liddiment. They decided against it. Liddiment was later to describe this as his 'Beatles moment' – a gracious reference to the celebrated time in the early sixties when the Decca record label turned down the Beatles. This left Channels 4 and Five, the former a government-owned network and the latter whose majority shareholder was Marjorie Scardino's Pearson.

The director of programmes at Channel 4 was Tim Gardam, a cerebral figure with a first-class degree in history from Cambridge University. He was nevertheless charged with running a channel whose remit was to be creative, innovative and diverse. Gardam had already seen a tape of the Dutch *Big Brother*, brought to him by one of his team: 'I felt there was something about the intimacy and the claustrophobia. And also the strange rhythm of the editing where you followed them, via the cameras, from room to room. You were more immersed in it than you were in a cut-about documentary. I was very excited by it.' Gardam's counterpart at Channel Five was Dawn Airey, also with a Cambridge degree but who was notorious for having jocularly described the output of her channel as 'films, football and fucking'. I was also receiving insistent telephone calls from Alan Yentob at the BBC wanting to pitch in as well. Yentob was my neighbour and, with our sons in the same class at school, we even shared a school run. But I was convinced that the BBC would suffer several collapses of nerve before getting *Big Brother* to air. The Corporation's colossal and impenetrable web of competing committees would scrap over the format and its ethics, eventually emasculating it.

Airey offered us a nightly prime-time slot and £3.5 million. Gardam pitched an 11 p.m. slot and £4.5 million. Channel 4 had been lacking a genuine, internet-related attraction and he saw this as their own sort of *Blair Witch Project*. I cautiously preferred Channel 4's late-night slot. As to the money, I was in a dilemma. Endemol had told me that we had to use their entire Sony kit and that the budget would be in the region of £6 to £7 million. Endemol was trying to help Sony recoup their investment in the Dutch production, but I did not, at the time, believe I could sell a television series at that price. So, risking de Mol's wrath, I asked our production managers to cost *Big Brother* from scratch, including reinventing the technical rig that would be necessary. They told me that it could not be done for £3.5 million but that it *might* be do-able for £4.5 million. Gardam added one more argument which I considered an asset: 'Our commissioning editors will be bloody difficult and question everything. That will make a better programme.' Indeed, Gardam had already concluded that the British version should be shorter, sharper and more flamboyant, with an eviction every week rather than every fortnight. In any event, Channel Five declined to offer any more money and the decision was made. In the UK *Big Brother* was going to Channel 4. In the US a Greek tragedy was about to unfold.

On 15 October 1999 a phone call was made to Time Warner's head office in New York. It was a call that would kick off the biggest deal of the internet boom, one whose vaulting ambition made many lesser deals possible. Hubris was the order of the day. Steve Case, chairman of AOL, wanted to talk to Jerry Levin, chairman of Time Warner. AOL's stock market valuation was twice Time Warner's, yet its revenues were only $5 billion, a mere fifth of Time Warner's revenues of $25 billion. That was the insane premium the market was putting on internet companies at this time and it emboldened Case to make the biggest play of his life: 'We should put our two companies together. What do you think? Any interest?' Levin appeared doubtful but promised to think about it. Case sweetened the proposition by suggesting that Levin was the man to be chief executive of the new, merged entity. Case said he was content to be chairman.

In fact Levin was a good deal more interested than he let on. He was struggling with the low valuation of Time Warner. He was desperate for a real internet story to excite the market. He also wanted to parley with Case for the moment to stave off something worse – the distinct possibility of a hostile bid from AOL. Levin and his closest colleagues agreed that he should meet Case. It was agreed they would have dinner in New York on 1 November. Case's honey trap was set. To avoid prying eyes and wagging tongues the two met in a private room of the Rihga Hotel in Manhattan. Was it the power of mutual admiration or the properties of vintage red wine? Something happened over that dinner table that sealed Time Warner's fate. By the end of the evening Case had persuaded Levin that together they could create the first and surely the most powerful converged media company in the world. Time Warner's movies, TV shows, books and magazines would be delivered electronically to AOL's online subscribers in a marriage that would redefine a new, digital millennium. Secret negotiations then began between the two companies. As with Endemol and Pearson, a successful deal would depend on agreement about how much of the new company the respective share-holders would own. This would take two and a half months to settle. But there was already a sense of inevitability about the proceedings – Levin now saw it as his destiny.

A few days after the Case–Levin tryst *Who Wants to Be a Millionaire?* gave away its top prize for the first time and it was in America not Britain. A tax inspector called John Carpenter reached half a million dollars without even using all his lifelines. In accordance with the rules he could look at the million-dollar question before deciding whether to risk going for the top prize. If he then had a go and got it wrong he would only take home $32,000.

The lights go down and Regis Philbin asks Carpenter: 'Who was the American President who appeared on *Rowan and Martin's Laugh-In*? Was it Richard Nixon, Jimmy Carter, Lyndon Johnson or Gerald Ford?' Carpenter looks blank. He decides to phone a friend, in this case, his father. The clock ticks down as his father admits he does not have a clue. There is a further silence. Then, in a cool and mesmerisingly confident voice Carpenter announces to Philbin: 'I just want to tell you that I'm going to be a millionaire, because I know the answer to that question.' The audience gasps. He had known all along – the call to his father was just a wind-up. 'The answer is Richard Nixon.'

John Carpenter became a dollar millionaire at that moment. His wicked sense of drama was worth much more to Paul Smith. In this second run of *Millionaire* on ABC its audience peaked at a gigantic twenty-nine million, equalling the US's other top show of the time, *ER*, on NBC. ABC's overall ratings were 30 per cent higher than they had been the year before. Thirty-second commercial breaks during *Millionaire* were costing advertisers $600,000, again rivalling *ER*'s hitherto unchallenged slot value. The result of this was a rights payment to Smith and his partners of $12 million. *Millionaire* was already sold to fifty-two territories around the world, a statistic which was expanding by the week. But the American deal, as ever, was the major money earner. With *Big Brother*'s growing success, it was now time for John de Mol to have another go at selling his format into the most lucrative media market in the world. And there was already interest from the US.

The first executive to get in touch with Endemol, at about the time Bart and Sabine were consummating their relationship, was Stephen Chow from the cable company USA Networks. He had helped Rupert Murdoch launch the Fox TV network in the 1980s. He had pioneered early reality series such as *Cops*, using the police force's own footage, and *America's Most Wanted*. His reign at Fox came to a premature end when he delivered a speech about censorship. To make his point he had a woman strip beside him as he spoke. Rupert Murdoch was in the audience. No problem there; after all, he had been popularly known as the Dirty Digger in Britain after spicing up the *Sun* and the *News of the World* with 'Page 3' nudes. But Murdoch's wife was with him and it was said she was offended. Others speculated that Dick Cheney, the future Vice-President and also an attendee, was unamused. Murdoch does not like to alienate powerful politicians. Chow was sacked. Now working for cable TV he was still hungry for new ideas. He arranged to visit the *Big Brother* house in Holland.

Gary Carter and Paul Romer showed him around in November 1999. They took him down the darkened camera runs and he experienced the sense of intrigue and guilt that everyone did when they spied on the housemates for the first time. Chow loved it and was desperate to buy the rights for the US. Carter and de Mol took him to dinner in a Japanese restaurant that de Mol owned (he liked sushi so he thought he would have his own private supply). Carter worried about taking Chow there: 'It was a terrible restaurant. I could see Stephen Chow's Asian sensibilities curdling as he was presented with this Dutch interpretation of sushi.' Chow made no complaints. The real problem was that he, like so many of the potential buyers in Europe before him, could not afford the show. US cable stations simply did not spend that amount on their programming. Chow was followed that month by executives from other American networks. It became clear there was now real interest. Taking advice from the agents William Morris, the plan was to try to seal a deal at NATPE, America's equivalent to Mipcom – an annual TV market. Carter arranged to travel to its New Orleans location in January 2000. De Mol said to him: 'If you can sell this show at NATPE . . .' 'Yes?' said the hard-dealing Carter. 'If you can do the deal . . .' began de Mol again. 'What, what if I sell it?' interrupted Carter again. 'I'll take you for a drink,' said de Mol smiling, finally finishing his sentence. Carter looked at him with a raised eyebrow and said: 'All right, if I can choose the bar.' De Mol knew what Carter had in mind. He had no desire to be recognised in a gay bar in the heart of Amsterdam. 'OK, so long as it's not in Holland,' countered de Mol.

De Mol had more on his mind than selling *Big Brother*. His hunch about breaking off negotiations with Pearson had proved entirely justified. Endemol now had an approach from Holland's national telecommunications company KPN. The prevalent theory at the time, inspired by the talk of convergence, was all about telephone companies and their networks. Since it was becoming possible to transmit far more than speech down their pipes they were being told by the legions of internet gurus and web soothsayers that they should own the producers of this new programming too. Music, film, television – telcos were being advised to buy into the lot. Here on KPN's doorstep was not only a highly successful producer of content, Endemol had now invented a single show that had viewers glued to their televisions, voting via telephone calls and scrambling to get online as well. De Mol had succeeded where Jerry Levin of Time Warner had failed. His company now had a credible internet association.

Big Brother appeared to be the ultimate piece of convergence. It certainly looked that way to Nina Brink at World Online, a second suitor for Endemol. She had seen users flocking to the *Big Brother* web site she was sponsoring. She liked it so much that she wanted, as the saying goes, to buy the company that made it.

Ruud Hendriks and Aat Schouwenaar agreed to hold talks with Brink. She was still planning her IPO, like all self-respecting internet service providers at the time. But Schouwenaar was sceptical of her business model: 'As with many similar companies she was losing money like crazy – it was really terrible.' Hendriks also had doubts about her personally: 'She had a huge energy level which became irritating. She was very chaotic.' Hendriks and Schouwenaar distrusted the value of the World Online shares that any buy-out would be based on. But these were strange times and it was best to keep talking, partly just to see what sort of crazy deal might be on offer and partly to keep KPN hungry.

On 2 November 1999 the NASDAQ broke through 3000 for the first time. It would break through 4000 as well before the end of the year. The markets of the Western world were on amphetamines. Endemol's share price, long dormant, suddenly caught the mood. At the beginning of September, just before the launch of *Big Brother*, it had stood at €27. As the full significance of the nation's obsession with Bart and Sabine began to percolate the world of the despised financial analysts, so sentiments about Endemol began to change. By 19 November it pushed through €40. On 30 December, the eve of the new millennium, the romantic Bart emerged from the *Big Brother* house as the winner. Fireworks burst spectacularly up from the path as he ran towards the studio, a hero. He was given the winner's cheque of £70,000. But that seemed unimportant compared to the adulation of a huge audience which had voted this regular guy number one in what was essentially a popularity poll. That night Veronica – the channel whose historic share was, of course, 8 per cent – won a 74 per cent rating. This included 96 per cent of the six- to twelve-year-olds and 90 per cent of the thirteen- to nineteen-year-olds watching that evening. Over the hundred days of the series there had been nine million telephone votes cast and the web site had received more than fifty-two million hits. New Year's Eve fell on a Friday that year and was a working day. The stock market was open and trading. Endemol's share price finished the year with a leap – €53, double what it had been in September. It was heading strongly up. And it had only just started.

In New York, the first ten days of the new millennium were frenetic for Jerry Levin of Time Warner and Steve Case of AOL. On 6 January the two finally settled on an (extraordinary) merger value of 55/45 in AOL's favour. They toasted the agreement with a bottle of 1990 Léoville-Las-Cases from Case's cellar. As Bordeaux lovers will know, this is a noble, second-growth wine from a great year and they were drinking it somewhat prematurely. But the deal came in the nick of time for Steve Case. By the time his shareholders finally got to vote on the proposition, in June 2000, AOL's stock value had halved.

On 10 January Case and Levin held a celebrated press conference in Manhattan to announce their $250 billion 'merger' – widely seen as, in reality, a takeover by AOL. Famously, Case, the internet entrepreneur and guru of the new economy, tried to go 'straight' by wearing a suit and tie. By contrast Levin, the conventional businessman with $6 billion of solid cash flow, wanted to embrace the new economy by appearing casually in khaki with an open-necked shirt. 'Two shits passing in the night,' as one wag observed. This spectacular deal was the high water mark of the 'new paradigm'. It was internet-connected and it offered entertainment content down telephone lines. Case trumpeted that old convergence magic: 'We're at the cusp of what we think will be a new era as the television and the PC and the telephone start blurring together.' Case's boast was an almost perfect description of *Big Brother*. De Mol had something ideal for this market. Endemol should be eminently sellable too. But time was running out for him to capitalise on it. By the end of the year 2000 the NASDAQ was to have halved. Within three years AOL/Time Warner would be a fifth of its current value.

In early January, Gary Carter flew to New Orleans, as instructed, for NATPE. With the considerable incentive of a beer to be bought for him by de Mol in a gay bar (*outside* Holland), he was charged to sell *Big Brother* to the Yanks. Before Carter left he checked that Endemol actually had the rights to sell. In 1999 de Mol had given a three-month option for *Big Brother* to Fox. He was negotiating a lucrative output agreement with a Fox-owned station in Germany and sweetened the deal with the *Big Brother* rights. Luckily for Endemol, Fox had no idea of the value of what they had. Carter had had one telephone conversation with Fox's US programming boss, Mike Darnell, about the option. But it was clear he was not yet across the *Big Brother* phenomenon. The option had quietly expired towards the end of 1999. Carter now had complete latitude.

New Orleans has a picturesque reputation – the old French town, the Dixie jazz bands, the Cajun dishes. In fact, beyond the eighteenth-century settlement it is a sprawling, industrial port intersected with a few Disneyland-style concrete hotels. And the much-vaunted gumbo is, without doubt, the most disgusting concoction ever cooked up in the name of food. Carter made his way through the modern streets to the conference centre hosting the market. There could not be a bigger contrast between NATPE and Mipcom. The first thing that greets you at NATPE is a ceiling-to-floor display of each network's main stars, magnified cruelly, each one a living testimony to Prozac and plastic surgery. The throng of buyers and sellers perform two essential techniques to perfection: first, you must walk with steely purpose, even if you are merely on your way to the toilet. Second, you have to master the art of the 'look-thru'. A cheery hello, how-are-you, have-a-nice-day is reserved for everyone on the up, with good ratings or a new commission. But with anyone who has recently suffered a setback it's crucial to look straight through them. To acknowledge anyone with the merest taint of failure is perilous – after all, the contagion could spread to you.

Luckily for him, Carter did not have to walk into this cauldron alone. The premier agents William Morris had been engaged to hold his hand. The downside to working with William Morris is that on any given project it turns out, by coincidence, that the only appropriate US producers and presenters for it are also represented by the agency. The upside is that they genuinely do have the ear of the networks. No more so than Mark Itkin, William Morris's Mr TV. Itkin is short, extraordinarily stocky, gravely voiced and has a messianic confidence in any project that he is selling. Not a man to be trifled with. It was Itkin who greeted Carter with the news that there were to be meetings with all the major networks, save NBC, and a goodly number of cable stations too. The word had got around: following the barnstorming success of *Who Wants to Be a Millionaire?* and the buzz around the *Survivor* commission, here was yet another, a third, innovative entertainment property from Europe.

Almost immediately Carter saw Stephen Chow from USA Networks, the man who had braved Dutch sushi to try to get the *Big Brother* rights the previous November. He went down on his knees in the aisle and publicly kissed Carter's foot, saying: 'What do I have to do to get the show?' Carter replied tersely: 'More than kiss my foot, Stephen.' The truth was that Chow could still not afford the show. The real game was between ABC, CBS and Fox. Like the practised illusionist he is, Itkin had organised three simultaneous breakfasts at all of which Carter was meant to be present. Carter attended the first, Itkin went to the second, assuring those present of Carter's imminent arrival, and the hosts of the third were allowed to sweat for a while. At the Fox breakfast Mike Darnell, the man who had let the option slip the year before, was now determined to win this auction: 'He was all over me – treating me as though I had invented television,' Carter recalls. ABC wanted to maintain the momentum they had generated with *Millionaire*. And CBS, who already had *Survivor* scheduled for that summer, were seeking a companion reality show for it. Most of all, none of them wanted their rivals to have *Big Brother*.

Over two days, as negotiations continued, Carter frequently consulted de Mol at his holiday home in Portugal: 'I had carte blanche to call him day or night. He was smoking a lot, I could tell. And he was going for frequent walks in his garden, sighing and saying – it is going to happen, it will happen, won't it?' Between them they began to favour CBS. It was seen as a family channel and therefore, defensively, a good home for a controversial programme. Fox, by comparison, was known for wilder, more louche entertainment which could give *Big Brother* a trashy profile from the outset. In addition, CBS had already acquired Parsons' rival reality format, *Survivor*. Surely it would be better to be on the same network as *Survivor*, rather than pitched against it from, say, ABC? Carter now had to meet the new boss of CBS, Leslie Moonves. He was trying to drag CBS into the new century faced, as he was, by the more outrageous Fox, ABC with *Millionaire* and the super-confident NBC with its long-term bankers *Friends* and *ER*. Carter was pushed by Itkin into a sales booth to await the great man: 'There were empty chairs around a table – it looked like a set up for a terrible office run-through of a chat-show pilot. In walked Moonves – short, well-built, good-looking. And I thought to myself – you're an ex-actor, so am I. If you can do this, I'm bloody well sure that I can.'

There were three issues – how the show would be cast, who had creative control and how many years the deal would be for. These were settled swiftly to Carter's satisfaction. The price was agreed too – a healthy $22 million. One issue that was not raised was the pending court case between Parsons and de Mol. Apparently Moonves had figured he would leave that to the Dutch courts – he had the two shows and if, in the end, it turned out he was buying both from Parsons, so be it. Carter then, not without an element of theatricality, announced he was flying out within a couple of days and hadn't time for a long negotiation. The contract had to be confined to just four pages. The lawyers in the room swallowed hard and then departed to try to achieve that. Carter shook hands with Moonves and went off to phone de Mol. He had no idea what time it was in Portugal but de Mol answered immediately. 'CBS for $22 million,' announced Carter breathlessly. De Mol responded instantly: 'Can't you get $23 million?' He was making his characteristic last attempt to tighten the vice. On this occasion Carter said firmly, if not a little histrionically: 'No I can't, John!'

Shortly after he put the phone down Carter was called by the lawyers. They told him that a car would be there for him in one hour. He was to get into it and talk to no one. He must fly immediately to LA. They had heard that ABC were about to leak the deal early, presumably in order to make it look as though they had walked away from the auction (which they hadn't) rather than lost it (which they had). To avoid the hungry entertainment press pack gathered at NATPE, Carter was now to go into purdah in LA. Arrangements were also made for de Mol to fly out to the West Coast in the first week in February to sign and announce the deal. Prior to that he had the pleasure of taking a call from Mike Darnell in his car in Holland, pleading for him to reopen negotiations and give *Big Brother* to Fox. A sweet moment for the man who had been ignored by the US networks for so long.

On Sunday 30 January the *New York Times* published an article headlined: 'Television's new voyeurism pictures real-life intimacy.' It predicted the imminent announcement of a deal with CBS for *Big Brother*, charting the new dominance of the European formats led by *Millionaire* and *Survivor*. The piece revealed that a disappointed Darnell was about to hit back with a new Fox reality show, *Who Wants to Marry a Millionaire?*. Fifty pretty, gold-digging young women were to be whittled down in a beauty pageant to a short list of five. All of them would wear wedding dresses for a compliant millionaire to pick one as his bride for a live wedding to take place on television. As usual, de Mol had been there first. But this was the first sign that the American networks were getting into gear with the new, non-scripted, reality genre. From now on the ideas would get more extreme. The *New York Times* also referred to Parsons' legal case against *Big Brother*. It was hanging over Endemol and would not get to court for another three months.

A week later John de Mol arrived at Los Angeles International Airport, twenty-two years on from the crippling snub he had received from John Denver's manager, Jerry Weintraub. This time he and Thomas Notermans were met by a sleek black limousine and a Mexican driver, George, with a shiny cap and immaculate white gloves. They were driven to the Four Seasons, Beverly Wilshire, made famous by Richard Gere's top-floor seduction of Julia Roberts in the movie *Pretty Woman*. De Mol could not reach the bed in his suite for all the flowers awaiting him. Notermans was handed the interview bids from network shows such as *Entertainment Tonight* and *Sixty Minutes*. De Mol would do them all – he was relishing every moment of his return: 'How can you describe a feeling like this? You are drunk or full of drugs.'

De Mol could not sleep in his hotel room in the early morning before the Monday ceremony with CBS – the result of a combination of jet lag and excitement. He called his trusted colleague, Ruud Hendriks at Endemol, back in Holland. It was 6 a.m. LA time and three o'clock in the afternoon in Holland. De Mol started to describe the feeding frenzy around *Big Brother* in the

US. Hendriks, of course, liked what he was hearing because he still had his 2 per cent shareholding in Endemol. He was, as ever, on the internet in his office, tracking the share price in real time. When their conversation started the price was €86. The deal with CBS was not yet announced but rumours of it had already leaked into the Dutch stock market. The price was climbing by the minute. Hendriks told de Mol to keep talking because of the magical effect their conversation seemed to be having. In forty minutes the share price rose from €86 to €96. At the beginning of the call their company had been worth €2.9 billion. At the end the value had gone up to €3.2 billion. The shares were suspended briefly by the Dutch market authorities who called Endemol to ask what was going on. Within twenty-four hours they were able to announce the US deal for *Big Brother*. At that point the share rose even higher, breaking through €100 for the first time ever. The company, for which there had been no takers at $1 billion just five months before, was now valued at three times as much.

Later that morning Notermans and de Mol asked their driver George to show them round the Los Angeles area. In Santa Monica they decided to stop to buy a camera so that they could record their triumphant progress through Hollywood. In the shop Notermans suggested buying the latest digital camera. It cost $500 but, then, who was counting? De Mol upbraided him. There was no need for such extravagance. He insisted they buy a secondhand model for $25. They then went on to rejoin Gary Carter and meet Les Moonves at CBS. Notermans remembers the scene: 'It was a typical Hollywood executive's office. The wall was covered with photographs of Les with famous people, including President Clinton. We signed the contract there. John kept on smiling to himself – maybe he couldn't believe his luck.'

Carter and de Mol went outside for a smoke. They were leaning against a wall outside the CBS lot with the classic Hollywood sign on the hill behind their heads. Carter said:

'You're nervous, aren't you?' De Mol replied: 'All my life I've wanted this, all my life.' Then he stubbed out his cigarette and went back in to face the press.

De Mol and Moonves had organised the press conference for fifty handpicked entertainment and media correspondents. With great charm Moonves said how excited CBS were and introduced John de Mol, looking very sleek in a dark-blue suit and a sober tie: 'I feel like the little country boy in the big city for the first time, being, to be honest, a little bit nervous. But this is a dream come true.' Was de Mol really nervous or was this a carefully calculated act? People present felt it was a bit of both. De Mol certainly went on to deal with questions about cruelty, nudity, bad language and all the other habitual *Big Brother* issues with great assurance. He was asked, tellingly, how *Big Brother* was different from *Survivor*, Moonves's other commission and its rival in court proceedings. De Mol pointed to *Survivor*'s island locations and games, arguing that it was, in effect, a reality game show. With *Big Brother* he contrasted its twenty-four-hour coverage of the participants at all times and the fact that they were cut off from all outside human contact, even cameramen. They rounded the press conference off with de Mol adroitly saying he preferred the term 'curiosity' to 'voyeurism' when describing the motive of the viewers watching *Big Brother*. And Moonves predicted a decline in traditional, scripted American entertainment from now on as reality television started tightening its grip on prime-time TV. The final question they had to answer was: 'What if it doesn't rate?' Moonves diplomatically replied: 'We don't expect that. But John and I would talk.' 'We'd put a rope around our necks,' corrected de Mol.

While de Mol was in the United States Ruud Hendriks and Aat Schouwenaar had been in contact with a third suitor for Endemol, in addition to KPN and World Online. The principals of Endemol's two Spanish production companies had introduced officials from Spain's massive telecommunications company, Telefonica. They had visited Endemol's headquarters in Hilversum and made it clear that, as a telephone company, their interest was motivated by the same philosophy as KPN's – the dogma of convergence. But how genuine were Telefonica? That depended on the sentiments of just one person, their chairman Juan Villalonga.

The man who had risen to run Spain's largest company, assisted by his friendship with José Maria Aznar, the Prime Minister, was now in danger of squandering his political capital. His love life was to blame. On New Year's Eve 1998 he, his wife and children had celebrated at dinner with Aznar and his family. Concha Talleda Villalonga remained best friends with Ana Botella, the Prime Minister's wife. There had been rumours of her husband having an affair. That night Villalonga assured Aznar his marriage was in good shape. But by 1 a.m. he was on Telefonica's corporate jet bound for Miami and the arms of his lover of three months, Adriana Abascal, a former Mexican beauty queen. When they met Villalonga was forty-five and Abascal twenty-seven. She had previously been married to the owner of Mexico's biggest television network, a man named Emilio Azcarraga. When he died he left Abascal 40 per cent of his fortune. This was contested by the rest of his family. She finally agreed to leave Mexico with a controlling interest in Azcarraga's $45-million-dollar yacht and possession of three other properties. She had already met Villalonga at a dinner her husband had hosted in New York before his death. She sought him out again in Madrid and they started an affair. It was mostly conducted in Miami, where Telefonica had an office. During 1999 Villalonga and Abascal became fixtures on the glamorous Florida East Coast party circuit, mixing with the likes of Gloria Estefan and Julio Iglesias.

From this point Villalonga spent more time in Miami than Madrid. He was prone to making virtual appearances at

Telefonica board meetings, via a tele-satellite connection, in a freshly laundered, pink polo shirt. His business dealings, like those of all corporate tyros of the late nineties, grew more expansive by the month. He had bought 5 per cent of Pearson. When Marjorie Scardino courteously invited him to address her firm's 1999 conference in Washington he delivered a blistering call for better performance – as though he owned a majority of the company. Scardino was white with anger. He often invited the long stream of those who wished to deal with Telefonica to attend him in Miami rather than Madrid. A visiting posse of merchant bankers was once ushered into the white marble boardroom of Telefonica's sharp, modern office there – its style was more *Miami Vice* than Mies van der Rohe. Villalonga bet them they didn't know who was in the next room and made each member of the delegation place $20 on the table to enter a sweepstake. He then revealed with a flourish that it was Thomas Middlehof, chairman of the German media giant Bertelsmann, owner of publishing and TV interests. The two were ostensibly discussing various internet deals but Villalonga's ultimate fantasy was to merge Telefonica and Bertelsmann. Had it happened, this would have been Europe's version of the AOL/Time Warner deal, both in terms of scale and hubris.

By February 2000, Aznar and Villalonga were barely on speaking terms. Not only did the Prime Minister and his wife strongly disapprove of Villalonga's extra-marital adventure, the exposure of a controversial Telefonica share scheme had also caused a huge political storm. Stock options, which were now worth $500 million, had been granted to senior management at Telefonica. This arrangement had not been declared to the company's shareholders – against the law elsewhere in Europe but permissible in Spain. When Villalonga had floated Telefonica's ISP, Terra, the previous November its share price had trebled in the first day. This alone had added $100 million to the covert management pot. Now revealed, the socialist opposition were making hay exposing all this capitalist greed. A general election was just a month away and Aznar instructed Villalonga to dismantle the scheme. His old school friend completely ignored him. Juan Villalonga was a master of the universe and no longer needed to heed prime ministers. This was the man Endemol had to reach and test out as to whether a deal was a realistic possibility.

De Mol, Schouwenaar and Hendriks turned to their chairman, Ben Verwaayen. Having worked at KPN before joining Lucent Technologies in the US he had had dealings with Villalonga. Verwaayen called Villalonga and asked if he was interested in Endemol. Whether or not he had previously heard of Endemol or *Big Brother* is unclear. But the answer was yes anyway. In his four years at Telefonica Villalonga had carried out one hundred mergers and acquisitions. He was not going to stop now.

Endemol was in play and, to the huge advantage of its founder shareholders, it was to be an auction between two telecommunication giants, KPN and Telefonica, with World Online to add a little colour from the sidelines. The NASDAQ was powering on nicely towards 5000 and the fever that the markets had been experiencing had now given way to an even more powerful emotion: mania.

CHAPTER NINE

To Withstand the Highest Bidder

Few men have virtue to withstand the highest bidder.

GEORGE WASHINGTON

When John de Mol failed to sell *Big Brother* to the German station Sat 1 in 1999 the directors of other networks agreed that they would not commission this disreputable programme either. Their solidarity did not last long. Once *Big Brother* had been seen to transform Veronica's fortunes in Holland there was a market for it in Germany. The RTL group, a majority shareholder in Veronica, did a deal with de Mol for their RTL2 channel in Germany. It was due to launch in early March 2000. The house was under construction for only the second production of *Big Brother* anywhere in the world. But what had been controversial in Holland was shocking in Germany. The Sat 1 executive who had so reviled the idea of locking individuals in a televised house, likening their treatment to that of an underclass (*Untermenschen*), was only the first to articulate a profound disquiet. When Endemol producers unveiled the basic design of the house, with its high fences, barbed wire and security lights, they were told this could not be done in Germany. Its connotations were too painful. The Dutch were at pains to point out the security was essential to keep intruders out, not the housemates in.

In mid-January de Mol attended a press conference in Cologne to launch *Big Brother*. Helpfully Holland's winner, Bart, also attended. Not only did he profess to being the happiest man in the world, he also caused laughter when, pressed as to the sheer inhumanity of the project, he said he would crawl from Cologne to the *Big Brother* house at Almere in Holland to do it again. Germans were by no means convinced. The following Sunday Kurt Beck, the Prime Minister of the Rhineland-Pfalz region, gave an interview to *Bild Zeitung*, Germany's biggest selling newspaper. He questioned whether *Big Brother* should not be banned. The Association of Catholics in Business issued a press release saying *Big Brother* displayed a contempt for humanity and RTL2 should be boycotted. A public letter from a Catholic, Christa Becker, spoke for the older generation: 'How can we have got to the stage where someone thought up a programme like *Big Brother*? What kind of person is he? Why does a TV company produce something like this? Why are there young people who are prepared to go into the container? Why are there millions who follow the events avidly on TV? Whose was the sick mind which infected all the others? Because all this does indeed seem to be a infectious disease – and one which is worse than BSE.' The Catholic Countrywomen's Association presented a petition demanding *Big Brother* be closed down. The campaign culminated in questions being asked in the Bundestag, Germany's federal parliament. And the Interior Minister, Otto Schily, declared that *Big Brother* violated articles of the country's constitution protecting human dignity. In the debates and newspaper articles that followed even the Holocaust was invoked. Producers at Endemol received death threats. They were advised by the police to remove *Big Brother* stickers from their car bumpers for fear of reprisals.

Many looked to the television regulator to put a stop to *Big Brother*. One of the regional directors was Dr Norbert Schneider. His views, like those of so many, were coloured by the history of the twentieth century: 'I grew up in the early forties of the last century and I saw what happened when people who are not allowed to come in my private area, do what they want and take away the privacy, take away the shelter, take away what is my personal meaning. Everyone needs a room or space where he is not observed, where he is not under the camera.' This could have been a speech from Winston Smith, the central figure in Orwell's *Nineteen Eighty-Four*, so acutely did Schneider summarise the nature of totalitarianism. Paul Romer, the man who had realised *Big Brother* in Holland, was in Germany training up the production team. He was baffled by this collective soul-searching. But the Dutch did not live with the constant fear that somewhere in their corporate psyche there might be lurking a corrupting, fascist instinct which could one day reassert itself. There was now only a month to go before the first transmission, unless the programme's gathering opponents could find a constitutional way to prevent it.

The heartfelt ethical debate raging in Germany failed to cause so much as a ripple in the world of corporate finance. This was a period when deals were announced daily and fat fees were available to middlemen. The ethics of television did not come into it. Merchant bankers were punting mergers and acquisitions as fast they could think them up and recommending them with all the relish of waiters in a three-star Michelin restaurant. To find out more about Endemol, Juan Villalonga could have asked any of a hundred banks in Madrid, Frankfurt, Paris, London or New York. All of them would already have had a ready-made plan for a merger – that was their job at the time, to sit in their glass towers and fantasise. Villalonga had recently set up Telefonica Media, to manage all his TV and radio assets. Following Ben Verwaayen's call he instructed José Antonio Rios and Juan José Nieto from the new division to appoint London's Deutsche Bank office to act for them and investigate an Endemol deal. Rios was a rotund, jolly former TV executive from

Venezuela. Nieto was more reserved, handsome, olive-skinned with a similar banking background to Villalonga. Deutsche's Guy Hayward-Cole and Bruce MacInnes were asked by Rios and Nieto to prepare a dossier on Endemol and a rationale for Telefonica to buy it. They codenamed it Project Eden. Eden stood for Endemol and a list of exotic fruit supposedly from the Garden of Eden supplied the other names: Tangerine for Telefonica, Mango for Telefonica Media and Tangelo for its internet service provider Terra.

This was a time of macho deal making. Wizard codenames, the more swashbuckling the better, were very much in vogue. Villalonga had launched 'Operation Veronica' shortly before, in January 2000. He had already invested in four Latin America telecom companies. Now he wanted to take control of them – 'Veronica' referred to the sweep of a bullfighter's cape and perfectly captured the machismo of the moment. Villalonga's expansion of Telefonica into South America would come to be seen as a brilliant strategy. But there is no recorded instance of a telco buying a content production company with anything other than regret in the end. Thankfully for the bank balances of John de Mol and his colleagues, this was not how it was seen at the time. Hayward-Cole and MacInnes sat long into the night at Deutsche Bank's huge corporate headquarters on London Wall in the City of London. They were preparing a detailed description of Endemol and a bullish analysis of how it might fit in with Villalonga's drive towards convergence. He wanted to best AOL and Time Warner – Endemol would help him do that. Before long de Mol's entertainment formats would become neatly encapsulated digital packages winging their merry way down Villalonga's telephone wires to his subscribers in two continents. That was the theory, anyway.

Deutsche Bank's view of Endemol had long been that it was an interesting company but overdependent on its two substantial output deals with RTL in Holland and Germany. They also remembered the company's problems with Sport7 and the risky theatre division. These were the factors that had held Endemol's share price down at around €30 for so long. But in the last week of February, as Hayward-Cole and MacInnes prepared their document, Endemol's quote was hovering nicely above €90, three times its historic value. The difference, as the bankers pointed out, was simple: *Big Brother*. A world-beating format, already sold in the US and, even better, internet-connected. An idea that at one time only de Mol had believed in, an idea his colleagues distrusted and no broadcaster wanted to touch, was now propelling the entire company forward on a wave of market enthusiasm. Endemol had a preliminary meeting with Rios and Nieto. Hendriks and Schouwenaar took them to watch Holland play Germany in a 'friendly' football match on 23 February in Amsterdam. Holland won 2–1 and the Spanish pair were able to cheer them on. There was already some serious bonding going on.

Deutsche Bank's description of Endemol was exactly what Villalonga and his Telefonica Media colleagues hoped to read. They arranged to meet Endemol and their bankers, ABN AMRO, in Amsterdam on 29 February. Deutsche Bank was to prepare Telefonica's presentation for the meeting. Rios and Nieto from Telefonica Media and a delegation from Terra, their ISP, met Hayward-Cole and MacInnes in the Sheraton Hotel at Schiphol Airport on the morning of 29 February for a briefing. They then moved on to ABN AMRO's offices to meet Endemol at three o'clock that afternoon. Rios, urbane, genial, with very good English, outlined a glowing future for a Telefonica/Endemol marriage: growing Endemol's business in the Americas, convergence with Telefonica's internet and mobile businesses, opportunities with Telefonica's terrestrial and digital television businesses. It sounded convivial, exciting and eminently achievable. Indeed, at this point in the media business, anything seemed possible. Endemol, led by Ruud Hendriks and their mergers and acquisitions specialist, Hubert Deitmers, then presented their plans for growth over the next five years. Everyone felt it had been a superb meeting. But Endemol pointed out they had seven companies interested in bidding for them and time was of the essence. Seven may have been a mild exaggeration, but this was a negotiation and Endemol needed to get an auction underway between Telefonica and KPN. World Online would be allowed a supporting role in order to encourage the others.

In Germany *Big Brother* succeeded in going on air on 2 March with an introductory programme. On 3 March the twelve housemates then entered their home for the next hundred days, which the German press had taken to referring to as 'the container'. Among them were a carpenter, a restaurateur, a student, a telephone hooker and a Macedonian mechanic. As in Holland, *Big Brother* immediately propelled RTL2 into the front rank of German channels, more than doubling its share of fourteen- to forty-nine-year-olds. But RTL and Endemol had a genuine fear that Germany's television regulator would succeed in banning *Big Brother*. The pressure continued to grow. On 1 March the Association for German psychologists had issued a statement: '*Big Brother* is a group experiment which shows contempt for humanity and is also an undreamt of extension of exhibitionist TV. A programme like this, disguised as exciting entertainment with the opportunity to help decide the fate of the participants, can function as a model for behaviour, particularly among the young, and can only enhance the growing tendency towards loss of values and the brutalising of society.' This was followed by a Catholic Association press release: 'People undergo merciless camera surveillance, which degrades them and makes them the object of a spectacle in which their personal life and individuality are subjected to the public's mockery and lust for sensationalism. We wish to protest against this irresponsible series and demand that those responsible at RTL2 immediately cancel this miserable project. We appeal to advertisers to ... prevent this kind of immoral voyeurism by withdrawing their TV commercials.' In fact, the opposite was happening. As the ratings continued to rise advertisers, at first hesitant, were coming forward to exploit the valuable young audience *Big Brother* was attracting.

RTL2's local regulator, LPR Hessen, had decided that they should ban *Big Brother*. But they were faced with opposition from more senior television regulators. Professor Wolf-Dieter Ring, president of a national watchdog for the protection of children, said they did not want to become the nation's morality police. He confessed he found it difficult to argue that human dignity was being abused when the contestants were taking part voluntarily and could leave whenever they wanted. And Dr Norbert Schneider, who had made such strong links between fascism and the lack of privacy in the *Big Brother* house, acknowledged that younger Germans had a different perspective: 'I learned that young people, they have no problem with it. They say – we want to be seen, we are eager to go on screen. We open up whatever we can show. We show our feelings and whatever we can offer to the public, we do. They had no bad experiences.' Schneider told the local regulator that if they attempted to ban *Big Brother* on the grounds of protecting human dignity, RTL would challenge them in the courts. He did not think the regulator would win. Schneider then brokered a compromise. RTL and Endemol agreed to turn the cameras off in the bedrooms for one hour a day, so that housemates could preserve their privacy and dignity for that brief period if they wanted to. The housemates resented this change to their regime and ostentatiously avoided the bedroom during the statutory hour every day. The pen pushers at the regulator's office used to monitor the transmission on the *Big Brother* web site closely. They would telephone and complain if they saw even a flash of the bedroom during this designated period. But having discharged their official duties they would then start to gossip about the goings-on in the house and fish for extra information about how the voting was going.

Telefonica Media and Deutsche Bank began March by preparing more detailed plans for the Endemol acquisition. MacInnes and Hayward-Cole speculated that Endemol's other suitors might include Pearson, Deutsche Telecom, a couple of cable television companies and World Online. But they never guessed that their real opponent was KPN. KPN had also unfurled their plans for Endemol to the company's management. They wanted to merge various of their media assets, including their ISP, Planet Internet, into one company and keep it quoted on the Dutch stock exchange. For both cultural and patriotic reasons many of the senior Endemol executives were very attracted to KPN. But the charm and the enthusiasm of the Telefonica team was also very seductive. On 6 March another meeting took place between the Endemolites and the Telefonicans which culminated in a very friendly dinner. Now Deutsche Bank had to assemble the elements of a bid for Villalonga's approval. Endemol wanted to know exactly what Telefonica and KPN were offering. It was time for everyone to lift their skirts.

Back in London Hayward-Cole and MacInnes ran the figures. On Monday 6 March Endemol's share price touched €98. So the market was saying that the company was worth €3.4 billion. There were three other ways of valuing Endemol. The first was via discounted cash flow. This predicts future performance based on a set of assumptions. The answer you get from this is only as good as the guesswork that is fed into the calculation. On this occasion Deutsche Bank thought that discounted cash flow could justify a bid of up to €3.5 billion, close to the current market value. The second method involved looking at recent sale prices of other comparable companies. This was imprecise because there were none sold recently that were identical. But an analysis of other TV companies that had recently changed hands, such as King World and All American Fremantle in the US, led to a much lower valuation of €1.7 billion. Then, confusingly, the third approach yielded a massively higher figure. This scrutinised how the market was valuing other companies with similar trading figures. Of course, entities such as AOL were being given hyperinflated valuations. And so this third method said Endemol could be worth a staggering €7 billion. On top of this Telefonica was involved in an auction. How high might they have to go to see the other bidders off? This was what they had to discuss with Villalonga. They had an appointment with him on Thursday 9 March. Conveniently the chairman of Telefonica was due to be in Madrid rather than Miami that week, even though his consort Adriana Abascal was now pregnant with their child. Hayward-Cole and MacInnes were due to confer with Rios and Nieto on the Wednesday night before going in to present their conclusions to the man himself the following day. Various changes were suggested, necessitating revisions that had to be made overnight.

Bleary-eyed, having had no more than a couple of hours sleep, Hayward-Cole and MacInnes joined Rios and Nieto at eight o'clock on the Thursday morning to rehearse the presentation before their appointment with Villalonga at nine. They were then ushered through a number of anterooms and into a beautifully panelled room with an antique octagonal table at its centre. By this time, the bankers' nickname for Villalonga was the Sun King. He had indeed become an absolute monarch and getting access to him, through a succession of rooms, was not unlike an attempt to penetrate Versailles for an audience with Louis XIV. They took their seats at the table and waited for fifteen minutes. Rios then scuttled into Villalonga's office and re-emerged, beaming, a quarter of an hour later: 'Good news. He is in an excellent mood this morning.' It was Villalonga's custom to host as many as five or six of these takeover talks simultaneously in various satellite rooms. Only he kept track of the deals, frenetically touring the

The young disc jockey, John de Mol, at the controls in his early days at Radio North Sea International, 1972. (Wim Sonius)

Joop van den Ende (centre) and John de Mol (right) shake hands on the announcement of Endemol's stock market flotation, selling one third of the company to the market, 1996. Aat Schouwenaar, van den Ende's chief financial officer, is on the left. (Endemol)

Webcam pioneer Jennifer Ringley. Jennicam went online in 1996, using cameras in the twenty-year-old's apartment to record the intimacies of her daily life.

The Truman Show, released in 1998 but written in 1995, whose protagonist, Truman Burbank (Jim Carrey, *pictured*), is the unwitting star of his own television series. Every aspect of Truman's life is available to viewers but his town (a huge TV set) and his friends and family (all actors) are an artificial creation of the show's omnipotent producer. (Band/Uppa.co.uk)

Edtv, also ready for release in 1998, in which video-store assistant Ed (Matthew McConaughey, *pictured left*) agrees to have his life filmed twenty-four hours a day and broadcast live on a TV network. (Uppa.co.uk)

Paul Smith, the single-minded champion and, later, producer of *Who Wants to Be a Millionaire?* (Rex Features)

Doug Van Gundy (left) on his way to a quarter of a million dollars on the US version of *Who Wants to Be a Millionaire?* It was in the very first week of the show and made it a sensation. Host Regis Philbin (right) had been one of the few to see the potential of the idea right away. (Getty Images)

Passionate, innovative and litigious – Charlie Parsons, the man behind *Survivor*. (Rex Features)

The very first cast for the US version of *Survivor*, January 2000. The series' eventual winner, Rich Hatch, stands in the back row, fourth from the left. (CBS/Getty Images)

The idyllic South China Sea island of Pulau Tiga, setting for the show. (Terence Lim/wildasia.net)

'All my life I've wanted this, all my life.' A jubilant John de Mol with Leslie Moonves, the president of CBS, answering questions from the media after announcing the deal to bring *Big Brother* to the US, June 2000. (Endemol)

John de Mol's house in Blaricum – where Endemol's inner circle met secretly on 13 March 2000 to decide which multi-billion deal to go with. (Leo Vogelzang)

The colourful Juan Villalonga, chairman of Telefonica, with John de Mol, after agreeing to buy Endemol for 5.5 billion Euros. It was the first time they met. (Endemol)

A promotional shot of the first line-up for *Big Brother* in the UK, which began on 14 July 2000. The winner, Craig Phillips, is on the extreme right and 'Nasty' Nick Bateman is fourth from the right. (Amanda Searle)

Housemates, led by Craig Phillips, confront Nick Bateman with evidence of his attempts to influence the *Big Brother* evictions. 'Nasty Nick' was subsequently thrown out of the house. (Endemol)

Bart and Sabine, *Big Brother*'s first 'couple', in the first ever series, Holland, 1999. (RTL Nederland)

The original Dutch *Big Brother* house under construction, and (inset) its control room. (Endemol)

Zlatko, German *Big Brother*'s first 'trash hero', signs autographs after his eviction from the house in April 2000. (S. Gegorowius/Endemol Deutschland)

Sebastian Florek, *Big Brother Poland*'s last-minute addition to the show and would-be politician. (Forum)

The housemates from *Big Brother Africa*, the first pan-African version, May 2003. Cherise Makubale, the Zambian winner, is in the centre, crouching.

Islamic demonstrators outside the *Big Brother* house in Bahrain, February 2004. The Arabian production was screened for just nine days before being suspended amid waves of protest. (AFP)

'John de Mol is in the diary room.' On a visit to *Big Brother Poland*. (Endemol)

negotiations like a plate-spinning vaudeville entertainer. Shortly afterwards Villalonga made his entrance and they got down to business. The Deutsche Bank pair took him briefly through all their calculations as to the possible value of Endemol, though it was, in truth, a case of 'think of a number'. Each of their models gave such different answers. But they made great play of Endemol's prospects with its new hit *Big Brother*. Villalonga was a man heading a company that had telephone, internet and television interests. He was being told about an entertainment property that drove voters to the phones, fans to the internet web site and viewers to the television. At that time, in that market, this must indeed have seemed like the philosopher's stone. Villalonga cut short the presentation: 'This is a unique asset. We need to have more contents.' (The Spanish always talked about 'contents' with an s, as though they were referring to a can of beans.) He went on: 'I want you to buy this company. And you must pay what it takes. Project Eden must succeed. The right place to start is a premium of 60 to 70 per cent.' There was silence in the room as Rios, Nieto, Hayward-Cole and MacInnes took in what he was saying. Endemol's share price that day was around €94. He was instructing them to take the company out at between €150 and €160. That valued Endemol at upwards of €5.5 billion (more than £3.5 billion). Villalonga knew he was entering an auction and he intended to win it with a knock-out blow – a piece of pure, Spanish tumescence. But given Endemol's profits at the time, this was a multiple three times higher than any production company had ever been valued at before. These were the team's instructions – they were to prepare an offer letter and get it to John de Mol personally.

March 2000 was an unusually cold month in Holland. Since the New Year de Mol had done the *Big Brother* deal in America, struggled to launch *Big Brother* in Germany and found himself in constant meetings about Endemol's future. He was tired and decided to fly to the Algarve for a weekend of warmth and golf.

If the Telefonica team were to see him on Friday 10 March they would have to fly to Portugal. When de Mol heard that they wanted to talk to him that day he told the Endemol team that they had better be there too. So on that Friday morning Hendriks, Schouwenaar and Deitmers, along with their ABN AMRO advisers, all flew down to Faro Airport in the Algarve. At the same time Rios, Nieto, Hayward-Cole and MacInnes piled into one of Telefonica's corporate jets in Madrid, also bound for Faro. As they sat in the deep leather armchairs, being served a luxurious breakfast, Rios was racking his brains to think of any other deal sweeteners they could come up with to win the auction. He had (correctly) guessed that other bidders might offer about the same, crazy though the sums of money seemed. Rios suggested they propose an additional €100 million bonus pot for the majority of Endemol employees who did not hold shares in the company. It was a clever idea to win the hearts and minds of as many Endemolites as possible.

They met in the Hotel Quinta do Lago, at Vale do Lobo on the Atlantic coast. They were unaware that 10 March was turning into an historic day in the US. The NASDAQ had broken through 5000 the day before and that Friday it held on to the gain and rose slightly. It turned out to be the very top of the market. It had taken a bull run of seventeen and a half years to reach this point and it was about to fall catastrophically. By mid-April it would have plunged by 25 per cent. Within a year it was to have sunk back as far as 2000. There was no time like the present to deal. March's market values would be revealed as laughable within weeks. The emperor had had no clothes for some time. Within days he would be seen to be naked.

The Telefonicans handed over their offer letter. It was effusive, pointing out how Endemol and Telefonica shared a common understanding and vision for this tremendous opportunity for a union between their companies. Telefonica's convergent range of distribution assets throughout the Hispanic world would provide Endemol with unparalleled opportunities. Their opening bid for Endemol was €150 per share. The letter pointed out that this was a premium of 60 per cent over Endemol's share price on the previous day and an 86 per cent premium over the average price during the preceding six months. The special bonus was also set out. De Mol was in his element. This was a game he could play. Better still, it was a competitive auction.

By the end of their hotel meeting de Mol and his team had pushed Rios and Nieto all the way up to €160 a share – the upper limit that Villalonga had authorised. This constituted an offer for Endemol in excess of €5.5 billion. Telefonica would pay with an element of cash but mostly with shares. The atmosphere was convivial. Endemol said they would let Telefonica know which way they were going to jump on Monday evening, after a board meeting. On their way back to Faro Airport, Hayward-Cole and MacInnes noted what the Endemolites already knew. During the afternoon the Endemol share price had leapt from €94 to €100. Had there been a leak? Was some insider trading going on? This was something that, in due course, would be investigated by the Dutch authorities, but the Telefonica team jetted out that night feeling they had done all they could to win the auction. Their task now was to prepare the details of the amended offer for approval by a Telefonica board meeting the following Monday. In between, on the intervening Sunday, was the small matter of Spain's general election. If the socialist opposition were to win, the top management of Telefonica, from Villalonga down, was likely to be sacked and the deal would be in ruins.

On the same day that Endemol and Telefonica were negotiating in Portugal and the NASDAQ was peaking in New York, the final members of a vast television crew were flying into Borneo in south-east Asia. No fewer than eleven cameramen, ten sound men and an army of producers and support staff had assembled.

They were led by the former paratrooper Mark Burnett. This was the start of the first US production of *Survivor*. Unlike *Big Brother*, which is virtually live, *Survivor* is shot and edited like a documentary, well in advance. The location Burnett had selected was a tiny tropical island called Pulau Tiga, forty miles off Borneo's coast in the South China Sea. It was heavy with vegetation and infested with snakes and rats. The sixteen contestants were taken to within a mile of the shoreline in a Chinese junk while Burnett directed a helicopter to circle above taking dramatic, panoramic shots of the scene. Then the sixteen hopefuls were 'marooned' on the island by being cast overboard and made to swim for the shore with as many rafts and boxes of supplies as they could throw out of the junk. Over thirty-nine days they were to compete for $1 million by voting each other off the island every three days. Among the contestants were students, a dairy farmer, a basketball coach, a biochemist, a lawyer, a retired naval officer, a neurologist and a truck driver. As ever with the new breed of 'reality' shows their reasons for taking part were more complicated than any of the show's detractors imagined. The contestants were usually condemned as attention-seeking wannabes desperate for fifteen minutes of celebrity. That was undoubtedly the motivation of some (and not necessarily a crime, as it was pointed out). Others were in it for the money and nothing else. And a third category were people who, fed up with their lives, were looking for a change and a bit of adventure. On this occasion they had come to the right place.

The sixteen were divided into two rival tribes and sent to live on different beaches. Within minutes the cameras would catch them bickering, arguing, sulking and struggling to dominate each other with their own ideas for shelters, latrines, fishing traps and so on. The tropical island looked idyllic. But before long the flies, the rats and the humidity prompted one of the contestants to bemoan the loss of her hermetically sealed New York apartment with its air conditioning and shiny bathroom.

The first challenge between the two tribes was for each to propel a raft across the water, lighting paraffin flares as they went. The Tagi tribe lost out to the fitter, more aggressive Pagong tribe. In particular, Sonja Christopher, a recovered cancer sufferer, aged sixty-three and from San Francisco, stumbled and slowed her team down at a critical moment. The losing tribe had to march immediately to a jungle clearing and vote one of their number off the island. Rudy Bosch, a didactic, former Navy officer received three votes. But evicted on this occasion, with four votes, was Sonja, ruthlessly labelled as a liability. Burnett and his team were delighted. Already this had become a Darwinian struggle – only the fittest would survive as these sixteen learnt the laws of the jungle the hard way.

Survivor was due to start on CBS on 31 May. This was a month earlier than its great rival, *Big Brother*, was to premiere on the same channel. They were already being set up as major competitors in what would be the first season of blockbuster, reality formats on US television. As this rivalry developed Charlie Parsons became more determined than ever to have his day in court. It had been set for 20 April in Amsterdam. There his lawyers would argue that *Big Brother* was no more than a copy of *Survivor*. The verdict was critical. Telefonica were aware of the action and would make their offer for Endemol contingent on its winning the case and establishing an unchallengeable right to the growing revenue from *Big Brother*. This was one of the many factors that Deutsche Bank and Telefonica's lawyers had to include in the document they were preparing for the main board's approval. But the more pressing question in Spain was whether that board meeting would take place or be postponed. It was all down to politics.

The Spanish government no longer obviously controlled Telefonica. But they held a 'golden share', meaning they still had considerable influence. Telefonica remained Spain's largest company and the make-up of its board was a highly political issue. In the preceding six months Villalonga's controversial share options scheme had been revealed, to the unease of the Aznar's centre-right government and the indignation of the socialists. If the opposition were to win on Sunday 12 March things – and personnel – would change very swiftly. The socialist leader, Joaquin Almunia, had specifically accused Prime Minister Aznar of cronyism, allowing his personal friends to enrich themselves. Villalonga was the primary target for this attack. Aznar held a 4 per cent lead in the final opinion polls on Saturday 11 March, but he needed a substantial lead in order to secure an overall majority. If he failed all sorts of things could happen in the horsetrading that would follow.

Guy Hayward-Cole and Bruce MacInnes flew into Madrid with their presentation and calculations at teatime on the Sunday. When they arrived at Telefonica's headquarters they found the six executives with whom they had to discuss the figures prior to the meeting with Villalonga and the board the next day. All were chain smoking and watching the television, waiting for the election results. None of them could concentrate on the Deutsche Bank pair until they knew that their jobs and their share options were safe. Just before 10 p.m. the first results came through. Aznar's centre-right party had exceeded all expectations and secured an outright majority. There was huge relief in the room followed by much back slapping. It was only at this point that they were willing to concentrate on the presentation. They asked the bankers to rework several parts of it. They rushed to do this overnight, emailing quantities of data back and forth between Madrid and their London office.

When the plan was presented to the Telefonica board, on Monday 13 March, it was approved. Villalonga demanded as much. But Deutsche Bank received one surprise later in the day. Telefonica's chief financial officer, Fernando Abril-Martorell Hernandez, had apparently known nothing of the negotiations to buy Endemol. He was furious and attempted to blame

Deutsche Bank for not telling him. His real target, of course, was his chairman who, by this time, was setting up deals almost daily on his own initiative. In normal times this would have been highly irregular but these were not normal times. Despite their internal disagreements, however, Telefonica were now officially ready to deal. What about Endemol? They had gone to ground in a wealthy village near Hilversum called Blaricum.

In 1976 a Dutch art collector called Pieter Menten fled to Switzerland to try to avoid prosecution for war crimes. It was alleged he had assisted in an SS massacre of Jews at the Polish village of Podhorce in 1941. Switzerland eventually expelled him and he was brought to trial in 1977. While he was in custody vigilantes burnt down his forty-room mansion in Blaricum. His wife Meta had to move into the coach house. Although he was acquitted on technical grounds he was eventually retried and sentenced to fifteen years in gaol. He emerged in 1985 and died in 1987. For some years his ruined mansion lay derelict. No one came forward to buy the land, regarding it as tainted, if not cursed. But in the early 1990s a newly wealthy television producer with a stronger stomach finally acquired the plot to redevelop it. John de Mol razed any trace of Menten's property to the ground. Then he and his partner Els replaced it with a simple, rather beautiful white cottage, thatched in the Dutch vernacular style. Although de Mol's home looks modest from the outside, inside it is very spacious with an enormous basement. This was the house in which Endemol's inner circle met on the evening of Monday 13 March to ponder their company's future. They had to decide between KPN's offer and Telefonica's bid, both of which would make them extremely rich. It was the kind of dilemma most people pray for.

At the large, circular dining-room table sat John de Mol and Joop van den Ende, Endemol's controlling shareholders. With them were Ruud Hendriks, Aat Schouwenaar, Hubert Deitmers and Alex Oostvogel, Endemol's finance director. Also there to advise was a banker from ABN AMRO. In the middle of the table was an enormous vat of caviar. Beside it were chilled, opened bottles of the choicest Mersault from Burgundy. They had a big decision to make and they needed to fortify themselves. De Mol asked Hendriks to summarise the main points of KPN's and Telefonica's offers. Hendriks then reminded everyone that KPN had offered marginally more money. But they weren't as international as Telefonica and they wished to maintain a share quote. World Online had offered the most – north of €6 billion. But for everyone in the room, Nina Brink's punt had a strong whiff of fantasy about it.

De Mol then went round the table and asked everyone a simple question: 'Shall we go with KPN or Telefonica?' The first to respond was the numbers man, Alex Oostvogel. He knew that KPN's proposition was to create a larger company by merging Endemol with other media assets. They had made it clear that they would give this group a new finance director. Oostvogel said he didn't wish to lose his job so he was voting for Telefonica. Hendriks also voted for Telefonica – he liked their deal terms more. Then it was Schouwenaar's turn. He was almost neutral since he explained they were both good offers. But when pressed he added: 'I'm 51 per cent in favour of KPN and 49 per cent in favour of Telefonica. If you really want me to make the choice I will choose KPN because the cultural future for our company is probably better Dutch than Spanish.' Hubert Deitmers opted for KPN too – he liked the idea of their internet business being folded into Endemol. So far those in the room were evenly balanced between the two offers But this was not a democratic vote. Van den Ende and de Mol were the majority shareholders.

Joop van den Ende was known to favour the Dutch solution. But he was also planning to stand down from the day-to-day running of his old production company. 'Can I have a word with you outside?' he asked de Mol. The two left the room and van den Ende said: 'John, listen, I'm leaving the company. You are not. So tell me what you want. You make the decision and, whatever it is, I will support you.' They went back into the room.

For de Mol there were several factors that made him prefer Telefonica. First their offer was to buy Endemol outright and remove it from the stock market and the detested analysts. KPN wanted to maintain a share quote. Second, de Mol was genuinely impressed by Telefonica's international scale; KPN was parochial by comparison. Third Telefonica was offering a clear route by which de Mol and the others could realise monetary value – he would be able to sell their shares on the open market at an agreed point. KPN's proposed structure was more complicated. Van den Ende addressed his colleagues first: 'John will head this company in future. I will agree to John's choice and I will not vote.' Everyone looked at de Mol. 'Gentlemen, we will go with Telefonica,' he announced. There was relief all round the room that they had a decision at last. Several of those present noticed that at this point de Mol, the hard man of Dutch television, had tears in his eyes. Were they tears of joy at his approaching fortune or distress at finally letting go of his baby?

At around midnight they telephoned Rios at Telefonica who was waiting in Madrid for their call. He was delighted. Now he discovered that in any deal de Mol always turned the screw a bit further. He would be receiving an element of cash but mostly Telefonica shares in payment for his Endemol shares. The Dutch told the Spanish that they wanted a 'collar'. If Telefonica's share price fell by more than 10 per cent in the weeks it would take formally to complete the deal, then they would be compensated with extra shares. The Spanish agreed. When the markets did, indeed, plunge within weeks the collar arrangement was activated and saved the Endemol team millions of euros.

Next they had to call their chairman Ben Verwaayen with their decision. They found him in another time zone crossing a different continent in Lucent Technologies' corporate jet.

Verwaayen would personally have preferred KPN, his previous employer, but he congratulated them and flew on. He was involved in a high-tech adventure of his own. Lucent's shares had peaked the previous December at $82. In January the company's quote had plummeted to $52 in a day when their financial results were lower than expected. Two and a half years later it would be trading below $1. Some time before that Verwaayen had moved on to run British Telecom.

Finally Endemol had to call KPN with the bad news. By this time it was 3 a.m. They were extremely shocked and very disappointed. Their chief executive, Paul Smit, retorted: 'This is a football match. Maybe the ninety minutes are over. But we think we are in for extra time and maybe some penalties. We should still negotiate.' Hendriks told him: 'Listen, we've done the deal. How would you feel if we'd done it with you and were continuing to negotiate with Telefonica. We can't do that.' But Smit turned up at de Mol's house the next day to persuade him to reconsider. De Mol and Hendriks stood firm. Some weeks later Hendriks and Schouwenaar were visiting Telefonica in Madrid. They met Paul Smit and a KPN colleague in the lift. Then it dawned on them. Throughout their negotiations with Telefonica, Villalonga had also been trying to buy the company he was negotiating against, KPN. The simple truth was that, in this final week of the dotcom boom, everyone was trying to buy everyone else. It was an orgy.

De Mol's colleagues drove away from his house in the early hours of Tuesday 14 March tired but happy, and very wealthy. De Mol had made a billion pounds sterling. Van den Ende was now worth more than a billion euros. And the others had shares and options that would be redeemed for handsome sums – in Hendriks's case, potentially over €100 million. At the time none of them questioned how an alliance with a Spanish company might work. Northern Europe and southern Europe are culturally very different. The Dutch had fought a number of bitter wars with the Spanish colonists in the seventeenth century. 'At that point,' Schouwenaar says, 'nobody mentioned those conflicts. But they did later on.'

Endemol and Telefonica agreed a schedule for the rest of the week. The due diligence, allowing Telefonica's bankers, lawyers and accountants to inspect Endemol's books, could not be completed in three days. But they would do as much as they could. De Mol and Villalonga would still announce the deal and sign the contracts on Friday at ABN AMRO's offices on the edge of Amsterdam. Hayward-Cole and MacInnes from Deutsche Bank, tired as they were, accepted that they would not be able to go to bed for another three nights. Speculation was rife in the newspapers as to which company might be buying Endemol. KPN and World Online were among the purchasers suggested, but no one guessed the identity of Telefonica. Not even when a huge telecommunications van with a satellite dish and a massive Telefonica logo pulled up outside ABN AMRO's offices on the Wednesday morning and started to cable up. It was there to transmit the signing live back to Spain. But, amidst all the gossip and rumour, no one seemed to notice it. Speculation was also rife on the Dutch stock exchange as investors piled into Endemol, now an identified takeover target. On the Tuesday its share price rose to €108, by Wednesday's close it was €118 and Thursday saw it reach €124.

As the week wore on the advisers continued number crunching. There was one issue that many at Endemol thought Telefonica might want to return to – that of handcuffs for the company's senior executives. As things had been left on Monday they were only requiring de Mol to stay for five years. The others were not tied in in any way nor did they have any onerous conditions requiring them to hold their Telefonica shares for a long period, as de Mol did. This was extraordinary since in a creative company its major asset is its executives. But Telefonica did not seem to care as they rushed towards completion. The only change during the week, for technical reasons, was an agreed adjustment of the purchase price down to €158 per share.

Endemol held a supervisory board meeting on the Thursday to approve the deal formally The heads of the major holdings abroad also gathered to be told about the sale. José Velasco was the founder of Zeppelin, the Madrid-based production company Endemol had bought two years before. He pointed out to de Mol a photograph of Villalonga in a Spanish newspaper he had brought with him. All the managing directors were amazed when de Mol laughed and said: 'So that's what he looks like.' They realised that the man who was buying Endemol for €5.5 billion had never even met de Mol. That would only happen at the signing the next day.

On the Thursday evening van den Ende threw a party at his home in Baarn for his leading presenters, actors and producers. In an emotional speech he announced his own retirement and told them about the deal with Telefonica. The press were outside photographing all the famous faces coming and going. One of the presenters could not contain himself and as he left he told one journalist who the purchaser was. So *De Telegraaf* had a scoop the following morning on their front page. Nobody yet knew, though, the magnitude of the price.

On Friday 17 March Ruud Hendriks travelled early to ABN AMRO's modern, high-rise office block beside a busy motorway outside Amsterdam. He was to be master of ceremonies. First Endemol briefed all the analysts on the deal as the press release announcing the purchase was simultaneously released on the wires. The news quickly spread across the dealing screens of Europe. At Pearson's headquarters in London's West End John Makinson read the figure and had to read it again: 'We were absolutely gobsmacked by the price. We thought the world had gone mad at that point.' At Schroder Investment Management in the City of London there was a loud cheer and they punched the air – their remaining investment in Endemol shares was now going to realise five times what they paid for it originally. A fund manager there recalls how nerve-racking that week was: 'We were climbing a wall of fear. We knew the end was coming but we didn't know when. To cash out one investment, however minor, was a bonus.' Down the road, at the headquarters of Rothschilds, the merchant bank which had touted Endemol without success the year before, the reaction was different: 'We were absolutely gutted. This was one of the biggest fees we'd missed in our entire life. Then our second reaction was – this is barking, this is not going to last. It'll end in tears.'

At around noon Villalonga touched down at Schiphol Airport in one of Telefonica's corporate jets. Hendriks was told he was on his way to the signing, where de Mol was already in place. At that moment Hendriks received a call on his mobile. It was the excitable Nina Brink from World Online. Within a couple of hours she was launching the IPO of her own company on the Dutch stock market. But having read of the deal she still found time to call Hendriks and insist he introduce her to Villalonga. If she couldn't buy Endemol from de Mol and van den Ende any longer she would buy it from Villalonga. In Europe, this was the most insane moment of the dotcom boom. And it came just hours before everyone was to discover the market had turned and it was over.

Villalonga greeted de Mol warmly. They signed the official documents and smiled for the cameras. Hendriks was puzzled as to why Villalonga also seemed to know ABN AMRO's chief executive, Jan Kalff, so well. Later he speculated that, on the other side of a Chinese wall, ABN AMRO had been advising Villalonga as he tried to bag KPN. After the ceremony was over everyone went back to van den Ende's house where he held a second dinner, twenty-four hours after the first. This time the members of Endemol's supervisory board were present, along with Villalonga, Rios, Nieto and all Telefonica's key advisers.

Guy Hayward-Cole and Bruce MacInnes had barely slept for a week. MacInnes had cancelled a skiing holiday in Canada with his fiancée in order to complete the deal. He no longer knew if she was still his fiancée. Also at the dinner was Sylvia Toth, the member of Endemol's board who was wealthy in her own right having sold an employment agency some years before. She cut a flamboyant figure in Dutch business circles with her taste for haute couture and sports cars. She was attending with a personal guest – the chief executive of the Philips electronics group, Cor Boonstra. Everyone remembers his presence now because it later transpired he had bought a tranche of Endemol shares only a few days earlier and therefore benefited from the hike in value when the company was sold to Telefonica. Both he and Toth denied it was insider trading. Although he was investigated no action was ultimately taken against him. But the following year he retired from Philips and resigned other board positions.

For Villalonga, Rios and Nieto this was a dinner of welcome. But for Toth and Ben Verwaayen, who was also present, it was a farewell. They would be leaving the supervisory board when Telefonica took over. Both van den Ende and Villalonga made generous speeches and the evening ended happily. A good deal happier than how Nina Brink felt that evening. The IPO of World Online had not gone well.

World Online, Nina Brink's internet service provider, had been talked up by the markets for some weeks. Its growing sub-scriber base, by now more than 1.5 million across Europe, saw World Online labelled as AOL's main continental competitor. There was talk of the share being twenty times oversubscribed. The familiar model at this time was, of course, for internet flota-tions to double or even treble in value on their first day of trading. World Online's shares were placed at €43. Enthusiastic traders were speculating that they would at least double to €80. But by 2 p.m. on 17 March they had risen to a mere €50 and then settled back right away to the launch price of €43 before the close. By the standards of the market this was a failure. It followed two other less than spectacular IPOs that same week – in London (lastminute.com) and Norway (Stepstone). Somebody somewhere was finally questioning how companies with no profits and meagre cash flow could possibly be worth more than conventional businesses with both. Within a month it was to be revealed that Brink, who had offered World Online's shares to the public at €43, had not long before quietly sold her own shares to a US fund manager for a mere €6. So much for her confidence in the float. She was forced to resign from the company and the shares collapsed to €17. Everyone at Endemol had correctly read the form of this particular rider in the dotcom stakes.

Friday 17 March marked the week in which the NASDAQ peaked and the bull market became a bear market. Fear replaced greed as the dominant sentiment. John de Mol had ridden the dotcom wave perfectly with a television format that encapsulated the spirit of the times. Better still, he sold out only hours before the wind changed. He was now one of the richest men in Europe. That would remain the case unless, of course, he lost a certain legal action – *Big Brother* versus *Survivor*.

CHAPTER TEN

A Very Good Case

If your lawyers tell you that you have a very good case, you should settle immediately.

RICHARD INGRAMS

Big Brother had just unlocked a treasure chest of Spanish gold for the Dutch. But it is difficult to appreciate just how much of a punt everyone involved in the Endemol sale was taking on the success of this idea. In March 2000 it had only been fully produced once, in a small country. What if it did not catch on elsewhere? By the time Villalonga and de Mol shook hands *Big Brother* had also been on air in Germany for two weeks, albeit with the cameras disabled for an hour a day. In fact, to everyone's relief, *Big Brother* Germany was following a very similar pattern to the Dutch version.

The German series generated thirty thousand press articles during its run. While the regulators, the Church and the politicians agonised over the maintenance of human dignity, German newspapers had something else on their mind: sex. They told and retold the story of Bart and Sabine with relish. When were the German contestants going to get it together? They did not have to wait long. Two of the housemates, Kerstin and Alex, had clearly been taking an interest in each other. After three weeks *Big Brother* gave everyone a party. The alcohol may have rendered them less inhibited. They crept under a duvet in the girls' bedroom. Another housemate read poetry out loud to sanitise, if not sanctify, the proceedings. The duvet rose and fell rhythmically and Alex's face, when it could be seen, was fixed in an expression of masculine pleasure. As with Bart and Sabine, it was visually a non-event, obscured by bedding. The members of the production team concluded the goings-on owed more to the application of the mouth than the missionary position. But the papers had their story. *Der Spiegel* tried to label the broadcaster RTL2 as salacious and hypocritical: 'The example of Alex and Kerstin shows most clearly what RTL2 thinks of the candidates. They enjoyed showing their intimacies, but referred to them demurely. "Pillow talk" or "cuddling" was how *Big Brother* described the event. However, if you put the word Kerstin into the search on the official *Big Brother* site you come across a page whose title presumably was not meant for public consumption. Here the cuddling is referred to prosaically as "Kerstin/Alex bonking".'

On 27 March *Der Tagesspiegel* picked up on the incident: 'So RTL2 has managed it at last. The programme is being talked about everywhere ... And from the regulators, at first so outraged, there is now hardly a peep.' The regulators were reflecting public taste. Over twenty years European society had become much more tolerant of sex and bad language (whereas hostility to the depiction of violence remained as high as it had been two decades before). Unlike Holland, though, Kerstin and Alex's romp was by no means the biggest talking point of the series. That was provided by Zlatko Trpkovski, a car mechanic aged twenty-three and originally from Macedonia. His best friend in the house, Jürgen Milski, described him in a book he later wrote: 'The first thing I noticed was his enormous neck with three rolls of fat. What a guy, I thought – I bet he weighs 105 kg and wants to lose a bit of weight here in the house. But he'll also be after the prize money of 250,000 Deutschmarks, I thought to myself.

And he admitted that without any pretence, which endeared me to him straightaway. All the others came up with some kind of claptrap about being fascinated by the project and wanting to test themselves.'

Zlatko was ill-educated, prejudiced and he didn't mind who knew it. Early on a remark of his became nationally celebrated: 'Who was William Shakespeare? If you were to ask me what he did – words, films or documentaries – I'd have no idea.' His sense of refined tolerance was also much debated. He was not sure precisely what 'homosexual' or 'heterosexual' meant, but he knew what he liked: 'Adam and Eve. Man and woman. He didn't write Adam and Adam. I don't care what men shove up their arses but leave me out of it.' To complete the picture of almost cartoon-like stupidity Zlatko demonstrated a fetish against his own body hair. But he did not have a razor. He proceeded to attempt to remove his growing chest hair with a pair of nail scissors. This was not only painfully laborious it was also hazardous. He persistently cut himself and then cursed in surprise.

One of Germany's television presenters, Stefan Raab, called Zlatko 'The Brain'. A newspaper then dubbed him a 'trash hero'. Then on Sunday 9 April Zlatko was due to leave the house, having been evicted by the popular vote. The day before there was a presentiment of the mayhem that was to follow when a light aircraft flew over the house trailing a banner reading: 'Everyone loves Zlatko – read all about it on Monday in "Bunte".' *Bunte* is a sort of German *Hello!* magazine. He may have been voted out in a straight choice with another housemate, but Zlatko was now a celebrity.

The German *Big Brother* house was situated in the small town of Hürth, outside Cologne. Its population was only fifty thousand. Ten thousand *Big Brother* fans descended on the town to attempt to witness Zlatko's eviction. They had their ready-made banners. One summed it up: 'Zlatko, the man what should be President!' The fans tramped through people's front gardens, they urinated against the walls – they did all the things that large crowds do when there are no plans or facilities for them. The local mayor, Walter Boeker, was besieged by angry residents and had, with Endemol, to come up with a ticketing system so that this could never happen again. Zlatko was truly *Big Brother*'s first 'trash hero'. There were to be many more around the world. He was offered record contracts, personal docu-soaps, chat shows and numerous commercial endorsements. His rise and fall is documented later in this book. Some German commentators were depressed that someone so ignorant could become so celebrated. Others were appalled that such a person could get on to television at all. Their reaction partly explains 'Zladdi's' popularity. That someone could honestly admit to crushing ignorance on television had its appeal – such people had not really been seen before on their own terms. And with his crude, politically incorrect opinions German viewers also found his honesty refreshing. Zlatko was saying publicly what they themselves sometimes thought but felt constrained from expressing.

Big Brother was unscripted, it was making heroes of painfully ordinary people and it was being followed by millions. Its number one fans were the executives of the hitherto fringe German channel – RTL2. Like Veronica in Holland, *Big Brother* was transforming its fortunes. It won more than 25 per cent of younger viewers right from the start. It gained almost half of all viewers with its programmes in the final week of *Big Brother*. And, once again, the television and the internet had established a symbiotic partnership. By the time the winner, John, emerged in June the *Big Brother* web site had recorded 190 million hits – an extraordinary statistic for the time. As yet, not many had the technology to be able to receive the live, streamed pictures from the house. But anyone with an internet connection could enjoy the news pages and the chat rooms where they were able to pursue their own obsessions with fellow fans. Was it serendipity or shrewdness that brought *Big Brother* on to television screens at exactly the time mobile telephones and the internet became widely available? The same can be asked of Elvis and his harnessing of the electric guitar, transforming it from an obscure jazz instrument to a popular teenage icon. Or of the Beatles bursting on to the scene in the early sixties at the same time as the transistor radio and cheap vinyl discs. The technology enabled the idea but the idea also drove the technology. In any event, this was a different way of using television. It was proving both popular and lucrative. Endemol Germany made more than €10 million profit on this first series alone. The Spanish at Telefonica were delighted. Charlie Parsons was not. His aim was simple. To take possession of all those revenues.

April the twentieth was the appointed day for the court hearing between Charlie Parsons and John de Mol. The verdict would come later. In a district court in Amsterdam John de Mol was represented by his lawyers, along with Paul Romer and Gary Carter. Charlie Parsons came in person with his two co-owners of the format, Waheed Alli and Bob Geldof. There had been a war of words in television trade journals in advance. Parsons was quoted as saying: 'The most important thing in life is to own your own thoughts and nobody should be able to steal those.' Thomas Notermans, the Endemol spokesman, in the same article had re-emphasised that *Big Brother* and *Survivor* were totally different shows, confiding that John de Mol thought that the owner of *The Wheel of Fortune* would be more likely to win a lawsuit against him.

Parsons, Alli and Geldof were there because they felt so strongly about the action, particularly Parsons: 'This was very important to us and we didn't feel we should let them get away with it.' But it was a strange experience for him: 'So we go to court . . . there were the three judges, they're in court already and this is very weird because in England you sit in the court and the judge comes in. And the second thing, obviously, which is weird is the whole proceedings are in Dutch. It's not surprising but it's extremely hard to follow.' What Parsons couldn't know was that his lawyer had introduced the three plaintiffs rather elaborately, placing great emphasis on *Lord* Alli and *Sir* Bob Geldof. This led to a farcical exchange where one of the judges responded, a little curtly, that he had never heard of Sir Bob Geldof. The implication was – get on with the case. It was a comic moment reminiscent of the sixties British judge who reportedly asked: 'Who are the Beatles?' So Parsons may have been right when he suspected that one or more of the judges was not a rabid fan of television: 'One of the judges I can remember yawning all through the proceedings. I distinctly had the impression one of the judges felt – as lots of people do, let's face it – what's this TV about? It's not really important – TV, it's rubbish.'

Parsons' lawyers had built on the charge faxed through to Mipcom the year before. They were throwing every possible legal weapon at *Big Brother* that they could come up with. *Big Brother* had infringed *Survivor*'s format. In a wrongful act Endemol had stolen the *Survivor* format and then taken advantage of Parsons' creativity, hard work and investment. This is a Dutch law known colloquially as preventing anyone from benefiting from the sweat of another man's brow. Further, it was unjust enrichment via the profits derived from the wrongful act. Finally, Endemol had infringed Parsons' moral rights, changing and broadcasting the *Survivor* format without his consent and without crediting him. Parsons had been advised that he had a reasonable case. He was going to give it his best shot. And litigation in Holland was, helpfully, much cheaper than in his native UK. Among the evidence they brought to court was the original selling tape for *Survivor* voiced by Gary Carter when he still worked for Parsons. Coupled with the fact that they sold an option for *Survivor* to Endemol in the mid-nineties, they argued that Endemol had armed itself with their ideas in order to come up with *Big Brother*. Endemol went once again through their defence. They argued that these were very different programmes and that Gary Carter had played no part in the conception of *Big Brother*. To the Brits the rehearsal of these arguments was not only long but completely impenetrable. Indeed, so excluded did Bob Geldof feel he started to read a newspaper rather than attempt to affect interest.

When the judges had heard both sides they reserved judgement until June. John de Mol and his colleagues would have to wait another two months to discover if their deal with Telefonica was intact. Parsons may not have known quite what was at stake for Endemol, but he was asking the court for all *Big Brother* format revenues so far and in the future, damages and an end to any further unauthorised sales. As *Big Brother* took off around the world its revenues would exceed half a billion pounds. So there was plenty at stake for him too. The next territory to strike *Big Brother* gold was Spain, in Juan Villalonga's backyard.

In his rush to buy Endemol one of the many factors Villalonga seemed to have overlooked was that *Big Brother*, the jewel in the crown, had already been sold to a rival television network in Spain. Telefonica owned half of Antenna 3. Endemol's Madrid affiliate, Zeppelin, had already done a deal with another commercial channel, Telecinco. But the head of the affiliate, José Velasco, managed to pull off a groundbreaking arrangement that did, in the end, benefit Telefonica too. Digital television services were just being introduced into Spain in early 2000. Three rival platforms were vying to establish themselves. To help pay the enormous production costs of *Big Brother*, Velasco made an agreement with two of the platforms for a twenty-four-hour *Big Brother* channel. This took the streamed video offered, somewhat jerkily, on the web site and turned it into a pure, television-standard feed. If you were so inclined you could now watch your favourite housemates awake and asleep, all day, all night and on your TV. When one of the digital platforms failed to launch, the benefit of this idea went solely to Viadigital, in which Telefonica was a shareholder. Hundreds of thousands signed up to pay a monthly subscription to see uninterrupted *Big Brother*, live from the house whenever they wanted it.

This was a revolutionary moment in television – it was the first time that a programme had offered its rushes, its raw material, in high-quality pictures. Viewers could now do what small numbers of web users in Germany and Holland had already done. They could form their own view as to what the most significant events in the *Big Brother* house were. Normally everyone has to rely solely on the edit of the rushes into a transmitted programme. In this exercise – carried out to create a narrative – 90 or 95 per cent of the material is discarded by the production team. It is a subjective process – no two producers would ever edit the material in the same way. Now viewers were being empowered with the whole picture. *Big Brother* fans often complain about one or other of the characters being unfairly edited and inaccurately portrayed. The reason they can enter such an argument is that, for the first time in television, all the rushes have been made available to them. *Big Brother*, like *Penn and Teller*, was gradually revealing the tricks of the trade.

But whether *Big Brother* continued to be a success, in its third territorial roll-out, was the most important thing of all for Telefonica. They need not have worried. The show was an even bigger hit in Spain than either Germany or Holland before it. The pecking order in Spain in early 2000 had the state broadcaster, Television Espanola, at number one, as it had been for at least forty years. Telecinco lay in second place with a 20 per cent market share, with Telefonica's Antenna 3 trailing in third place. Within just three weeks of *Big Brother*, Telecinco had overtaken Television Espanola to claim the top spot. This was a more dramatic achievement than boosting the shares of the fledgling networks of Veronica and RTL2 in Holland and Germany. That Endemol achieved it owed a lot to their new producer in Spain, Gilda Sentana, whom they had recruited from Cuba. There she had learnt how to plot compelling storylines when producing the steamy, melodramatic soap operas so beloved by Latin audiences – the *telenovelas*. Gilda appeared to be the only person in the Spanish production team who had read Orwell's *Nineteen Eighty-Four* and she had had to do it clandestinely. The book remains banned in Cuba to this day.

Sentana ignored the, by now, usual debate in the Spanish press and national parliament about the ethics of the project. Spanish television showed clips of Bart and Sabine from the Dutch *Big Brother*. Some picked up on the invasion of privacy of the housemates, others argued that this would be a highly manipulated exercise in pornography. But Sentana was casting ten young Spaniards for romance, not sex. She knew that fiery passions and smouldering looks were what made *telenovelas* irresistible to Latin audiences, not explicit congress. Sentana needed relationships to develop. They went on air on 23 April 2000. She had to wait till 26 April – all of three days.

On the second day, one of the housemates, Maria José, revealed that she wanted to win the prize money because one of her daughters had a brain disease and she could then afford the best medical treatment for her. Other housemates decided that the nomination system was unfair, that they didn't wish to judge each other when they all had personal reasons for wanting to win the money. The public should decide. They dismantled *Big Brother*'s rule book and stitched up the nominations so that they all came equal. Everyone was up for eviction and the public vote alone would decide who went. By day three in the Spanish house they had all bonded closely, but some more closely than others. Maria José and Jorge formed the first couple. They took to a bunk bed together. As in other houses it was entirely unclear what, if anything, took place. Speculation in Spain was rife. The biggest issue, though, was not the suggestion of sex. The press was convinced that the entire production was a setup and that the mistress of the *telenovelas*, Sentana, handed the housemates their daily scripts secretly every night. No one believed that such relationships could develop spontaneously.

The pact between the housemates was soon suspended. On 3 May Maria José was evicted by a public vote, having been nominated by her fellow contestants. This left the lovesick Jorge on the inside. Jorge's favourite saying became: '*Dios! ¿Quien me pone la pierna encima?*' (God, and now who's going to put her leg on me?). This was a reaction to the loss of Maria José's affectionate, Harpo Marx-like gesture, draping her leg over his knee. It became the *Big Brother* catchphrase of the series. A late-night show made by Endemol's other production company in Spain, Gestmusic, turned this phrase into a popular rap song.

There were a few surprises to come. On 22 May a popular scandal magazine, *Interviú*, broke the story that Maria José had once been a prostitute. They had even found the personal ads she had placed in a newspaper. Her new boyfriend, Jorge was, like Bart, a former solider. Bart had cried when Sabine left and threatened to walk out too. But he had eventually got a grip and stayed. Jorge reacted differently. Over the three weeks he pined for Maria José. The joker of the house became the moper. By the weekend of 20 May Jorge was determined to leave and be reunited with Maria José. Normally the production team would have done their utmost to dissuade him. But they now knew *Interviú* would be exposing Maria José in two days' time. They called Jorge's mother and Maria José to the house on Sunday 21 May and organised Jorge's departure. He spent the Sunday night in a hotel with her so she could reveal and explain her past before he read it the next day. Their relationship survived the revelation and they were together for six months (before a spectacular and public falling out).

The producers were accused of knowing all about Maria

José's secret, though, in fact, they did not. But from this point the Spanish *Big Brother* developed from drama to tragedy, and finally into farce, all accompanied by unprecedented ratings. To cast one prostitute could be seen as an accident, to cast two is bordering on the sensationalist. But this was Latin *Big Brother*. Nothing was done by halves.

While the Maria José story was unfolding one housemate left to attend the bedside of his dying father. Another of their number, Silvia, also walked out because the man she had become attached to, Israel, was being evicted. The production team had to top up the house from their list of reserves. They chose Monica. Eleven days later *Interviú* had another exclusive story: yes, Monica had also once worked as a prostitute. The day before publication she talked to the producers from the diary room. Would she like to stay and brave it out, or come out and deal with the revelation in person? Monica cried. She exclaimed: 'Forgive me because I have lied to you about my past!' She hovered, decided to stay and finally decided to leave. Unlike other housemates she then ceased attending the live eviction night programmes and disappeared from the public eye. Her particular attempt at celebrity exposure proved to be an experience that ran out of control. That was the tragedy. Now for the farce.

Big Brother became, even more than in Holland and Germany, *the* national talking point in Spain. So much so that a famous clown, Leo Bassi, attempted to lead a backlash. He set up a rival web site which, loosely translated, was called 'aload-ofbollocks.com'. Here Bassi railed against *Big Brother*: 'It cheapens democracy . . . what faith can we have in the wisdom of a population that is so easily manipulated?' Bassi enterprisingly leased the plot of land directly adjacent to the *Big Brother* house. He erected a platform supported by a tall pole and, armed with a megaphone, took to treating the *Big Brother* house to amplified readings from the original *Nineteen Eighty-Four* by George

Orwell. It took him six days to read the entire book out loud. When he had finished he resorted to blowing a cast-off Polish ship's fog horn to try to drown out the next live eviction show. The publicity that flowed from his filibuster drove *Big Brother*'s ratings even higher. At this point Bassi accepted defeat with an appropriately clown-like shrug of the shoulders and a doleful expression. He had set out to satirise the popularity of *Big Brother*. He ended up increasing it.

At one point, on 9 May 2000, Real Madrid were playing Bayern Munich at home in the semi-final of the Champions' League. Endemol executives were Telefonica's guests at the match. This was a national event for a football-mad country, but *Big Brother* achieved higher ratings that evening. Then, when it came to the last night, Telecinco achieved a massive 70 per cent share of the television audience. This was delivered with the customary multi-million phone voting, the country's biggest web site and, of course, a very popular pay-TV digital channel too. *Big Brother* had taken root in Anglo-Saxon northern Europe. Now it had taken off in a Latin culture. As John de Mol had predicted and Juan Villalonga had hoped, it was beginning to look like a truly international hit.

After securing Endemol, Villalonga kept up his relentless pace of acquisitions. The market had turned but at the time who could tell whether it was merely pausing for breath or beginning a long-term decline. In early May 2000 Telefonica's internet arm, Terra, bought Lycos, the American ISP, for $12.5 billion. It was a company the bulk of which Telefonica would sell off in 2004 for just $90 million. Villalonga's exuberant belief in the new economy at a time when others had become bearish now helped contribute to his downfall. His biggest obsession at the time was to complete his merger with KPN, Holland's former nationalised telco and his rival in the battle for Endemol. The ambition was to create a group with a combined value of €150 billion. This would have put Villalonga at the top of a company ranked fourth in Europe's telecommunications sector, behind Vodafone/Mannesman, Deutsche Telekom and France Telecom. But Aznar's government did not like the deal because it thought the Dutch politicians still had too much influence over KPN. They had promised to sell off most of their 43 per cent holding in the company but had so far failed to do so. Other Telefonica shareholders simply did not like the deal, period. Villalonga attempted to persuade his board to go ahead. But he was talking to them via satellite from Miami where his partner Adriana Abascal was shortly to give birth to their first child. It is difficult to exert influence when not physically present. The board members, conscious of the opposition of the government and some key shareholders, finally asserted themselves and voted the KPN deal down. This was the beginning of the end for Villalonga.

Sensing a wounded man, *El Mundo* then published allegations of illegal share dealing by Villalonga. These were based on information supplied by bitter former executives who had been ousted by the dictatorial Villalonga over the years. He strongly denied them. The press speculated that the board and the government had the next chairman already lined up. By July 2000 he was finally ousted and withdrew to Miami to concentrate on his second fatherhood. Villalonga left Telefonica six times the size it had been when he became chairman in 1996. His expansion into Latin America proved to be of immense and long-lasting value to the company. His acquisition of Endemol, however, like that of Lycos, appeared an expensive diversion. This was not yet to worry de Mol and his colleagues – they had the Telefonica shares securely in their possession. Some, like Ruud Hendriks and Joop van den Ende, had taken advantage of the laxity of the Endemol deal to cash out a good portion of their Telefonica shares already. While appearing a little hasty, this turned out to be a profitable decision. Telefonica's shares slid during 2000, like the rest of the market. But those who, like John de Mol, kept their shares for the moment had the comfort of the negotiated 'collar'.

By this time, in addition to Holland, Germany and Spain, *Big Brother* had been sold to the UK, USA, Portugal, Switzerland, Sweden and Belgium. The head of Endemol's production company in Rome, Marco Bassetti, had been finding it difficult to complete a deal. Mediaset, the major commercial network, owned by the Prime Minister, Silvio Berlusconi, had held back, not convinced the format would work in Italy. But when they saw it dramatically turn around the fortunes of Telecinco in Spain, another Latin country with a Catholic tradition, they wanted to deal. Bassetti then had to devise a strategy to deal with the programme's opponents, as Endemol producers were now doing in a range of territories. In Italy he reckoned, correctly, that the two key constituencies he would have to handle would be the left and the Church. He had a personal understanding of the left since his father-in-law was Bettino Craxi, the former socialist Prime Minister. Bassetti agreed with Mediaset that it would be good to provoke the left for advance publicity. But the broadcaster preferred to attempt to appease the Catholics.

So, in May 2000, Bassetti found himself travelling to Rimini, on Italy's Adriatic coast, to meet the eighty-three-year-old Cardinal Tonini. This highly educated old man was an influential figure at the Vatican, known as the confessor to the Pope and an unofficial media guru for the Catholic Church. Instead of residing in luxury in Rome he lived simply in a settlement he had founded for poor and homeless people. Bassetti, accompanied by a Mediaset executive and his assistant, sat down to discuss *Big Brother* with this man. They were not precisely looking for his blessing but hoping to explain the format before the newspaper onslaught began. On the table in front of the Cardinal in his bare room were the daily newspapers of the world in several languages. He had already read about *Big Brother* and he made it clear he was concerned. But Bassetti set out to argue it was a soap opera not a sex show: 'We tried to explain to him that we are not going to make any bad scene, it will be very soft, we will cut every bad word. To defend *Big Brother* is not so easy but we began to be in a better position because he was a little bit relaxed. He understands we're not mafia.' But then Tonini widened the discussion, saying that so much of the new television was bad. He gave them an example – he had seen a show in which children, twelve year olds, interviewed adults, sometimes about salacious subjects. He had seen a mere boy ask an actress why she had shot a nude calendar. There was silence in the room. Bassetti had produced the show and Mediaset had broadcast it. Then the Mediaset executive pointed at Bassetti – as if to say: It was all his doing, let him answer for it. Bassetti felt that now he was cast as the devil who was trying to tempt the pure broadcaster away from the straight and narrow.

They spoke for three hours that afternoon. The Cardinal did not give the project his blessing but he thanked them for coming to discuss *Big Brother* and from then on he kept in touch with Bassetti. The format was to start on air in September 2000 and would be made annually thereafter. As the various relationships took root between the housemates the Cardinal's main concern, expressed forcibly on the telephone to Bassetti, was that the diary room should not be referred to in the Italian show as 'the confessional'. He also wrote several newspaper articles arguing that recording people for twenty-four hours was like stealing their souls. In between man and God should be a priest, not a camera. Even the Pope weighed in to condemn *Big Brother*. Bassetti persisted with twenty-four-hour filming – that was the format. But he eventually promised the indefatigable Cardinal that they would rename the diary room and drop the word 'confessional'.

Bassetti had established a dialogue, a bridgehead, with the Church. Now for the intellectual left. Its members are seen as the great conservatives of Italian society. When Italy was about to convert from black and white television to colour they were the ones who opposed it – they preferred their politics in black and white. In the summer of 2000 Mediaset announced that *Big Brother* would be on air in September. They then waited for the left-wing newspapers to pick up the baton. On Sunday 18 June Bassetti was out for a jog early on a Sunday morning. As he passed the newspaper stand he could see a bold headline on the front page of *La Repubblica*: '*Grande Fratello*' (*Big Brother*). Was this it? Had the second front opened? Bassetti had no money in his tracksuit pockets but managed to snatch a glance at the main article: '*Big Brother* is still making an impression, by Eugenio Scalfari.' There followed the most deliciously Italian stream of consciousness that anyone could hope to read. It started as it meant to go on: 'I am aware how important it is . . . to continue looking for someone to lead the centre-left to recovery . . . to finally put an end to market liberalism and start on the high road to true and solid Federalism.' Scalfari asked whether new, converged broadcasts such as *Big Brother* would spell the end for traditional journalism, cinema, theatre and even the novel. Most appalling of all was the risk to poetry: 'Will this "reduct ad unum" [reduction to one] not risk burying poetry as well?' He then shrewdly cited *The Truman Show* and the innocence of its central character compared to *Big Brother*'s housemates who had 'chosen to be filmed and are under contract'. This he called a 'double fiction which is passing off a fictitious reality as true'. He pointed out that, on Mediaset, it would be coupled with brainwashing advertising, too.

Scalfari concluded with a call to arms: 'However, poetry remains . . . quite a few young people are open to poetry . . . perhaps we should be organising poetry readings at home or even in theatres while TV is transmitting *Big Brother*: at a time of non-violence it would be a way of putting up resistance. Brigades of partisans who read poetry. It's a thought: let's talk about it. One thing gives rise to the next.' Bassetti called his head of publicity from the street that Sunday morning to tell him the media debate, as they intended, had begun.

In the US *Survivor* went on air on 31 May 2000. Mark Burnett had completed the shooting in Borneo in April and the winner had remained a scrupulously guarded secret. On a Wednesday on CBS, after a huge marketing campaign, American viewers saw the sixteen castaways hit the island of Pulau Tiga. At the end of Episode One, Sonja was voted off the island. The entire programme was shot glossily like a movie. It had well-defined characters and they were involved in a clearly delineated game. The American public loved it. The first, hour-long episode gained 15.5 million viewers. Episode Two proved that people were hooked. The audience rose by a further three million. More crucially for the elderly CBS, it was gaining the network a younger audience. On 12 June *Variety* pointed out that *Survivor* was getting a better demographic profile than *Who Wants to Be a Millionaire?*, the other European format sensation that had, by now, been on ABC for eight months. The *Variety* article said that CBS executives hoped *Survivor* would help boost *Big Brother*'s ratings when it launched in July. That was not how Charlie Parsons felt. But for the moment he would celebrate. It had taken him six years to sell this show. He had been knocked back many times. Now, like Paul Smith, he finally had a lucrative hit in the biggest, richest television market in the world. This was a mountain John de Mol had yet to climb. But Paul Romer was working on it for him.

Paul Romer, the man who created *Big Brother* for the first time in Holland, had moved with his family to Los Angeles to oversee the first series for the US. He was finding it hard going. Despite advance publicity and an accessible web site, only eleven hundred people had applied to take part. The casting department of CBS were bitter that Endemol had insisted that they would do this alone. They could see the house taking shape in the middle of CBS's studio parking lot but they were not allowed to be involved. CBS, though, had given Romer some strict guidelines as to age, geographical spread and ethnic background.

Having made a short list of twenty candidates Romer arranged to present their video profiles to Leslie Moonves. This was a crucial meeting and John de Mol flew over from Holland to be present. Also in the room were twenty other CBS executives, including the casting department. Romer took them through each candidate. Moonves smiled encouragingly as he did so. He then came to the end knowing that he had no back up – these twenty were the only suitable people from the meagre application. After he completed the profile of the twentieth he sat down to wait for comments. Still smiling Moonves said simply: 'It's a bunch of crap. It's all a bunch of crap.' The casting department nodded. John de Mol said nothing. Romer swallowed hard and began to sweat: 'I tried desperately to limit the damage by making Moonves talk about them one by one. In the end he had to admit he was OK with about nine of them.' He only needed ten for the house so the situation was now manageable. But on the way out, in the lift, Romer was drenched in perspiration. He turned to de Mol and said: 'You asshole, why didn't you say something?' De Mol replied: 'But you did well. I didn't have to say anything.' In the end the members of the production team felt that, with CBS's sense of concern, they ended up picking a cast that was too middle of the road, too 'milk toast'. With similar caution they decided to make Julie Chen from CBS News the host – they didn't want *Big Brother* to look too self-servingly showbiz. This proved a popular choice with Moonves. In time he left his family and moved in with Chen.

On 14 July *Big Brother* went on air in the UK. It had a larger, more modern looking house and a music mix by one of Britain's top DJs. And evictions took place every week rather than every two weeks. But otherwise, it was the same format. Within three days the housemates had diverted a clay pot-making task in a new direction. Six of them stripped and smeared themselves with wet clay. As the series progressed, though, it was class and not sex that would provide the major scandal.

'Ghastly, cynical, dissipated, distasteful, a new low, tedious, desperate, seedy, voyeuristic, a sham, pointless, sad and pathetic, creepy, inane, barrel-scraping, phoney, gross, tacky, skull-crushingly dumb.' Those were the British critics. 'The creation of a human zoo where the human beings are trapped in a confined space . . . its obsession with imperfect personal integrity failing to disguise the underlying collective lynch mob morality of the whole experiment . . .' That was the Church of England. All the usual, tough questions, asked with particular urgency of *Big Brother* whenever it made its first provocative appearance in a country. But, as ever, an analysis of the critics shows that the vast majority of them were male and over fifty. Men have little sympathy for soap operas with emotional storylines, whether scripted or unscripted. The middle aged and elderly, meanwhile, not only dislike the younger generation's relaxed attitude to nudity, sex and 'bad' language: many of them are baffled by it. So Salman Rushdie attacked *Big Brother* early on: 'The television set, once so idealistically thought of as our window on the world, has become a dime store mirror instead. Who needs images of the world's rich otherness, when you can watch these half-familiar avatars of yourself – these half-attractive half-persons – enacting ordinary life under weird conditions? Who needs talent, when the unashamed self-display of the talentless is constantly on offer?'

By the time *Big Brother* US launched, a week earlier than the British version on 6 July, *Survivor*'s ratings were rivalling those of *Friends* and *ER* on NBC, America's two most popular series. By contrast, there seemed to be no spontaneous enthusiasm for *Big Brother*. The truth was that the production team had to pay the whooping, screaming first-night crowd to turn up – the hoopla was a strictly commercial transaction. On 10 July the *New York Times* helpfully published an article headlined: 'CBS's *Big Brother* fails in the TV ratings.' It made unflattering comparisons with the hits of Paul Smith and Charlie Parsons: 'After a weekend of sharply declining ratings, CBS's *Big Brother*, the latest effort in the reality television trend, is falling far short of the phenomenon status reached by two other European imports, ABC's *Who Wants to Be a Millionaire?* and CBS's *Survivor*. Indeed . . . *Big Brother* runs the risk of becoming a hugely expensive flop.' *Big Brother* had, of course, been here before, in its first week in Holland. Its audiences were small compared to *Millionaire* and *Survivor*. But it was delivering a young audience to the hitherto elderly channel. And it was doing it daily. Under pressure at a press conference, Moonves was asked whether he would be as welcome with his golfing chum, President Clinton, after *Big Brother* as he was before. Facetiously, Moonves replied: 'With Bill Clinton? He already called me about some of the people on *Big Brother*.'

He was put right two days later. In an interview with ABC News President Clinton attacked *Big Brother*: 'How can these people, particularly the parents, abandon their families and children for a chance at money and disgrace.' The interviewer pointed out that certain events in Clinton's life had unfolded in public. He retorted: 'That's the problem. Privacy should be protected. My lack of privacy is a direct result of my position as President of the United States. But privacy shouldn't be auctioned off to the highest bidder. These people are prostituting themselves to media conglomerates. It's very troubling.' This was, perhaps, the turning point for *Big Brother* in the US. Now that the older generation had condemned it, as heartily as Elvis Presley had been condemned in the 1950s, it would gain credibility with the younger generation. Then three of the housemates turned out to be more interesting than CBS had bargained for. One was revealed as a former gun-toting black militant. Another had killed a man in a hunting accident and a third had been a stripper. Gradually, day by day, at a modest but sustainable level, *Big Brother* helped bring down the average age of the CBS audience. Towards the end of its first series the usual battle lines were drawn up. The *Denver Post* spoke for the older generation: 'The most phenomenally boring television series in history will have its resolution Friday night . . . *Big Brother*, the show that illustrated why *Survivor* was a hit.' The *Nation* had a different take. In an article headed '*Big Brother* perfectly captures America's psyche', Neil Gabler argued: 'More than one wag compared it to watching paint dry. But sometimes you can watch paint dry and end up seeing a mural . . . For those who watched enough episodes it may have been the most revelatory program on television in years and the one that was closest to the grain of contemporary America. If *Survivor* was pure TV hokum, full of bombast, *Big Brother* was Proustian.' Gabler was in a minority. But what everyone agreed on was that *Survivor* was the biggest US hit since *Millionaire* the previous year. The whole nation seemed to be preparing for the final show on 23 August, with special viewing parties organised across the fifty-two states.

An extraordinary one in six Americans watched the *Survivor* final. The rating, at fifty-two million, was the highest audience on CBS since 1994 and its highest ever recorded audience in summer. They were all glued to the remaining four castaways fighting it out for the prize of $1 million. First Susan, the truck driver, falls away in a vote. Then, in sonorous tones with a heavily orchestrated underscore, the presenter tells the final three: 'Take everything you've become and channel it into one powerful experience.' Three remain: Rich, the gay corporate communicator, Rudy, the grizzled retired Naval officer, and Kelly, the young female river guide. Kelly gets the chance to send Rudy packing, which she does. Now, in the blue-lit jungle clearing, it is Rich versus Kelly. A jury of ex-castaways, already voted off, has to decide on the winner. Speeches are made. Kelly: 'Judge me on the person that I am.' Rich: 'It's about who played the game better. I hope you think I did.' The vote gets to three-three. Rich says: 'I need water and oxygen' and holds his head in his hands. The last vote goes to Rich. He is the winner. The closing credits with lush strings and Rich's voice-over have the tone of a movie like *The Shawshank Redemption*. Unlike *Big Brother* this was crafted, not live. The participants in the game voted, not the public. And the game dominated the show, rather than the relationships between the contestants. It was perfect for the American audience.

In the battle of the ratings *Survivor* was a clear winner over *Big Brother*. But what of the most important contest of all, the legal one in Holland? This was to decide whether all *Big Brother*'s worldwide revenues were to go to Charlie Parsons instead of John de Mol. A decision against Endemol would also completely unstitch the epoch-making deal done with Telefonica the previous March. The three judges of the Amsterdam court promised to deliver their verdict on 7 June. And this they did, in a fax to Endemol's lawyers. They in turn then had to call Jelle Wieringa, the in-house lawyer at Endemol who had overseen the case. When their lawyer came on the line Wieringa tensed himself: 'Jelle, we won all the way. All claims denied. Congratulations.' His task was now to call John de Mol, who was at home: 'Often when I call John I wind him up and say – bad news, John, and so on. I didn't feel like making jokes this time. There was tension in his voice. He said, good morning. I said, good morning, John. Good news. We won all the way.'

Parsons was to continue appealing for another four years. But de Mol and everyone at Endemol now felt secure. Paul Smith had his international hit, *Who Wants to Be a Millionaire?*. Charlie Parsons finally had resounding success with *Survivor*. And John de Mol had established that his world-beating format, *Big Brother*, was entirely his.

Who Wants to Be a Millionaire? sold to the most countries and earned the largest revenues. *Survivor* introduced the elimination contest and was the biggest hit in the US. But neither matched *Big Brother* for controversy or revolutionary use of new technology. And neither cornered the elusive but invaluable younger audiences so comprehensively as *Big Brother*. Smith, Parsons and de Mol created a revolution in television entertainment and taught the past masters of the art, the Americans, a lesson. Each had an idea that was derided but none of them ever gave up. Each became rich, but only de Mol became super-rich. He was the only one for whom the deal was even more important than the idea. His idea, meanwhile, was beginning to take on a life of its own.

PART II

CHAPTER ELEVEN

Civilisation As We Know It

Reality television is not the end of civilisation as we know it, it *is* civilisation as we know it.

GERMAINE GREER

In June 2000 British Telecom were tasked with laying the special fibre optic cables to the *Big Brother* studios in east London. Only new links could enable the TV signal, the internet and the telephones to converge, as advertised on the *Big Brother* box. They came. They dug up the ground. They laid the cable. With five days to go it emerged that they had laid the cable to the wrong studio. They came back. They dug up the ground again. They relaid the cable. Chris Short, the head of interactive services at Endemol UK, was tense but now confident he could launch live video streaming on the web on schedule. He had promised this to the broadcaster, Channel 4. The new web site's sponsor (Terra, the subsidiary of Telefonica) had been persuaded to invest more than a million pounds in extra capacity. Expert consultants were concerned that, without it, the web site would not be the only thing to collapse. There was a real possibility that Britain's entire telecommunications network would seize up.

The ten housemates chosen for the very first *Big Brother* house in Britain swept into the studio complex in a fleet of black-windowed Mercedes. Chris Short had his webcams trained. This was the moment the site would go live. They switched it on. Nothing. The screens were blank. The technicians looked at each other. Incomprehension bordered on panic. They checked every connection and every camera. There was nothing wrong with them. They should have been functioning. Then one of them looked more closely at the bank of computer monitors in their Portacabin. They had come from America. He looked at the back. They were all switched to NTSC, the standard US television signal. He flicked all the switches to PAL, the British standard. The picture burst into life. Chris Short gently put down the telephone receiver with an irate voice from Channel 4 still in full flow. The web site was live, just two minutes before the housemates walked into the house.

Between the first and second week the number of hits on the *Big Brother* web site doubled from seven to fourteen million. These figures rather perplexed the *Sun*, which announced that seven million people were watching the streaming. In fact the internet was still in its infancy in Britain. There were probably no more than 250,000 people taking the streaming, but they were accessing it so often that the number of times it was 'hit' ran into many millions. At least the *Sun* was alive to the new phenomenon. The technology editor of a broadsheet newspaper could not get to grips with the streaming at all. He telephoned Chris Short. He said the whole thing was a hoax. He accused Short of a massive deception along the lines of *Capricorn One*. There were further accusations of fraud when the defining moment of the first British series occurred. And the incident was driven dramatically by the new technology embedded in the *Big Brother* format.

Nick Bateman was thirty-two when he applied to take part. He had been at Prince Charles's old public school, Gordonstoun, and afterwards had had a broking job in the City. Craig Phillips was twenty-eight, born in Liverpool and the owner of a small building firm in Shropshire. He suffered from dyslexia and had difficulty reading and writing. He was five inches shorter than Bateman. On his application form he was unable to specify a favourite book (he only recalled reading one, a biography of Sylvester Stallone). Bateman named Milan Kundera's *The Unbearable Lightness of Being*.

Bateman decided to play the game to the maximum, flouting the rules by surreptitiously recommending his fellow contestants to nominate particular victims from week to week. The public and the British tabloids, who were witnessing his tricks, became highly exercised that the housemates appeared blind to it. Finally the illicit notes that he would flash covertly in front of participants' eyes were discovered. He was unmasked and confronted by Phillips. Characteristically for the British, their *Big Brother* flashpoint concerned class rather than sex.

Tribune-of-the-people, Phillips, challenged the house toff, Bateman, in a hastily convened kangaroo court. The hits to the web site leapt into millions and the site almost collapsed. The news of this live event one Thursday lunchtime spread across Britain's web like a virus. By the end of the week *Big Brother*'s internet traffic had doubled again to thirty million hits. The *Guardian* called it the birth of the net as a popular medium in Britain. That night *Big Brother*'s television audience also doubled. What was, in effect, merely a skirmish in a television game show took on the proportions of a public trial, a *cause célèbre*. I even had to appear on BBC Television News. I polished up all my arguments in defence of *Big Brother*, but all I was asked was whether the story had been fixed. Nobody believed it could have happened spontaneously.

Following the confrontation the producers decided to evict Bateman for breaking the rules. But they were alarmed as to whether he would be safe – the newspapers were conducting a hate campaign to match what they took to be the public mood. In a piece of memorable hyperbole he was dubbed 'Nasty Nick' and 'the most hated man in Britain' and freely compared to fictional villains such as Dallas's J. R. Ewing and Heathcliff in *Wuthering Heights*. As it happened, the only danger to Nasty Nick turned out to be the pack of tabloid reporters intent on running him to earth after his eviction. He was met covertly behind the house by the executive producer, Ruth Wrigley. Endemol UK and Channel 4 had put together an evasion plan. They hired a former member of the SAS and a security expert whose most recent assignment had been organising protection for President Clinton on a visit to Britain. They had three identical Mercedes, black with smoked-glass windows, and several 'chase' cars – vehicles that would appear to chase the Mercedes but actually slow down and hinder pursuers. Two of the Mercedes zoomed off from the front of the studio with Fleet Street's finest in pursuit. In the third Mercedes Wrigley took Bateman to a secluded hotel in Potters Bar, a few miles north of London. There he had sessions with a media trainer as well as the programme's psychotherapist Brett Kahr.

The next morning Nasty Nick was on the front page of every paper except the *Financial Times* (which had him on page three). He was also the lead story on all the breakfast television shows. His face was now as well known as the Prime Minister's. And by 11.00 a.m. they realised his presence had been leaked. Outside, at the back of the hotel, they heard the sound of helicopter rotors. Not one but two choppers landed in a field directly behind the hotel. Only the *Ride of the Valkyries* was missing. Out spilled seven reporters, six photographers and two television crews. Barred entry to the hotel they congregated in the hotel car park. A wedding reception was due to take place there at twelve. The father and mother of the bride, in full wedding tackle, chose this moment to appear. The father was heard to exclaim: 'Dorothy, I said only one photographer! Have you gone completely mad?'

Bateman sold his story to the *Sun* for £75,000. He acquired an agent. On the day his personal story filled the front page of the *Sun* the tragedy of Russian sailors drowning in a crippled submarine was relegated to the inside pages. He had certainly achieved celebrity status. The *Sun* had given him a pair of fake devil's horns in a big photo spread so Bateman came out to give a press conference as a fully fledged pantomime villain. He predicted the furore would die down, and indeed it did, within days. *Big Brother* moved on to its next drama and, in time, its next series.

In *Big Brother 3*, in the UK, Jade Goody became Britain's first 'trash hero'. She was large, she had a snub nose and a strong Cockney accent. She thought chickpeas came from a chicken, that Cambridge was in London and that East 'Angular' (Anglia) was abroad. Jade got drunk and stripped, she had a sexual encounter with another housemate and she cried when she thought she had caught a verruca. Britain's tabloid newspapers, in a class of their own for demotic rabble rousing, dubbed Jade 'Miss Piggy'. But they didn't stop there . . . a fishwife, a slag, a Michelin woman and (astonishingly) one of the most hated women on TV. The producers at Endemol UK thought they had picked a brassy, bubbly, provocative Cockney girl: they discovered they had what felt like a full-scale, public lynching on their hands. Mark Lawson, writing in the *Guardian*, held them responsible: 'Participants who seemed to have been chosen to be disliked were then edited to be detested while taking part in stunts which . . . appeared calculated only to humiliate. The national demonisation of Jade Goody . . . made me fear for the first time that a reality game show will one day provoke a suicide.'

But then the tide turned. The celebrity magazine *Heat* revealed Jade's background: a father who had been in prison and a drug-addict mother whom Jade had to look out for, even as a young child. Jade became demonstrably popular since she made it to the final week of the series. And the tabloids, partly out of guilt and partly to ensure they were reflecting public sentiment, started to back her to win. Jade eventually came fourth but proved the most enduring of that year's instant celebrities. Her earnings for personal appearances, interviews and celebrity endorsements since 2002 have exceeded £1 million. The ups and downs of her personal life still feature regularly on the covers of celebrity magazines. With Jade, the critics of *Big Brother* mistook her ignorance for stupidity. She was undoubtedly ill-educated but, nevertheless, extremely shrewd. Mark Lawson, writing in the *Guardian* two years on, had changed his mind: 'Jade Goody's life is certainly more fun for her now than it would have been without *Big Brother*.' Lawson also took to referring to *Big Brother* and other shows as 'humiliation TV'. Its fans thought 'embarrassment TV' was nearer the mark. The housemates were making a contract with the viewer – we'll expose ourselves physically and emotionally for your entertainment and in return we'll gain notoriety and, with luck, money.

Big Brother, like other television shows of the era, was dogged by the lazy epithet 'reality TV'. This gave rise to abstruse debates about how real it was. The simple point was that the trash heroes and pantomime villains it elected were vivid enough. They revealed plenty about human nature to the show's fans. But it was still an entertainment, a pantomime. Was it shocking for such people to be on television? Or was it more shocking that people such as Jade had not been featured in this way before? When I asked that question I was called an 'intellectual rat fink' by a media professor, Brian Winston. To him *Big Brother* was not only exploitative but coarsened and degraded television's output. He accused *Big Brother* of portraying Jade as a 'scrubber': 'They're constantly . . . making these rhetorical arguments in favour of tat. Let them make all this tat but can't they get some really serious stuff on?' Others went further and concluded that such demonstrable ignorance meant that society was more ill-educated than ever before. In fact, it would have been easy to find ignorant, illiterate individuals at any time in television's first fifty years. But there was no room for them in the one- or two-channel-television culture. The arts broadcaster Melvyn Bragg was intrigued at the new development: 'Big Brother appears to be very close to the ultimate take over of the most democratic channel ever invented by "ordinary" representatives of that democracy. Everyone has a life worth putting on television ...' And Germaine Greer, initially hostile to *Big Brother*, warmed to the programme's human dramas with her ironic but affectionate aphorism about civilisation quoted as the epigraph to this chapter. In 2005 Greer furthered her love/hate relationship with *Big Brother*. She appeared in a celebrity version and then walked out early, accusing *Big Brother* of being a bully.

The *Big Brother* guinea pigs had agreed to be watched. Millions wanted to watch them, the more intimately the better. But how much intimacy should be allowed on television? In July 2003, the director of programmes at Channel 4, Tim Gardam, was in a London taxi on his way to his office at 8.30 a.m. Halfway down Park Lane his mobile rang. It was Channel 4's commissioning editor Peter Grimsdale: 'We've had a blow job. But don't worry, it's all under control.' He said they were now viewing the rushes to decide what could be shown. Bleary-eyed and with strong coffee in hand, Julian Bellamy from Channel 4 and Phil Edgar-Jones from Endemol had to watch a drunken encounter between two housemates, the controversial Jade and a trainee solicitor, PJ. Edgar-Jones was particularly tired since he had been called at home at 2 a.m. to be given the news. In fact, in tabloidese, whether PJ had had a BJ was by no means clear, the couple having been under bed covers. But, when the covers fell away briefly, what was clear was PJ's proud erection being vigorously manipulated by Jade.

This much was edited out right away. They were then momentarily distracted by another housemate, Sandy, who was on the roof of the house intending to walk out of *Big Brother*. He was not jealous – this was an unrelated incident. Returning to the edit they agreed to cut the sequence down to two minutes, not to be explicit in any way but to let the audience know the truth – an encounter had taken place. This sequence was duly completed and sent down the fibre-optic connection to Channel 4 for Gardam to approve. A technician at Channel 4 flicked the wrong switch and as it was played into his office Gardam recalls the sexual encounter also appeared, in real time, on five hundred TV screens around the Channel 4 building, including reception: 'There was this great moment when I realised no one at Channel 4 was doing any work at all.' Gardam viewed and re-viewed the material with a lawyer. Eventually he asked for two small cuts. In one PJ was apparently saying: 'Give me head.' In the other, what Gardam calls 'the rictus moment on PJ's face' was deemed too explicit: 'Most people disagreed with me – but if you show the humping bit you throw away something of the tension ... the producers desperately wanted PJ's face put back in ... I said, we can't show a come shot – even if you can't see it – on terrestrial television.' The shortened programme was broadcast that evening and to this day Jade and PJ have not revealed precisely what happened beneath the *Big Brother* duvet.

By this time the doubts I had expressed about the *Big Brother* format in 1998 had evaporated. I felt shamefaced that it had taken the Dutch to shatter the cosy consensus about what was possible or acceptable on television. If we had had the guts to think up *Big Brother* we wouldn't have dared pitch it. If we had pitched it no British broadcaster would have had the guts to commission it. Holland led the way. But I and others, like Tim Gardam, soon realised the power of the idea. Gardam's view of *Big Brother* from the beginning was, 'In all its raunchiness it revealed the truth of a generation ... it was the first programme that really laid open what all the marketing research, all the demographic research, all the cultural research was saying. You had a generation which was fundamentally different from generations before. They had no sense of propriety, no sense of

modesty. They were open, honest and candid with each other.'
That included, of course, uninhibited sexual encounters. These
were to reoccur, rather more red-bloodedly, around the world.

For this and other reasons, there has never been any shortage
of people who would like to see *Big Brother* shut down – from
politicians to priests, from regulators to the police, from intel-
lectuals to those simply too old to comprehend such public
goings on. Officialdom nearly put paid to *Big Brother 5* in the
UK. Wednesday 16 June 2004 became known as 'Fight Night' in
the *Big Brother* house. In fact there was no fighting to speak of,
but three separate rows blew up late at night. They were intem-
perate and certainly involved threatening words. Within minutes
the production team had cut the live television feed and sent in
the ever-present security team to separate the contestants who
were mostly angry or upset. Hundreds of viewers, fearing a serious fight, complained to the television regulator, Ofcom, about
the incidents. Two viewers took a different tack. They telephoned the police, one alleging that there had been a racist
incident. As it happens, there had not. One of the housemates,
Emma, was angry with another contestant, Victor, over remarks
he had made about her. Victor was of Afro-Caribbean origin and
the viewer had misinterpreted their row. The Hertfordshire
police arrived at the *Big Brother* site in the early hours of the
morning. They were assured all was now calm.

The police returned later with a request to interview the
housemates involved in the arguments. They had consulted the
Crown Prosecution Service and agreed that there was the possibility of a number of a criminal offences including affray,
threatening behaviour and assault. Had the incident been an
altercation in a pub they would have ensured that everything
had settled down, issued a warning and left. But this was *Big
Brother*, on the front page of every tabloid newspaper – still
Britain's most controversial television show. The police and government lawyers were anxious to follow the letter of the law and

to be seen to follow it. The suggestion of racism had also set a vast machinery of political correctness in motion. They told Endemol and Channel 4, the broadcaster, that they wanted to interview virtually everyone in the house, some as potential law-breakers, others as witnesses. They said they had a public relations strategy in place for this high-profile exercise. To the *Big Brother* production team this sounded a bit like the mayor of Pompeii claiming he had a health and safety policy for his citizens.

Channel 4 and Endemol desperately attempted to dissuade them. Interviewing all the housemates in an investigation would break *Big Brother*'s first rule – no contact with the outside world. Talk of the criminal case would thereafter dominate all the housemates conversations, ruining the programme but also rendering any sensible prosecution impossible. All the intimate details of the case would have been discussed by those involved in front of millions of viewers long before it came to court. This would make a mockery of the sub judice rules. And had *Big Brother* ceased production the police would have found them-selves at the centre of a frenetic media scrum. Had that been figured into their PR strategy?

Negotiations continued throughout Friday 18 June. The police remained adamant. The Endemol and Channel 4 teams went home at midnight convinced they had lost the series. For both of them this would have been cataclysmic: seven weeks of blank screens, massive losses of revenue and a terrible blow to the standing of the show. The following morning talks with the police resumed. Prash Naik, a Channel 4 lawyer, led for *Big Brother*. To begin with two enthusiastic, plain-clothes detec-tives continued to insist they had to remove the housemates one by one for interviews. More senior officers arrived. Endemol and Channel 4 kept repeating (and believing) that this spelt the end of the series. By lunchtime the police had soft-ened. We had explained the measures we were taking to prevent the reoccurrence of such an incident. The housemates were making up and one, Emma, was to leave the house. The police then, finally, relented. They agreed only to talk to the housemates when they were evicted. In the end no charges were pursued and a *Big Brother* collapse was avoided. *Big Brother* had been saved, to the delight of the record audiences watching it and, perhaps, the despair of those who found this latest series even more objectionable than its predecessors.

'The biggest freak show in history', 'a new low in spiritual degeneracy', 'downright obscene' – not, as it happens, descriptions of *Big Brother* but attacks on Elvis Presley in 1956 when he first began gyrating his hips in public. Elvis kicked off youth culture – for the first time children and parents no longer listened to the same music. And from that point on successful innovations in entertainment went through a cycle, appealing to the emerging generation and appalling their elders. The disgust of the latter guaranteed success with the former. In *Big Brother*'s case this presented politicians with a dilemma. Britain had no shortage of rent-a-quote MPs who condemned the show, usually admitting proudly that they had never watched it and would not dream of doing so. But by 2000 the country was experiencing record low turnouts among first-time voters. If these eighteen-year-olds were flocking to vote in *Big Brother*'s electronic polls, why were they absent at general elections? Could *Big Brother* have something to teach the politicos? This question taxed the Conservative Party most of all. They were reduced to a rump in the House of Commons and enjoyed a party membership whose average age was sixty-seven. The Conservative chairman at the time of Iain Duncan Smith's leadership was Theresa May. She telephoned me one day and asked whether I would serve on a 'non-partisan' commission to look into why fewer young people were voting. I said I might if it was genuinely impartial and if I was told who else was taking part.

Not long after, my telephone rang at 7.30 a.m. one Monday

morning. It was BBC Radio 4's *Today* programme. 'Will you come on this morning. You know why – the *Independent* news-paper is saying you've been hired to improve Iain Duncan Smith's image with young people.' This entirely erroneous news seemed, at the time, to be the greatest humiliation I had ever suffered. Duncan Smith was without doubt the dullest and least talented party leader since the Second World War. My name had become connected to his, it transpired, because the ambitious Theresa May had jumped the gun and announced her commission before several of us had even agreed to join it. I refused *Today*'s kind offer and contacted the Press Association to issue an immediate denial.

As the pantomime villains, trash heroes and their sexual antics filled the tabloid front pages, some may have been desperate to ban *Big Brother*. But this episode illustrated how others wanted to harness its success to their own ends. The pattern has been repeated many times in the countries colonised by *Big Brother*.

CHAPTER TWELVE

Trash Heroes and Pantomime Villains

The Dutch magazine *Privé* had lamented that ordinary people were becoming stars simply by appearing on television. Channel 4's *The Word* had had its deliberately banal feature, 'I'd Do Anything to Get on TV'. *Big Brother* took the principle and applied the stimulus of mass production. And Zlatko was one of the first off the production line – the car mechanic of Macedonian origin who participated in Germany's first *Big Brother*.

Zlatko had admitted he didn't know who Shakespeare was. He had famously tried to remove his chest hair, painfully, with nail scissors. He was thickset to the point of being squat and had a funny accent. What did *Der Spiegel* mean when they called him a 'trash hero'? For 'trash hero' read anti-hero. In the article whose headline translated as 'The bloke what should be President' the newspaper said he had been transformed from Simple Simon into an idiot with cult status. After Germany's most famous chat show host Stefan Raab dubbed him 'The Brain' he became nationally celebrated. When he left the Big Brother house he was lionised on television and, within two days, issued a CD. This was despite his having little sense of rhythm and being tone deaf. The CD went to number one and sold 800,000 copies. 'Zladdie' T-shirts shifted in hundreds of thousands and a beer was issued in his honour – 'Shakes-beer'.

Many older Germans were disturbed that such people could get on to television and horrified that they had become stars. They were about to get even more horrified. Zlatko had other hit records and a documentary made about him. Then he began shooting a movie as well. After a year of adulation he was entered into the heats for the German entry of *The Eurovision Song Contest*. He had to sing live but, of course, he couldn't sing at all. The crowd hissed and booed him. His immediate, public response was: 'You assholes, fuck off.' The microphone was still on. That was the end of Germany's love affair with Zlatko. He took his newly acquired Porsche and returned to live quietly with his mother. His movie was never released.

What was Zlatko's attraction? Why did so many celebrate his ignorance? Partly because his self-confidence, even insouciance, was funny and almost brave. Partly it was the sheer novelty of a thoroughly ill-educated person on television on his own terms. In fifty years of popular television you could find the Zlatkos and the Jades of the world as stooges in big-money game shows, or portrayed as social victims in documentaries. But never were they, in effect, given their own airtime.

In Brazil and Italy two trash heroes outdid Zlatko and went on to win the shows outright. Kleber was a none-too-intellectual body builder, bouncer and dancer. The producers of the first Brazilian *Big Brother* series found him, out of work, on the beach at Copacabana: 'I was the last one to go into the house and I asked God to let me be the last one to get out of the house and win the programme. You must see my bits on the videos, you must see my popularity! I was the first guy to kiss a girl in the house, to sleep with a girl in the first week. She didn't really want to have sex on television but I did. Everybody thinks that we did but we didn't. I put the blanket over us and I was moving my feet but it wasn't real.' Kleber became known as Bamm-Bamm, the character in the *Flintstones* who relies more on brawn than brains. As before, it was his simplicity that endeared him to Brazilian viewers. He had made a plastic doll out of odds and ends which he called Maria Eugenia. When it was removed from the house in a tidy-up he begged for it back. It was not returned. Having a limited vocabulary, at this point he simply burst into tears. After Bamm-Bamm won the *Big Brother* final he went on to be given parts in soap operas and formed his own dance troupe. His current ambition is to dance with Britney Spears.

Floriana won *Big Brother 3* in Italy. Her mother was a prostitute. She had been taken into care as a young child and brought up in institutions. She often ran away and finally escaped, working casually as a waitress. She is big, muscular, deep-voiced and has a working-class, Roman accent with which she took to addressing the viewers personally, straight to camera: 'Hello, Italy. Please vote for me!' As a result she became known as the Silvio Berlusconi of *Big Brother*. *La Repubblica* reported her victory on 9 May 2003 as: 'the 243,000 Euros prize money goes to the "vulgar girl from the backstreets"'. To some Floriana and Bamm-Bamm may have been trash heroes, but millions of viewers identified with their struggle to escape their humble origins and were charmed rather than shocked by their complete lack of intellectual ambition. This gave rise to the idea, in all the countries *Big Brother* is broadcast, that we now live in a celebrity-obsessed culture. It is argued that this obsession is something new. History tells us otherwise.

The word celebrity has been in use in English for around four hundred years and stems from Latin via French and Middle English. It originally meant 'the state of being famous or much talked about'. The idea that 'celebrity' was a semi-formal status conferred on someone emerged towards the end of the nineteenth century. But celebrity culture goes back further than that. It requires no more than an individual who wishes to be looked at or talked about and a group of people who want to do the looking or talking. In other words, it is about a performer who, by definition, needs an audience. Charles II's lover Nell Gwyn, the Regency dandy Beau Brummell, Nelson's mistress Emma Hamilton and the highwayman Dick Turpin were all famous for being little other than famous. Clara Bow, the first It Girl, and the pitiable Vicar of Stiffkey achieved the same in the 1920s and 1930s, as did the chinless debutantes at Queen Charlotte's Ball.

Big Brother is a popularity contest. It has proved adept at electing Turpinesque villains as well as Gwyn-like heroes. Germany's *Big Brother 1* included Manuela, an exceptionally pretty, twenty-three-year-old. Her ambition was palpable: 'My greatest wish is to hold a microphone in my hand and the whole world has to listen to me.' But before long the public took against her overtly flirtatious behaviour. Like the other housemates they felt that, when she was blowing up condoms to draw attention to herself, she was just trying too hard. On 18 April 2000 *Die Welt* published an article entitled 'Manu, the object of hatred. *Big Brother* candidate is made into scapegoat by fans'. The piece went on: 'Manu, you slapper! Manu out! Chants and placards like these could already be seen and heard when Zlatko turned his back on the *Big Brother* house. These battle cries have even been heard on the football terraces. There are moments when the reality soap becomes so absurd that it reminds us of Beckett, but at the same time disturbs and deeply touches us. The remaining candidates stood around looking lost as they listened to the mob and its curses. Manu must be absolutely terrified of returning to the real world.'

This was only the second series of *Big Brother* ever produced so they could not know that pantomime booing was to become a staple ingredient of the live eviction shows. In the following years some housemates went in specifically to provoke such a reaction and visibly milked the crowd's mock hostility when they emerged. But because they were real individuals rather than ugly sisters or wicked stepmothers some found it shocking, as they did in Britain when 'Nasty' Nick Bateman emerged.

Watching the Nasty Nick affair unfold in Britain was a visiting Australian entrepreneur Neil Balnaves. Balnaves was chairman of Southern Star, a production company specialising in drama and distributor of the soap *Home and Away*: 'I was absolutely floored. Eleven Sunday papers had Nasty Nick on their front covers ... we really needed to be in this business because it was taking off.' Balnaves negotiated a joint venture with Endemol in Australia, but no broadcaster would pay more than $10 million Australian dollars for the series. It was costed at eleven and a half. So Balnaves did a deal with the Dreamworld theme park to make the house a permanent attraction. Dreamworld agreed to cover the construction costs which meant Channel 10 could be given the series for $10 million. Channel 10 then got their own healthy share of trash heroes and pantomime villains.

Blair McDonough was a handsome twenty-year-old in Australia's *Big Brother 1*. A month after the series he was offered a screen test for Australia's premier soap opera, *Neighbours*. McDonough had no acting experience but aficionados of *Neighbours* will know that looks come before dramatic ability in that suburban saga of winsome looks and bronzed pectorals. He passed the screen test and *Women's Day* magazine featured his success: 'The spunky larrikin starts work in Australia's longest running soap ... to showcase the star-power that made him *BB*'s runner up.' Peter Abbot, *Big Brother*'s executive producer, then heard accusations of trashiness aimed at McDonough. 'There was a lot of resistance from the other actors ... you know – you're just a reality star – that kind of thing.' But McDonough managed to learn his lines, flash his body and was signed up for a second year in the soap.

The Australians also elected their own pantomime villain in the first series. Johnnie Cass took to hugging all his victims after he had confidentially nominated them for eviction in the diary room. This gesture came to be seen as a sort of Judas kiss, though the production team believed he was acting out of genuine guilt rather than a desire to dissemble. Queensland's *Courier Mail* soon nicknamed him Johnny Rotten and he became Nasty Nick's spiritual inheritor. A feature interview in *The Bulletin* just days after the end of the series showed how short-lived this pantomime villain status was: 'On reflection, Cass admits he became a little concerned that his cartoon villain image might prompt aggro in the real world – but when I saw that people on the street were supportive it was OK, he says.' The popularity contest proved so successful among ordinary Australians that the second series was subject to a bidding war. This time it sold for $25 million.

Most countries enjoyed their *Big Brother* villains as mock-hate figures. America has been the exception. The country which, in 2004, saw the moral majority re-elect George Bush, paradoxically appears to recognise and reward villainy on its own terms. Nasty Nick, Blair and Manuela never became winners. But the victor in the US *Big Brother 2* was a charming but deceitful doctor, Will. The winner of the first series of *Survivor* had been the equally scheming Rich. The American audience is, perhaps, the most sophisticated of all. They knew *Big Brother* and *Survivor* were games. They rewarded those who played most effectively.

A new breed of psychologists, who themselves were in the media limelight, started to capture headlines by speculating about the psychological damage that could result from these mind games. Dr Raj Persaud, a consultant psychiatrist at the Maudsley Hospital in London, said that *Big Brother* contestants were being portrayed as freaks and were subject to potentially dangerous levels of stress. Now that *Big Brother* has been produced more than eighty times across the world these warnings do not seem to have been borne out. Of the nine hundred housemates so far only one has been reported to be in serious mental difficulty. The winner of Portugal's first series was attended by an ambulance four years later after threatening to commit suicide. He complained that he had been dropped by the media and was now neglected. Brett Kahr, the psychotherapist who helped select and look after housemates in four British series, says that he has not seen any evidence of psychological damage. Persaud argues that you cannot make that judgement with confidence in less than forty years. But as *Big Brother* has gone along, and other reality formats have appeared, its proceedings do resemble less a public hanging and more a pantomime. Once the show is over, it's over. If this is true it is because of the precautions John de Mol and his Endemol team originally put in place – the careful sifting of applicants by trained psychologists or psychiatrists to weed out those too unstable or fragile to benefit from the *Big Brother* experience.

Brett Kahr spent weeks interviewing and screening applicants to *Big Brother* in the UK. He does not believe that every chosen housemate's motive was to achieve celebrity status. Some wanted an adventure or to escape their current lives, others were seeking new friends. But among those who did want to become well known he simply classifies the desire as a subset of something more general: 'Every single human being shares the exact same desire to be well known and recognised. Not necessarily to see his or her name in the newspapers. But it is a very, very basic human wish and also an essential human need.' Kahr also has a response to the charge made against those in the other celebrity constituency – the audience – that they are pursuers of the trivial and, at worst, voyeurs: 'By reading the newspapers on a daily basis we are voyeurs. By listening to the ten o'clock news we are voyeurs. By watching people in the street or on the train we are voyeurs. We find other people interesting and at the same time we hope that other people will find us interesting. All of human psychology is based on voyeuristic and exhibitionist strands.'

There are no new human instincts driving today's celebrity culture. What is new is the multiplicity of media channels via which it is possible to achieve fifteen minutes of fame or infamy.

In the past, only a few could succeed in capturing the level of public attention that Nell Gwyn, Beau Brummell and Clara Bow did. Now, as Warhol correctly predicted, everyone can – on terrestrial TV, on digital TV, on radio, in celeb magazines or on the world wide web. What is also new is that the media, which need fresh and frequent supplies of celebrities, are creating them to order rather than relying on the courtesans, highwaymen and film stars of the past. That has become one of the functions of *Big Brother*.

CHAPTER THIRTEEN

Sex Rears its Head

In Sweden three women masturbated in unison. In Britain two lovers built a nest under a heavily draped table. In Hungary an emancipated woman seduced the men whenever she felt like it. In Denmark a female housemate got pregnant when her male partner discarded condoms that were 'too small'. In Ecuador there was coupling almost every night. In Italy a bisexual woman appeared torn between a male and a female housemate.

Put twelve young people in a confined space for a length of time and there will be both sexual tensions and releases. But to succeed *Big Brother* needs relationships to develop. Sex is incidental – *Big Brother* remained popular in the US, Australia and the UK for several series without any instances of sexual intercourse. With the possible exception of the toilet camera, more is written by newspapers about the possibility of sex in *Big Brother* than anything else. But production teams are so busy following and encouraging the storylines that develop they give it little thought. Until it actually happens, that is. Then politicians and Church leaders are up in arms while regulators tend to be relaxed, so long as what happened is not too explicitly revealed on television. However, there has never been a television format before where sex is so routine and where the liaison can be so intimately recorded.

Sexual intercourse did not demonstrably occur in South

Africa's *Big Brother* house until their third series. But the producers had a foretaste of what the reaction might be the year before. Janine was a schoolteacher in her late thirties, highly liberated and, it transpired, obsessed with one of the younger, male housemates. In a 'talent contest' she decided to give a cucumber a rather assiduous blow job, partly for the hell of it and partly as a come-on to the man she had her eyes on. Unfortunately the Education Minister was made aware of the incident and, because Janine was a primary schoolteacher, Kader Asmal told the newspapers what he thought about it: 'lewd ... vulgar ... not funny ... not even erotic ... pornographic ... sluttish ... imbecilic'. When she emerged Janine lost her job as a primary schoolteacher, but her talents were later re-employed, as part of a team touring schools to lecture about safe sex.

Big Brother 3 was a pan-African edition, with contestants from across the continent. The Ugandan housemate Gaetano appeared to enjoy vigorous sex, under a duvet, with Abby from South Africa. As ever, no one knew precisely what happened or whether a condom was involved. But there were hundreds of telephone complaints, mostly about the issue of safe sex. It was hardly practical for Gaetano and Abby to sit up in bed, dangling a condom and say: 'Remember folks, safe sex pays!' before getting down to it. But the producers felt they needed to respond. They invited two of their most vociferous critics, Zambian pastors Nsoto Luboto and Chali Kasonde, into the *Big Brother* studio. Reverend Kasonde complained: 'What do we really want to achieve by this programming? Is it just mere entertainment? Why should we be entertained with something that is not bringing out the moral issue. The African morality, Zambian morality.' And, in relation to HIV Aids, Reverend Luboto argued: 'We are losing a generation! My cry is not for you to destroy MTV or whatever [i.e. youth entertainment]. My cry is – listen, be part of what we are fighting. Help us!' Luboto added that he was proud of the Zambian housemate (the eventual winner) because she wore her national flag as a scarf and sang gospel tunes – she set a moral example. The producers felt obliged to respond to their plea. They then promoted discussions about safe sex in the house. The housemates also held a televised party for children with HIV Aids.

There has never been gay sex in a *Big Brother* house, but there was a homosexual proposal of marriage. In Colombia's *Big Brother 1* they cast a gay man. This was seen as provocative since Colombia had as large a gay community as any other country but it was still mostly underground. He liked to help the women with their hair and make-up and loved doing the laundry. As a result he became known as Burbujita – 'little bubbles'. Despite the reservations of the local broadcaster he was allowed to propose 'marriage' to his boyfriend via the camera. His boyfriend was then filmed saying yes, at which point Burbujita burst into tears. Liberal Colombians felt this did more for gay emancipation than anything else that year. It was considered equally radical when gay men were included in *Big Brother Mexico* and *Argentina*. In every country where homosexuals were included initially dubious or hostile audiences discovered the humanity behind the sexual predilection. And the young fans of the shows demonstrated their acceptance of different sexualities. In 2002 a gay man won Britain's *Big Brother 2*. In 2004 the UK saw Nadia, a post-operative transsexual, win by a large margin. Elderly, mostly male commentators, believing the housemates were being held up to the public gaze for ridicule and profit, described the series as 'a freak show'. By the end of it *Big Brother* fans, clearly empathising with Nadia's quest to be accepted as a woman, regarded her as a person rather than a freak. Nadia originally came from Portugal, a country which embraced *Big Brother* more immediately than the reserved, Anglo-Saxon cultures of northern Europe.

Big Brother began in Portugal on 3 September 2000. The first seven weeks contained a full-blown love affair between Marco and Marta. The housemates were conducting themselves modestly, only ever taking showers in bathing costumes. But, despite that shyness, Marco and Marta managed to consummate their relationship, discreetly, beneath a duvet. This is how Marco explained the contradiction: 'We are rich people in terms of feelings and it's quite easy for us to fall in love ... and also to explode. To live passion without consequences.' Marco's relationship survived his being removed from the *Big Brother* house after he kicked another female housemate, Sonya. They had a late-night argument and she called his mother a whore. Marco lost his temper. He later apologised and many of the audience forgave what appeared to be unforgivable behaviour – they blamed Sonya for provoking him. Piet Hein Bakker, Endemol's managing director, turned on the television news that evening: 'They trailed the story immediately, at the top, and their ratings went sky high. So they ran *Big Brother* stories every day from then on.' It set off a furious debate about what was and was not legitimate news.

News of Marco's eventual eviction occupied the front page of several newspapers, relegating the announcement that Portugal's President was to run for office again to the inside pages. Marco was allowed to continue wooing Marta from outside the house, first, with a banner trailing from a light aircraft declaring, 'Marta, I love you! Marco', then he was placed in a mechanical hoist and lowered into the garden to present Marta with flowers. They married eight months later and now have their first child. A later series of Portuguese *Big Brother* actually saw a wedding conducted in the programme's studio for two of the contestants who had fallen in love.

In Latin countries *Big Brother* follows the rules of the local *telenovelas* closely – it is passionate, romantic and full-throttled. Colombia launched *Big Brother* in the summer of 2003. After three weeks one couple, Monica and Luis, fell in love. For a month they slept together and enjoyed covert, sexual relations virtually every night. This excited little condemnation from the press or the authorities. Then Monica's period was late and she became alarmed that she might be pregnant. Sex did not seem to be a problem – it was, instead, pregnancy outside marriage that was regarded as scandalous in this Catholic country. The priests now got into gear and condemned *Big Brother* for promoting such immorality on television. To make matters worse, Monica was already a single parent. Her period, or lack of it, became a running story in every newspaper. It was commonly believed that, although condoms were available in the house, the lovers had not been using them. Whatever the truth of it, when Monica finally menstruated, two weeks late, every newspaper made it front-page news as the nation heaved a collective sigh of relief. Monica went on to win *Big Brother*. The producers believe she would not have got close to winning had she committed the indiscretion of getting pregnant. Apart from that, though, she could apparently behave with abandon.

The *Big Brother* houses are, perhaps, the safest places on earth. The housemates are under the scrutiny of forty cameras, behind a guarded security fence and with a team of a hundred watching their every move. But this does not prevent the dark side of human behaviour emerging. In US *Big Brother 2*'s first week Justin, a twenty-six-year-old New Jersey bartender, was kissing Krista, a divorcée from Louisiana. He picked up a metal carpet sweeper and said to her: 'Would you get mad if I cracked you over the head with this?' She ignored this even when he swung it slowly at her. After more kisses he picked up a kitchen knife and asked: 'Would you get mad if I killed you?' He even placed the knife against Krista's throat before putting it away. It later emerged that Justin had been charged with assault more than once though this had not been discovered in checks before the series. Justin was removed from the house.

In Germany's *Big Brother 2* the threats were to the production team rather than one of the housemates. Two contestants fell for each other. Daniela was German and Karim was Moroccan. They had spent hours, if not days, in the jacuzzi and had also been to bed together. The relationship sustained and they became engaged. For several days the executive producer, Rainer Laux, received death threats on his home telephone from extremists who resented this high-profile, inter-racial affair. Nevertheless Laux agreed to be best man at their wedding after the series had ended.

Although older churchgoers may not always see the joke, sex is, of course, funny. In Belgium their first series of *Big Brother* was dominated by Betty 'Boob', a butcher's wife with a morning routine that included displaying her generous breasts. The housemates were underwhelmed by the performance but her resourceful husband adopted the nickname with relish and produced a special 'Betty Boob' sausage for his grateful customers. Betty then gave the plump sausage rather more publicity than even her commercially driven husband appreciated. One of the men was clearly infatuated with another, rather younger, female housemate. Betty jealously intervened by creeping into the boys' room in the middle of the night when he was asleep. What followed, recorded on infrared, night-time cameras, resembled a black and white silent movie. Betty raised his duvet, thrust her head beneath it and began to pleasure him orally. He stirred and moaned his appreciation, believing it to be an amorous response from his intended lover. Then, in a truly Chaucerian scene, he woke up fully and saw it was Betty Boob. He was furious and fought her off.

In March 2004, *Big Brother*'s broadcaster in Romania was fined by the national regulator for including footage of a couple in bed. When the production team persisted the regulator made the programme contain a still caption for a full ten minutes with the judgement as a punishment. But one of the few instances of sexual intercourse taking place openly, not under a duvet and in full view of the cameras, is down to the Hungarians two years

earlier. Evi came from a small town called Kaposvar in western
Hungary, where she worked in a café. She was not very educated
but expressive and warm-hearted. The Hungarian *Big Brother*
house was, for some reason, full of dogs as well as people and
she showed them great affection. She was a perfect *Big Brother*
'trash hero' and, in due course, went on to win. After just one
week in the house she had decided it was time for sex. She
selected the long-haired, romantic Renato. He was half-
Hungarian and half-Italian and loved to play the flamenco guitar
extravagantly. They made love, out in the open. An edited version of this was shown at 8 p.m. and an even more explicit
sequence in a late-night show. The act was shocking enough, but
that Evi had clearly instigated it was even more disturbing for
some. The Catholic Church and women's groups protested. The
regulator fined the broadcaster. And, for the first and only time,
Endemol in Holland intervened, strongly questioning the
wisdom of airing explicit sex. Endemol was acting to stop the
series being banned, but the company also wanted *Big Brother*
to remain a soap opera about relationships, not a porn show
about sex. Pornography is defined as a work whose primary
purpose is to cause sexual arousal. As far as Endemol was concerned that was not *Big Brother*'s purpose and the Hungarians
were so instructed.

In Sweden's *Big Brother 3* they had, as Swedes are wont to, a
rather wild sauna party. There was heavy drinking and some les-
bian clinches. One female housemate also appeared to have sex
with a man by sitting astride him in the bedroom. This was
shown on television and the broadcaster, Kanal 5, was made to
apologise. Kanal 5 is regulated by Ofcom in Britain because that
is where it is technically transmitted from by satellite. But in
Swedish *Big Brother 4* a more explicit sex scene in a bathroom
was, accidentally, allowed to go out as part of the streaming on
the programme's web site. This time no apology was demanded
because the web is largely unregulated. These much-debated

incidents, though, comprise no more than a few hours in a hundred days of television. The resident psychologist who worked for *Big Brother Italy* was Carlo Alberto Cavallo. There were several sexual incidents there too, but he was unmoved: 'Seeing a sex scene is absolutely not interesting. But seeing the love process . . . that's very interesting – seeing one person come close to another. Seeing the sex – it is boring.'

The Italian's blasé reaction was not shared in Islamic countries where even the merest peck on the cheek is *verboten*. February the twentieth 2004 was Day 1 in the Middle Eastern *Big Brother* house. One of the female housemates chastely kissed the cheek of the male Saudi Arabian contestant by way of welcome. This simple act set off a chain of events which involved the Bahraini Parliament, its police and its army, the Islamic faith, the King and the CIA. The *Big Brother* house had been designed with extreme care – there were completely separate sleeping quarters for the girls and the boys and separate prayer rooms too. The production team told the housemates that they should on no account hug or kiss or even touch each other at any time. But two of them, in their enthusiasm, breached these guidelines on the first day. Worse still, they were heard to boast about it later. Worst of all, another female housemate then wandered into the boys' quarters.

Arabian *Big Brother* had been discussed for three years. The Middle East Broadcasting Company (MBC) wanted to produce the show for its satellite service, beamed across the Arab world. MBC is owned by Sheikh Walid al-Ibrahim, the brother-in-law of King Fahd of Saudi Arabia. He appeared well connected enough to be able to work out the risks of such a production in Muslim countries. MBC had started broadcasting from an industrial unit in Fulham in the 1980s. It was legendary for the number of 'exercise' videos it transmitted – ladies in Lycra were popular in the Middle East. Now MBC was headquartered in Dubai. It was producing *Big Brother* from Bahrain, the island kingdom in the Persian Gulf connected to the Saudi Arabian mainland by a causeway.

The Bahraini Parliament, only two years old, was from the start dominated by Islamic conservatives – they constituted 95 per cent of the deputies elected. While the former Emir, now King Hamad, remained pro-Western, there had been several demonstrations against the Anglo-American invasion of Iraq the previous year. Perhaps with hindsight, the auguries were not good. The US Fifth Fleet is based in Bahrain but Western foreign policy was abhorrent to many. Before long, Western entertainment was to seem even worse. Examples were already beamed into the houses of Bahraini citizens every night. *Star Academy* was a pop talent contest in which the male and female contestants also lived together in a house. It was another Endemol format, produced in the Lebanon and now being transmitted across the Middle East on a rival satellite network. *Star Academy* was proving hugely popular with adolescent viewers. One of the reasons for its cred, no doubt, was that a Kuwaiti mullah had already declared a fatwa on it, forbidding Muslims from taking part or even voting on the telephones (as a result the phone lines in Saudi Arabia were withdrawn).

During the previous Ramadan there had been a minor riot in Bahrain in protest against a pop concert given by Nancy Ajram, a beautiful Lebanese singer. She wore skimpy costumes for her performances. The event was previewed in the newspapers and Sheikh Adel Al Maawada, a mullah and an influential deputy in Parliament, called for a ban. He was blamed by some for inciting the riot at which ten people were arrested. This he denied. As the launch of *Big Brother* (renamed *Al-Ra'is – The Boss*) approached, tension increased. The same Sheikh Maawada gave an interview to BBC2's *Newsnight* condemning the show: 'It doesn't suit our society at all. They said they have made sure that it would not go against our tradition and our religion. *The idea* of it is against our religion and traditions.'

Bahrain was also shortly due to host a Formula One Grand Prix. Bahrain had a reputation as one of the more liberal Gulf States, where alcohol was allowed and prostitution tolerated. But a condition had been that instead of models in bikinis draped across the cars all women should be wearing Bahraini national dress. The King's ministers had been anxious to encourage sport and television production so that they could develop a non-oil economy for the long term. With Parliament now dominated by Islamic conservatives, though, a battle was on for the soul of the nation. *Big Brother* was to be the field of conflict.

Anuska Ban was the Dutch plenipotentiary entrusted with training the local production team to make *Big Brother*. She took some of the producers to Athens to see the third series of *Big Brother Greece* as it was being made. There they heard about the problems the first series had encountered. The television regulator had forced the broadcaster to schedule the show in a much later slot, the national union of journalists had called for *Big Brother* to be banned and various left-wing groups had organised a demonstration outside the house. A Greek Orthodox priest had railed from his pulpit that if anyone's child took part in *Big Brother* their whole family would go to hell. Finally, garbage was dumped on the steps of the Greek broadcaster Antenna. None of this, though, prepared the Arabian production team for what was shortly to happen to them.

The site of *Big Brother*'s mullah-proof house was at the Amwaj beach. It had been built on a man-made spit of sand jutting out into the sea. As a precaution, the opening show was to be recorded and broadcast the following day rather than in its usual live form. The production team were already jumpy, working on such a controversial programme. The first night made them fear the production was jinxed. An unusually extreme tide capsized the traditional boats with which they had dressed the beach. All the houseplants in the *Big Brother* compound mysteriously died. And one of the camels hired to carry the housemates up to the house bit a member of the audience. This was followed by an unseasonal sandstorm and an almost unheard of shower of rain. So unnerved was the production team that they sacrificed a goat outside the compound, a ritual supposed to bestow good luck on a household. Despite such alarms they managed to edit an opening programme together and it was broadcast the following day, 21 February, on MBC2. This was the channel that already transmitted the pneumatic-chested *Baywatch* and the sexually explicit *Ally McBeal*. *Big Brother*'s first transmission merely showed the Bahrainis a kiss on the cheek. But this had been filmed on home soil in Bahrain, just the day before. Parliament sprang into action.

Its first target was the Minister of Information, Nabil Al Hamr. He had given MBC a licence to produce *Big Brother* in Bahrain. He had promised the deputies that he would set up a panel to monitor its progress. He hastily announced the panel as the series was starting but none of the leading opponents, such as Sheikh Maawada, were on it. They retaliated by composing a petition demanding four concessions: two completely separate houses for the boys and girls; rigid control of behaviour with absolutely no kissing, cuddling or touching; religious instruction included in the programmes; and supervision of the production team by a group of imams.

By now the local press were following this power struggle closely. The *Bahrain Tribune* reported the objections of the Islamic deputies but also commissioned an opinion piece accusing them of hypocrisy: 'To my knowledge contestants aren't doing anything harmful. There are other un-Islamic actions happening ... but I don't see anyone stopping that or trying to discuss it in the parliament ... kids, aged 12, that are seen smoking in the malls, women who are divorced and their children are robbed away from them during breastfeeding ... girls who are molested by their brothers, fathers, uncles ... to me these problems are more important than a TV show ... it is time to wake up and smell the coffee.' Another of the newspapers reported how it had been asked by some of the hostile deputies to describe *Big Brother* to them so that they could make specific criticisms. None of them had seen it.

On Day 5 MBC tried to improve the situation by inviting a religious committee of Shias and Sunnis to visit the house to explain to them how carefully the show was being made. They took the precaution of playing into the house the Muslim call to prayer. By this time only one of the housemates was praying regularly. MBC instructed the production team to tell the housemates that they should all go into the two special rooms with their Korans and pray. The effect of this staged piety was somewhat spoilt when four of the female housemates, in the intimacy of their bedroom, had a frank conversation about the injustices of Islamic divorce. One of them, an Egyptian contestant, was separated and argued that their male-dominated society had deliberately misinterpreted the Koran to create an oppressive law for women. The other three agreed. The ratings surged on this day. The visiting clerics countered by saying they could only endorse the continuation of *Big Brother* if the women covered their heads and if they were able to vet each programme before it was broadcast. Things were beginning to unravel.

On Day 6 one of the producers received a call from the team hired to telecast the imminent Grand Prix. She was offered a job on it. She already had a job, unless of course, they knew something she didn't. Anuska Ban was aware how nervous the team was. However, she was determined to see the project through. Ban had masterminded *Big Brother* around the world, including working with a twenty-four-hour, armed guard in Colombia. She had also been Endemol's consultant on the already controversial *Star Academy* being transmitted from Lebanon. But she now says that Bahraini *Big Brother* turned out to be the most bizarre production she was ever involved in. The housemate from Jordan was a salsa teacher. He showed the others his dance steps. The owner of MBC, Sheikh Walid al-Ibrahim, immediately called up and ordered that there should be no dancing. Ban thought that before long *Big Brother* in the Middle East would become a tableau of frozen statues. She finally concluded she had done all she could and was preparing to leave. Then two burly, heavily armed men burst into the production room, unannounced.

'Hello! Listen up everyone,' said the first to the startled team in an American accent. 'I'm Agent Joe – that's not my real name. He's Agent Ed – and that's not his real name. Where are your emergency exits?' Ban indicated them. 'Use them, now!' They all fled the building at which point they were instructed to go back inside again. Agent Joe explained: 'Now you know how to escape in a hurry if you have to. We are expecting a demonstration here tomorrow after Friday prayers at the mosque and you need to know your evacuation procedure. We are only a kilometre and a half away at our American base and we have you under satellite surveillance. We'll be here in minutes if there's trouble'. With that Agent Joe and Agent Ed – the CIA's finest – disappeared, never to be heard from again.

The next day, sure enough, a demonstration of several thousand arrived at the site waving banners and chanting 'Stop Sin Brother! No to indecency!' Bahraini police and a detachment of the army blocked their path down the causeway to the house. Among the crowd was Sheikh Maawada, the man who had led the campaign against the Lebanese singer Nancy Ajram. On this occasion the demo was peaceful and broke up without incident. A hostile petition was also prepared for the King. And next day a group of forty women protested outside the Ministry of Information. On both occasions the demonstrators were well covered by the cameras of the Al Jazeera satellite news station. The *Bahrain Tribune* quoted the views of a moderate Shia judge, Sheikh Mohsin Al Asfoor: 'Instead of protesting uselessly we have to be sensible . . . what about other places in Bahrain where boys and girls mix freely ... schools, universities? As regards some of the scenes, they are not as bad as those aired by local Arab and international media. There are evil books in Bahrain shops a thousand times more evil than *Big Brother*.' But his words were not heeded in an increasingly feverish atmosphere.

Speculation on the web was that Big Brother was now a top five target on the island for Islamic terrorists, others including the Grand Prix and the American naval base. There were clearly conversations going on between American intelligence, the King, the armed forces and MBC. On Day 8, 29 February of the leap year of 2004, the owner of MBC called the Bahraini Minister of Information. Sheikh Walid al-Ibrahim announced that he had decided to close the production down. The reason he gave was that his production team were frightened. The following after-noon the *Big Brother* crew were told that the house would close at 7 p.m. the same day. The programmes edited for that day were not broadcast. The housemates were to be whisked away to a secret hotel location, and the production team of two hun-dred were all out of a job. Sheikh Maawada greeted the news with great pleasure: 'When I heard the news I praised Almighty God, and prayed for him, because he is the real power that changes the minds of others and he's the real creator.' Another of *Big Brother*'s opponents in Parliament, Sheikh Mohammed Khalid, was at Mecca in Saudi Arabia: 'I had twenty-five mes-sages on my mobile congratulating me for stopping *Big Brother*.' He was ambivalent about whether King Hamad had personally intervened, first saying: 'As for us, we clerics, we went to the King and thanked him for stopping the programme.' But later Sheikh Khalid claimed he didn't know whether the King was personally involved. There were rumours of MBC receiving a payoff from the Bahraini government. They certainly found the money to compensate Endemol.

In the debates and recriminations that followed some charged *Big Brother* with being the embodiment of Orwell's oppressive, scrutinising society. Others accused the Muslim clerics themselves of being Orwellian in their campaign to close *Big Brother* down. The controversy over *Big Brother* was a power struggle – between Islam and the West, between the mullahs and the business-friendly regime of the King and between the older and younger generations. It might have started with a kiss; it is not clear where it will finish.

CHAPTER FOURTEEN

Bimbos, Bans and Boycotts

Across the world people didn't merely dislike *Big Brother*, they wanted it stopped. The European territory in which *Big Brother* provoked the most disquiet was Germany. A newspaper called it, with memorable eloquence, 'a cage full of shit'. Politicians, regulators and Catholics saw it as a return to the mores of the Third Reich. The battle lines in Germany had originally been drawn up when a senior television executive persuaded those from rival broadcasters to agree they would never commission this dangerous idea. The dirigiste pact did not hold but was perfectly echoed when Endemol tried to get *Big Brother* commissioned in France.

Stéphane Courbit runs Endemol in Paris, having sold a controlling interest in his production company to the Dutch in 1998. From the autumn of 1999 he tried to place *Big Brother* in France. The state broadcaster was not interested. But, more problematically, neither were the two leading commercial, free-to-air networks – TF1 and M6. He was frequently told that the format was trash and that reality TV was not for the French. By the end of 2000 the pan-European broadcaster RTL had had huge success with four series of *Big Brother* in Holland and Germany alone. RTL was the majority shareholder in M6 too. So in January 2001 Courbit and John de Mol met M6 executives for a secret dinner at the Hotel de l'Europe at the confluence of two canals in the heart of Amsterdam. It was a long dinner. But by 4 a.m. they had agreed a deal. Courbit's only problem now was that 60 per cent of his turnover was still with the rival TF1. Since the taboo was about to be broken he had to give them the chance to bid for *Big Brother* too. He managed to get someone from TF1 on the telephone by 6 a.m. He gave them till noon to make up their minds.

By nine, by ten, by eleven Courbit had heard nothing. During this time he flew back to Paris. Finally, at quarter to twelve, he received a call back from TF1: 'You can sign with M6. Do what you want. We don't want the programme.' Five minutes after that he was telephoned with an alarming message from M6: 'We refuse to sign an agreement for *Big Brother* because you delayed making a deal with us.' The delay had been all of eight hours, between 4 a.m. and noon. Courbit was amazed, depressed and embarrassed. Two weeks later he went in to see M6 and the whole story emerged of what had happened that morning. At 11 a.m. the top executives in both companies had managed to get together. They agreed that neither would commission *Big Brother* in France. M6 said that they were forced to go along with it because they knew that TF1 could always outbid them for the show. Instead of their commercial rival getting it, this outcome was at least neutral for them. They told Courbit they had to stick to their agreement: 'But,' they continued, 'if you were able to come up with a different format . . . say *Big Sister* . . . we feel we would be able to commission it.'

Courbit took the hint and, with Endemol's help, created *Loft Story*. This was a new take on *Big Brother* with a different voting procedure and two winners, a boy and a girl, winning a year in an apartment. It constituted a novel enough format for M6 to feel able to go with it. *Loft Story* went on air in April 2001 and was as big a hit as *Big Brother* had been elsewhere in Europe. TF1 then went on to a war footing. As the show started to take chunks out of TF1's ratings Courbit received lawyers' letters alleging he was in breach of his production agreement with TF1. This he was able to dismiss. TF1 then set a team to watch the *Loft Story* programmes and delivered a stream of complaints to the French television regulator about bad language. They also argued that elimination voting was an unfair infringement of personal rights. Neither of these ploys succeeded. TF1's case was not helped by the fact that they had already bought the rights to *Survivor* and shot the series – *Survivor*, of course, also contained the elimination procedure.

An intervention by the French government was altogether more serious for Endemol. Courbit was contacted by the Ministry of Labour. France not only had a mandatory thirty-five-hour week, there was also a rule prohibiting the working of more than fifty hours in a week, even if employees wanted to. The Ministry insisted on inspecting the contracts of employment of the production team. Then they announced they would move on to their real targets – the housemates. They appeared to be working for Endemol twenty-four hours a day. That was a 168-hour week – a clear and provocative breach of the law. But they are contestants in a game show, replied Endemol. No, they are employees, like actors in a drama, retorted the Ministry. If the government won this argument, Courbit knew the series was finished.

Officials from the Ministry of Labour said that this was a grave matter and they would have to interview each of the housemates. This on its own could have spelt the end of *Loft Story* because it would panic the housemates, destroy the atmosphere on screen and ruin the rhythm of the relationships already developing. Endemol had to defeat them and they came up with the means. They told the Ministry inspector that they would be delighted for him to interview the *Loft Story* housemates. His face brightened. But they could not leave the set – he would have to go in and talk to them. And one other thing: the cameras would, of course, continue rolling. All France would witness the Ministry bureaucrat attempting to prove these were, indeed, employees wickedly and wantonly breaching the fifty-hour week. He looked perplexed and immediately responded, as they guessed he would: 'I must call my chief.' Wiser heads at the Ministry did not think they wanted to be responsible for – and to be *seen* to be responsible for – closing down this hugely popular show. Endemol did not hear from the Ministry again, and within weeks they had a new output deal with TF1, with whom they still work closely and happily.

In Europe there is a tradition of clear and carefully worked out regulation for television. In Central America there is more a culture of taking the law into your own hands. This is what happened in Mexico in 2002 where *Big Brother* was due to launch on a channel owned by Televisa. Asociacion A Favor De La Mejor (i.e. The Silent Majority) was a long-standing campaign group formed in 1977 by Mexicans who wished to clean up the media. It had close links to the Catholic Church. When the Association heard of Televisa's intentions they immediately opposed them. They published their objections to *Big Brother*: 'It is a means to provoke conflict and controversy in which the bold and unexpected occur and in which people's most private aspects are on view. This method of entertainment is ethically unacceptable . . . this programme encourages in the basest way, the sickness of entertaining oneself by viewing other people's private lives . . . to make private lives a spectacle of entertainment is to begin an escalation of excess which is denigrating to society . . . Televisa is the promoter of this degradation, the participants are the voluntary protagonists and the society which watches them become their accomplices.' This was becoming a familiar litany from a generation that abhorred exhibitionism, nudity and street language. A newspaper journalist even argued that the housemates would be worse off than the terrorist suspects being held by the Americans in Guantanamo Bay because at least they had their privacy respected.

The Association achieved an early victory. They recorded Televisa's trails for *Big Brother*, slowed them down and then reissued them on video to demonstrate that there were indistinct images of a couple making love contained within the close-up pupil of an eye. Televisa dropped the trails. Strike one to the Association. But the main battle was to get *Big Brother* stopped. The Association hit upon the idea of an economic boycott. They would persuade major advertisers to withdraw their commercials from Televisa during *Big Brother*'s time slot. The campaign was led by a powerful businessman, Don Lorenzo Servitje. He owned Bimbo, the biggest bread and biscuits company in Mexico. He was now in his eighties and extremely conservative. Since most of Mexico's large companies are owned by around two hundred families Don Lorenzo knew whom he had to talk to. His first target was Banamex, a banking subsidiary of the US-owned Citibank. Banamex had been the sponsor of the *Big Brother* promotions on Televisa. Don Lorenzo told them that if they did not back out he would remove all his company's accounts from their bank. They immediately withdrew. Strike two to the Association. Don Lorenzo then concentrated on putting together a powerful coalition of the largest advertisers, all pledged to boycott *Big Brother*. He recruited the local franchise holders for Coca-Cola and Pepsi-Cola. He persuaded Proctor & Gamble and Kimberley-Clark to sign up as well. In all, thirty-seven companies joined the Association's boycott and this included seven of Mexico's largest advertisers.

There were now two weeks to go before *Big Brother*'s March launch. Televisa had made a five-year agreement with Endemol but they were faced with almost no commercial income for the prime-time, eight o'clock slot in which *Big Brother* was scheduled. The Association now met Televisa officials in the Marriott Hotel in Mexico City. They revealed the size of the boycott. In what they called 'a declaration of war' they demanded Televisa should cancel *Big Brother*. This was a clash of two different generations with vastly different social and moral outlooks: the elderly business men versus the young Televisa management. It was a tough call for their thirty-six-year-old President, Emilio

Azcarraga. Even his own commercial department was now pressuring him to axe *Big Brother*. But he remained cool and resolved to press on. A crumb of comfort for him was that one large company, Nestlé, had not joined the boycott.

Big Brother began on 3 March. Televisa nodded in the direction of the Association's campaign by shifting transmission later, by half an hour, to 8.30 p.m. The live, opening show lasted three and a half hours. The twelve housemates were given two bottles of tequila to help relax them – it was a tense evening during which the adrenalin flowed. The show was eventually completed successfully. At around midnight Pedro Torres, Endemol's Mexican executive producer, started drinking champagne with Televisa's officials. They were watching the housemates on the twenty-four-hour digital stream. Suddenly one of the boys in the house kissed one of the girls in the bathroom. It was just a kiss. Endemol had spent months preparing Televisa for some of the things that might happen in the house. They had seen quite explicit footage from other countries. But now it was happening in front of their eyes. Laurens Drillich was the Dutchman present from Endemol: 'The Televisa guys went crazy. They told me – "we don't care how you do it, they are not going to keep kissing. They are surely not going to screw tonight! It doesn't matter if you have to send in the police – it's not going to happen!" We then had to kill the party mood in the house immediately. We called the girl into the diary room and told her to drink three glasses of milk and sober up. We told her to change bedrooms to be away from the guy she had kissed. We were there till three in the morning. And it wasn't even a big kiss – in Holland they would have been disappointed.'

The ratings for *Big Brother Mexico* were the highest Televisa had ever achieved. They were partly helped by the advance publicity that the Association had engendered. It turned out that they were also assisted by the lack of advertisements. Mexican viewers, like Americans, were usually fed commercials about every six minutes. The novelty of a narrative programme stretching to half an hour without a break proved attractive. However it was not a habit Televisa wished its viewers to get into. By *Big Brother 2* advertisers had begun to drift back, unable to ignore such a ratings phenomenon. In later series *Big Brother* switched to a celebrity version so that the much-worshipped *telenovelas* stars could be included. The programme retains a solid and (now) lucrative 40 per cent share. Seven big advertisers still continue to refuse to support *Big Brother*. At their core remains Bimbo's owner Don Lorenzo, rock-solid in his opposition.

If the morality of *Big Brother Mexico* caused a commercial crisis, in Malawi it led to a constitutional crisis. South Africa's *Big Brother 3* began on 25 May 2003. It was far more ambitious than the previous two series in that it was pan-African. The twelve housemates – eleven black and one white – came from twelve different countries on the continent. The broadcaster, M-Net, delivers its signal via satellite to subscribers, most of whom are in South Africa. So that the series could be seen across Africa M-Net decided to give the daily edited highlights show to the terrestrial broadcaster of each country which had a contestant taking part. The careful casting had delivered a group of educated, cosmopolitan housemates. This provoked both approbation and debate. A Malawi newspaper, *Nation Online*, reflected this: 'In Africa, a woman is not supposed to appear in public with some of her sensitive parts in the open. But in *Big Brother Africa* women housemates walk about half-naked, kiss, touch and make love before the camera. Is this African? Wine and liquor flow like water and the housemates' knowledge of how to operate some of the gadgets in the house was awesome. Warona, the Botswana housemate, was the first to push in some buttons for opening the high-tech fridge.' Viewers of the twenty-four-hour digital streaming were treated daily to what became known as the 'shower hour', when the uninhibited housemates washed themselves communally, rather in the manner of a post-match rugby team.

But pan-African *Big Brother* had an unexpectedly galvanising effect. Here was a group of peoples constantly fed negative stories about their continent – HIV Aids, government corruption, poverty, starvation, genocide. And here was a television programme full of educated, confident, sophisticated Africans presenting a wholly different picture. It was widely recognised as aspirational and consciousness-raising. On a continent ravaged by civil wars it showed the representatives of twelve countries getting on in harmony. When the winner, Cherise Makabale from Zambia, emerged from the house she was dubbed the African Queen. Nelson Mandela asked to meet her and this was arranged. 'You're a really tall, beautiful young lady. How many boyfriends have you got?' asked Mandela. The various housemates returned triumphantly to their own countries where crowds as big as fifty thousand were waiting to greet them at airports. They were granted diplomatic status by their governments and several became unofficial ambassadors-at-large. However, *Big Brother* was not universally praised.

The President of Namibia, Sam Nujoma, condemned the show. He said that Namibia's national broadcaster should be showing programmes on the history of Namibia instead. But he did not take any action to try to enforce his views. In Malawi they did. The free, half-hour version of *Big Brother* was transmitted on TV in Malawi at 6 p.m. every night. Through the summer of 2003 Malawian churches were in a state of agitation. The Reverend Ian Longwe of the Word of Faith Church said that *Big Brother*'s erotic scenes were polluting the minds of the nation's youth: 'As far as I am concerned, with sexual antics, heavy boozing and puffing all sorts of cigarettes the *Big Brother* house is doing more harm to viewers than good. Perhaps instead of calling the reality show *Big Brother Africa*, they should have renamed it *Big Pornography Africa*.' The Reverend Daniel Gunya of the Church of Central African Presbyterian suggested that if the filming and broadcasting of pornography was an

offence in Malawi why should the beaming of housemates getting into bed together and kissing passionately be legal: 'How
are our youths benefiting from watching someone answering
nature's call in a toilet or removing his clothes to take a bath?
What is beneficial about people having sex or arguing about
who ate eggs or conniving in order to win prize money?'
Malawian fans responded vigorously to the debate in the newspapers, saying that if the prelates didn't like it they could switch
it off.

As the controversy developed there was an obvious and
growing confusion between the carefully edited, sanitised daily
digest given away free by M-Net to the local channel and the
digital, twenty-four-hour streaming of the pictures only available to satellite subscribers. This was more explicit and
included the fabled shower hour. When the debate spread
beyond the Church and the newspapers to Parliament it was
clear that many of the priests and politicians did not know the
difference. On Day 72 of *Big Brother Africa*, Tuesday 5
August, the Malawian Parliament held an impromptu debate
about the issue. The chairman of the Malawi Committee on
Media, MP Taylor Nothale, tabled a motion that TV Malawi
should stop transmitting *Big Brother* immediately. He claimed
the TV Malawi show beamed naked people (which it didn't)
and referred to 'horrible pictures which are corrupting the
morals of our children'. Malawian politicians, like their British
counterparts, watched little or no television but had an opinion
on every programme. Another MP said a ban would be too
hasty and that the Media Committee should investigate the
issue further. But then the leader of the opposition, Gwanda
Chakuamba, said the House should stop this nonsense on TV
right away. Another opposition MP, Dr Hetherwick Ntaba,
agreed. The government and the opposition seemed to be
speaking with one voice. The Deputy Foreign Affairs Minister,
Chimunthu Banda, announced: 'This is an issue of national

importance ... we are asking this House to petition the Minister of Information to instruct TVM to scrap the show before six o'clock this evening.' He was strongly supported by the longest serving member of the opposition, John Tembo, who referred to *Big Brother* as 'moral and cultural madness'. The motion was passed overwhelmingly, 80 per cent of the MPs voting in favour of a ban.

TV Malawi reluctantly bowed to Parliament's will and pulled *Big Brother* from their schedules immediately. Malawi now had a full-scale constitutional crisis on its hands. Could Parliament simply order the national broadcaster what to do, bypassing the Malawian Censorship Board and ignoring their contract with M-Net? Some said that it was a straight censorship issue and a return to the period when Malawi had a one-party system which directly controlled the media. Others accused the MPs of dual standards. They were suspected of being members of a small minority who could afford satellite TV and would continue to be able to watch uninterrupted, twenty-four-hour coverage. There were only seven thousand such subscribers in Malawi out of a population of twelve million. Everyone else would have their viewing decided for them. Finally, there were those who pointed out that, with twenty-nine MPs having died of HIV Aids in recent years, they were not inclined to take lessons in morality from them. For the director of domestic productions at M-Net, Carl Fischer, it was an overreaction: 'The half-hour show is very carefully edited ... we've had no direct communication regarding specific scenes that may have caused offence.' Fischer had been on a long journey with *Big Brother*. He was the man, when previously working for Endemol, who had spoken up for the idea when John de Mol had first presented it to the company's managing directors in 1998. At the time he had been the only one.

The controversy snowballed over the following week. Then, on 15 August, a 'concerned citizen', one Sam Mlanjira, applied to the High Court to have the parliamentary ban overturned. He was successful. On the same day the judge, Dunstain Mwaungulu, granted his application. The reasons were that Parliament had no mandate to ban *Big Brother* since they had not actually passed a bill – no Act had been signed by the President. There had been no consultation with the people of Malawi so the ban was undemocratic. Thirdly, there was a presumption that the people had a right to freedom of information and this had been infringed. TV Malawi had *Big Brother* back on air within twenty-four hours. But, judiciously, they now scheduled it at 10 rather than 6 p.m.

In the Malawian general election of 20 May 2004 there was an interesting postscript to the saga. The man who proposed the order banning *Big Brother*, Taylor Nothale, lost his seat. The member of the opposition who supported the ban, Hetherwick Ntaba, also lost his seat, as did his fellow MP and objector to *Big Brother*, John Tembo. Maybe it was coincidence. A number of Malawians argued it was not.

All these attempts to ban *Big Brother* illustrate how, from the start, television had been different. Its means of dissemination – spectrum – remained very limited for the first fifty years of the medium and largely under government control. Even in the 1990s its programmes were still a matter of public policy in a way that the contents of newsagents or bookshops in the more liberal world were not. But *Big Brother* arrived just at the point when, with multi-channels, content began to be driven more by popular taste than the dictates of a cultural elite. TV was no longer different or special, as it had been with only one or two networks. From the start *Big Brother* was different too. With its nudity, sex and bald language it was an extreme provocation to television regulators and governments. Across the world it became the catalyst for fierce censorship debates, clashes between Church and state and constitutional crises. No single television idea had ever had such an effect before. That *Big Brother* survived in all but one of the skirm-ishes shows how satellite television, like the world wide web, cannot be rigidly controlled by governments. Television is no longer different.

CHAPTER FIFTEEN

Vote Early, Vote Often

In January 2001 the politicians and civil servants of the Danish Parliament, the Christiansborg, crashed their entire internet connection. They were all logging on at once to watch the housemates of Denmark's *Big Brother 1* taking their morning showers. A year earlier a committee of the upper house of the Spanish Parliament decided to visit the *Big Brother* site to investigate the ethics of television game shows; they had to be dissuaded from this on the grounds that they would have looked a bit silly popping up on the *Big Brother* cameras. Not long afterwards a Basque separatist broke into the house to stage a one-man protest. The Spanish housemates were later challenged to memorise the European constitution. Politicians in several countries, alive to popular culture and its possibilities, were now starting to pay close attention to *Big Brother*.

On 3 October 2003 the Colombian *Big Brother* house was silently surrounded by armed government agents. It was not a coup, nor was it to close the programme down – far from it. The President, Alvaro Uribe, was about to make a surprise visit to the housemates. The producers had designed a task around an imminent referendum in Colombia. The housemates had to learn and then explain the fifteen different propositions on a ballot intended to reform the judicial and political systems in the country. They were to be neutral, encouraging people to go to the polling booths but pushing for neither a yes nor a no vote. The President, desperate to get the reforms through, decided that visiting the house could make all the difference. His advisers chose a Friday night – the day of the week with the highest audiences.

Big Brother ordered the housemates into a bedroom. President Uribe then took his place on one of the sofas in the living area. The executive producer, Juan Maldonado, watched the contestants' reaction once they were let out of the bedroom: 'They yelled and screamed and they just wanted to hug him. But they stopped and thought – hey, this is the President, you're not supposed to run and hug him! But they did, and he hugged them back.' For *Big Brother* this was entertaining television and guaranteed front-page coverage in all the newspapers. For President Uribe, however, it did not turn out so well: his reform programme was roundly rejected on the day of the referendum. The episode highlighted a complicated and ambivalent relationship that had developed between *Big Brother* and organised politics.

In every country *Big Brother* generated millions of phone votes – something that had political significance in itself. Britain's *Big Brother* alone has garnered eighty million votes over five series since July 2000. By contrast the UK general election of 2001 saw the lowest turnout since 1918. At 59 per cent it was a full 13 per cent lower than the preceding election in 1997. Meanwhile membership of British political parties is a fraction of its levels in the 1950s and 1960s. There have been many, mostly facile, parallels drawn between *Big Brother* and politics. In particular, we often hear that more younger voters participated in the television series than turned out for the general election. This is probably untrue since it confuses the number of telephone votes cast in *Big Brother* with the number of people voting. Those eighty million votes were generated by probably no more than seven or eight million fans doing what they are not allowed to do in a general election – multiple voting. Some simply put their telephones on redial for a while to ensure the candidates they loved or hated got their just desserts. But there is a connection between *Big Brother* and politics – both are essentially popularity contests. We often hear politicians intone: 'I don't want to discuss personalities. It's the issues the public care about.' This is nonsense. Politics is certainly about issues, but it is even more about personalities, particularly in the television age. People can vote for whatever reason they choose. As often as not it will be on a candidate's smile, hair colour or suit. The first *Big Brother* housemate to work out the affinity between the television game and the practice of politics was in Poland.

'He did genuinely have a real charisma. He had this sort of ability to listen and to look at you all the time and make you feel as though he was giving you some kind of special attention and focus.' This was the verdict of Endemol's managing director in Poland, Mike Morley, when he first met Sebastian Florek. Florek was thirty, the son of a university professor, an agricultural college graduate and the owner of a farm and a sawmill. But he had a taste, so he thought, for politics. He had been elected deputy-head of his school in his final year. Then, in 1998 in his rural community, he managed to oust the sitting local councillor, a veteran, by four votes. By 2000 Florek wanted to graduate to national politics. Without any party contacts he could not see how to achieve this. Then, in November 2000, he saw a television trail for *Big Brother* applicants. The series was to start in Poland in March 2001. He wrote a humorous letter of application about himself as part of a deliberate plan: 'I thought that if I could get on to the media in a positive way, this could help me make a jump to bigger politics. *Big Brother*, which is entertainment, would be considered something good. And the media, the press, would write about it.' Florek did not reveal his 'springboard' strategy to the Endemol team; he merely concentrated on making himself interesting. He did not succeed in being chosen as one of ten housemates who were automatically going into the house, but Morley could see he had something to offer: 'We had an older traffic warden, a tubby woman who was very funny, a Hell's Angel biker – I wasn't looking for a mild-mannered, husbandly figure ... but Florek was someone who would be a listener. He was also articulate ... he could be the peacemaker because I imagined there could be a lot of tension and vitriol flying around.'

Florek was made one of several candidates for the last two places, to be voted on by viewers. He and the others were then put through a bizarre ritual which, it transpired, was both compelling and shocking to this very Catholic country. They were each attached to a lie detector and asked ten questions based on the Ten Commandments. Had they honoured their father and mother? Had they committed adultery? Did they covet their neighbour's ass? Florek came through the third important election in his life successfully. Polish viewers warmed to him and he came top of the poll. His plan was working – at the eleventh hour he had gained admission to *Big Brother*.

Florek lasted thirty-two days in the house. He proved genial enough in late-night beer-drinking sessions; he was the best host of a weekly talk show they were made to enact; and he did not mind dressing up as Juliet to another housemate's Romeo in an elaborate sketch. The day of his eviction was 15 April. Poland had a general election scheduled for the following September: he had just five months to exploit his newfound fame and only one month to get his name on to the all-important slate of a party's candidates before it was closed. With only days to go he attended a May celebration being held by the Democratic Alliance Party which he knew its leader, Leszek Miller, would be attending. He had worked out it was Miller's birthday so he baked him a cake, which he managed to present to him in person. Florek immediately petitioned the party leader to adopt him as a party candidate in his home area. Miller agreed to use his influence – he could see how others at the party flocked around this new television star. And that is what happened. Florek managed to get the eighteenth and final place on the official candidates list for his region. His inclusion was a gift for the Democratic Alliance. During the campaign a local newspaper announced Florek would be meeting the voters at a small town near Olsztyn. For any of his fellow candidates this would have attracted an audience of ten, maybe twenty. Seven thousand people turned up to see him, there was a huge traffic jam and the town was paralysed.

Three days before the September general election Florek received an anonymous call from the state broadcaster. Their detailed poll was predicting that he would easily be elected a deputy. On 23 September 2001 it became official. Sebastian Florek had been elected as one of nine parliamentary deputies for Warminsko-Mazurski. His party, the Democratic Alliance, had also won the election and Leszek Miller was now the Prime Minister of Poland. Since 2001 Florek has taken an interest in agricultural and environmental issues. He attracted a good deal of satirical attention when he suggested Poland should grow willow trees for fuel, preparing for the day the world's oil ran out. He was also criticised for being lazy and not contributing much to debates in Parliament. Mikolaj Lizut, a journalist on Poland's biggest daily newspaper, *Gazeta Wyborcza*, has a jaundiced view of Florek's efforts: 'He's spoken twelve times. So that is not really much, nothing in fact. So it's concluded he doesn't work much in Parliament. Because of his fame . . . it was simply a short cut . . . he is just, you know, a young guy with a degree from a small town.' The man Florek replaced as a local councillor regained his position once Florek had gone to the national Parliament. He was quick to get revenge, in a *Gazeta Wyborcza* feature: 'I keep expecting Florek to finally do something for our town, but in vain. If only building a road – in the winter the bus is afraid to go on its route and children have to walk back seven kilometres from school.'

Florek tried to win a seat in the European Parliament but failed. Now he is to stand again for re-election in 2005 and hopes, finally, to become a minister. He feels that his *Big Brother* exposure has become a hindrance: 'Many people still criticise me for *Big Brother*. It's like a stamp on me, perceived in a negative way. Articles always start with – Sebastian Florek, ex-contestant in *Big Brother*.'

South Africa's first series of *Big Brother* began a month before Florek was elected, in August 2001. One of the housemates there decided to use his moment of fame to launch an entire political party. 'He was odd from the start. He struck me as the dark horse. I don't think anybody anticipated how dark he would be.' That was the judgement made of Brad Wood by one of the production team who had to interview the housemates before they went in. Brad Wood was a police reservist and ran his own security company, called 'The Organisation'. He was tall, bulky, liked guns and would drop hints that he had been involved with South African intelligence. A genuine operative or a juvenile fantasist? No one quite knew. Wood concentrated hard on establishing himself as the tough guy of the show. The production team planned to put a dog into the house. They lined up twelve mongrels that were due to be put down and asked the housemates to give one of them a reprieve by voting it into *Big Brother*. Wood threw a tantrum and said he would kick any dog introduced into the house. Hundreds of animal lovers besieged the broadcaster, M-Net, by telephone. Animal societies attacked Wood and *Big Brother* on the radio. Within a day the production team dropped the idea altogether. From now on Wood was dubbed Bad Brad by the viewers and the newspapers. He then tried to escape the house by unscrewing one of the doors. As an act of rebellion it didn't exactly rank with Hereward the Wake or Paul Revere. But it certainly caused controversy.

When Bad Brad was voted out of the house he enjoyed his customary few weeks of celebrity. He released a best-selling CD. A lady whose husband had left her because she watched so much *Big Brother* asked him to autograph her divorce papers. He even wrote a book about his experiences called *Living Lies*, in which he attempted to explore what he saw as the falsity of celebrity status. And he began to present himself as the tribune of law and order, boasting that, as a police reservist, he had shot a car hijacker dead in Durban: 'There was a whole big thing in the newspapers, and I sat back and I thought to myself – you know what, prevention's better than cure.' He also claimed that he was developing special security equipment on his own initiative: 'I made this police vehicle. It cost me over a million rand. This thing had cameras, and microwave and satellite connections. If they were chasing a car I could uplink the image straightaway . . . then Pretoria shut it down. They said, "No, you can't do it." So I lost money there. And I thought, OK, I've got enough money to go into politics. I discussed it with a lot of people, high-powered people, in the country, and they said, go for it.' During 2002 he seemed to court adverse publicity. He was arrested at an airport for carrying spent gun cartridges. He was then caught up in a restaurant brawl as a result of someone burning his Hugo Boss shirt. It continued in 2003 when he became embroiled in his neighbours' marital dispute, attempted a citizen's arrest on an armed robber and suffered a road-rage incident. Despite, or perhaps because of all this, he decided to try his hand at politics.

Bad Brad founded 'The Organisation Party' in May 2003 in order to contest South Africa's general election in April 2004. Its name bore a passing resemblance to that of his security company. His entry into politics got him sacked as a police reservist in Camps Bay. His party's manifesto demonstrated why. As revealed on his web site it demanded 'an efficient police force weeded out and free of all deadbeats'. The manifesto began like this: 'To the Citizens of the Republic of South Africa: The

Organisation Party is made up of South African Citizens who have no desire to be labelled as politicians, a title synonymous with empty promises, half truths, outright lies and corruption. We tell it like it is. Our campaign is simply to attack the disease, not the symptoms, that is eating away at the heart and soul of our potentially great country. South Africa is renowned for Table Mountain, diamonds, gold and its wildlife, as well as the infamous Big Five that are collectively destroying the country ... murder, rape, corruption, armed robbery, fraud.' Brad Wood went on to unfurl his two most controversial policies – the reintroduction of the death penalty and the erection of a fence on South Africa's border to prevent economic immigration from the rest of the continent.

Bad Brad was challenged by the newspapers as to whether the transition from *Big Brother* celebrity to politician was merely a ploy to keep him in the limelight. This he denied: 'I've been fighting crime for the last ten years and as a South African citizen I feel it is my responsibility to give something back to my country. I truly believe I'm the one person who can make a difference.' On the issue of trying to become a white MP in a predominantly black Parliament he had these sensitive words to offer: 'I would hope that people are not elected to office based on their race or gender. Representatives need to be chosen according to their abilities and what they have to offer the country. Besides, chocolate goes well with vanilla.' Shortly afterwards he revealed his two campaign slogans: 'Criminals, it's time you get fcuked' and, 'Child rapists and violent criminals, it's time we start fcuking you.'

Despite being regarded as a figure of fun by the media Wood managed to raise the requisite funds and support to qualify as contesting party for South Africa's general election. He was twenty-nine and the youngest ever party leader. At the hustings, where all the parties had to sign up to a code of conduct, Brad Wood met the head of the ruling ANC Party, President Mbeki.

'Oh, Bad Brad, what are you doing?' asked Mbeki. Wood was flattered the President knew who he was, though since Mbeki's younger brother is chairman of Endemol South Africa, it was not surprising. 'Are you aiming to go into the bigger House? Parliament is the ultimate *Big Brother* house,' joked Mbeki before wishing Wood good luck. He needed it.

In the election which saw another clear victory for the ANC, The Organisation Party received 8000 of the eleven million votes cast. Wood was not downhearted and announced plans to contest the next election too. An outspoken media commentator, Professor Michael Simpson, responded sceptically: 'Bad Brad has as much chance of getting legitimately elected into Parliament as I have of becoming the next Miss World.'

Neither Florek nor Wood won, or came close to winning, *Big Brother*. They merely capitalised on the passing notoriety their participation had given them. The key to winning the *Big Brother* popularity contest is, paradoxically, not to try. Time and again the eventual winner is a person who apparently has no strategy for the popularity game at all. They are just themselves. The young fans of *Big Brother* value this sort of authenticity above all else. They may be gay or straight, they may be black or white (in the case of *Big Brother 5* in the UK, they may be transsexual) – viewers appear to be blind to such characteristics. They elevate and reward individuals who appear guileless and who reveal themselves honestly. Bart, the very first winner in Holland, fell in love with Sabine. Craig, the man who triumphed in the UK's *Big Brother 1*, tackled and defeated the cheating Nasty Nick. After the second British series Janet Jones, a lecturer in media and communication studies at the University of Wales, polled 9000 fans. She found that, most of all, they wanted personalised narratives and real emotions. Jones asked them to consider this statement: 'I think the winner should be the person that is "true to themselves".' Ten per cent disagreed while 80 per cent agreed. As Jones puts it, 'they were policing the "genuineness" of the housemates'. They were confident they could spot false or fake behaviour, as became clear when she asked them to react to this: 'I think it is impossible for the housemates to fake it all the time for the cameras.' Nearly 70 per cent of the fans agreed or strongly agreed with that sentiment. Just to underline how strongly they felt about this, 84 per cent agreed that the winner should be the person who was just themselves while only 8 per cent thought it should be a person who played to win.

The viewers of *Big Brother* are more female than male and more young than old. What they are doing when they watch and vote is replaying the game that is as old as time among teenagers at school. First, it is an endless analysis of who is 'popular' and who is not. Second, and as part of the same exercise, individuals are rated as to whether they are 'fake' or not. Some would argue that this is a socially juvenile attitude and that as we grow into adulthood we realise that life has to become a series of white lies and strategic falsehoods. Others find something very positive about these idealistic instincts. Melvyn Bragg, who has been active in politics and television for forty years, is in the latter camp: 'I think one of the attractions of *Big Brother* is that here we have a group of very young people trying to establish a hierarchy. It appears to have nothing to do with "breeding", nothing to do with money and nothing to do with the old class categorisations, or even tradition. What emerges is a search for who is the most helpful and truthful and most sincere of them all. Quite heartening and quite new.'

As the world's academics piled into analysing *Big Brother*'s growing success, one of them had an unusual idea. Stephen Coleman is Professor of e-democracy at Oxford University, studying how new technologies can reinvigorate the democratic process. He isolated and polled two groups – political junkies (PJs) who were mostly older, more conservative and disliked or knew nothing of *Big Brother*, and *Big Brother* fans (BBs) who were younger and broadly not involved in organised politics.

What would their contrasting opinions teach us? 'The most persistent and overwhelming message from the BBs,' concluded Coleman, 'concerned authenticity. They regarded politics and politicians as somehow "unreal" and believed that opaque and devious construction of political imagery could be exposed through the lens of transparent media ... The discourse of authenticity (who is a "real" person) and transparency (being "seen" to be who one says one is) may well offer significant clues to BBs' reasons for distrusting and disengaging from politics.' Elsewhere this has been dubbed 'the death of deference' – that we no longer automatically believe and respect those in authority over us such as politicians, policemen, teachers and doctors.

Whether politicians really have something to learn from the clash between idealism and cynicism is a nice debate. Can being guileless really be a 'strategy' or is that a self-defeating oxymoron? Could there be such a thing as an ingenuous politician, and would we want it? John de Mol, the begetter of *Big Brother*, can never have imagined that his humble entertainment idea, hatched late at night in his office, might end up giving rise to such philosophical questions.

POSTSCRIPT

Billion Dollar Game is the story of three men and their formats. How have they fared in the years since they successfully conquered the American market?

Paul Smith's *Who Wants to Be a Millionaire?* still runs on Saturday nights in its native United Kingdom. The ratings are half what they were in its triumphant first year but that still makes it a winning show. *Millionaire* continues on ABC in the States as well, with special editions from time to time. At its peak it transmitted in more than a hundred territories. Today it is still being produced in over fifty of those – it remains a formidable engine of cash generation. Its sales revenue will shortly approach a billion pounds. Paul Smith now talks of taking it easier and perhaps spending more time on improving his golf swing. His colleagues say they will believe that when they see it.

Charlie Parsons cuts a more ambivalent figure, disenchanted by the world of television. In all, he spent five years pursuing *Big Brother* through the Dutch courts. On 16 April 2004 the Hoge Raad, Holland's Supreme Court, delivered the final verdict in the dispute. It emphatically dismissed all Parsons' claims against Endemol. In 2002 Parsons launched another set of proceedings, this time against Granada. He claimed that their reality hit, *I'm a Celebrity, Get Me Out of Here!* was also a copy of *Survivor*. This was met with scepticism by an American judge. Parsons was undoubtedly one of the most influential figures in the development of reality entertainment, but he was not to be allowed a monopoly on it. His compensation is the annual receipt of approximately £10 million that *Survivor* still earns from its highly successful productions in the US, Scandinavia and elsewhere.

Big Brother has continued to prove the adage that where there's money there's legal action. Endemol had to defend the format from a Dutch security company also called *Big Brother*. Then the owners of the film rights to Orwell's *Nineteen Eighty-Four* sued Endemol and CBS in the American courts. The confidential settlement is thought to have run to millions of dollars. And in Brazil Endemol turned plaintiff to take a channel to court which was broadcasting a 'badly disguised and rude' copy of Big Brother. These, though, were all minor skirmishes as the *Big Brother* cash continued to roll in. Its revenues are not far behind those of *Millionaire*. So-called reality shows – simply individuals scrutinised under pressure – have sprung up worldwide. Thanks to *Survivor* and *Big Brother*, the genre is here to stay. The bad formats (too tacky or too derivative) fail, the good ones command valuable audiences and will continue to do so.

Viewers have switched *Big Brother* on eighteen billion times. More than a billion votes have been cast via telephones and interactive TV. Six and a half billion page views have been recorded at *Big Brother* web sites. It remains the most perfectly converged piece of entertainment ever conceived. And it is monitored by legions of psychologists, psephologists, sociologists and technologists. While the format has undoubtedly entered the intellectual and popular mainstream there remain those who are resolutely opposed to it. The words of an ITV broadcaster from 1955 crystallise the argument perfectly. The Labour opposition, if returned to power, had promised to close down their vulgar new entertainment channel. Observing that ITV was an expression of popular taste the broadcaster retorted: 'It is not really television with which they are dissatisfied. It is with people.'

John de Mol's emergence as a master of the media universe

was officially endorsed in 2003 when he appeared on the cover of *Forbes* magazine under the heading, 'Sex, Money and Videotape'. He had become, perhaps, the most celebrated tycoon in Holland. His private jet was known as the costliest packet of cigarettes in broadcasting history – he acquired it partly to circumvent the smoking ban on commercial airlines. Rumours abounded about his love life, plastic surgery and his business affairs. But, unlike Trump or Branson, de Mol remained intensely private. Some in Spain still believed the sale to Telefonica was too good to be true. De Mol even had to give evidence to an ambitious Spanish magistrate trying to prove Juan Villalonga was corrupt. In fact, of course, Villalonga's only sin had been excessive exuberance at the top of the market. And all de Mol had been guilty of was matching that with exquisite timing.

In 2004 de Mol had a very public falling out with Telefonica. His Spanish shareholder was not happy with some of the deals Endemol had done to acquire production companies and imposed a new, Spanish chief executive on the group. In the Dutch newspapers de Mol alleged Telefonica had hampered the development of Endemol. He then exited a year earlier than his original deal decreed. By this time his own, sizeable private investment vehicle was taking strategic holdings in media, entertainment and sports companies. Talpa (the Latin for 'mole') earned international publicity when it bought and then sold 5 per cent of Manchester United, achieving a substantial gain.

The one-time producer and scourge of the networks has now leased himself a Dutch channel of his own and become a broadcaster. From September 2005 he is scheduling and programming Holland's Nickelodeon in the evenings. In preparation he has won the rights to the Netherlands' Premier League Football and to some international matches. A close colleague interprets this as pure revenge – he is intent on demonstrating to those who ridiculed his old Sport7 deal in 1996 how wrong they were.

Most unexpectedly of all, in January 2005, de Mol announced that he had bought *Survivor* for his new network. After all the enmities between Charlie Parsons and John de Mol they have now become the least likely partners in the television business. Peace in our time, albeit inspired by the commercial imperative.

John de Mol is determined to show the world and himself that *Big Brother* is not the end. He still wants to come up with one more world-beating format to prove that lightning can strike in the same place twice. He is extraordinarily rich. He could take it easy. But then, where's the fun in that? Money means little to him. He needs to take risks and do deals. It is a compulsion.

BIG BROTHER TRANSMISSIONS WORLDWIDE
1999–2005

COUNTRY	START DATE	END DATE	BROADCASTER
1999			
Holland	13 Sept	30 Dec	Veronica
2000			
Germany	1 Mar	9 June	RTL2
Spain	23 Apr	21 July	Tele 5
USA	5 July	29 Sept	CBS
UK	14 July	17 Sept	Channel 4
Portugal	3 Sept	31 Dec	TV1
Switzerland	3 Sept	17 Dec	TV3
Sweden	3 Sept	14 Dec	Kanal 5
Belgium	3 Sept	17 Dec	Kanaal 2
Italy	11 Sept	21 Dec	Canale 5
Holland 2	14 Sept	30 Dec	Veronica
Germany 2	16 Sept	31 Dec	RTL2
2001			
Portugal 2	21 Jan	20 May	TV1
Germany 3	27 Jan	12 May	RTL2
Denmark	28 Jan	10 May	TVDK2
Switzerland 2	28 Jan	13 May	TV3
Norway	25 Feb	31 May	TV Norge

COUNTRY	START DATE	END DATE	BROADCASTER
Poland	4 Mar	17 June	TVN
Argentina	10 Mar	30 June	Telefe
Spain 2	18 Mar	24 June	Tele 5
Australia	24 Apr	15 July	Channel 10
France (Loft Story)	27 Apr	5 July	M6
UK 2	24 May	26 July	Channel 4
USA 2	5 July	20 Sept	CBS
Argentina 2	4 Aug	1 Dec	Telefe
South Africa	26 Aug	9 Dec	M-Net
Denmark 2	26 Aug	6 Dec	TVDK2
Belgium 2	2 Sept	16 Dec	Kanaal 2
Poland 2	2 Sept	16 Dec	TVN
Portugal 3	2 Sept	31 Dec	TV1
Greece	10 Sept	31 Dec	Antenna
Holland 3	14 Sept	30 Dec	Yorin
Italy 2	20 Sept	27 Dec	Canale 5

2002

COUNTRY	START DATE	END DATE	BROADCASTER
Sweden 2	26 Jan	12 May	Kanal 5
Brazil	29 Jan	2 Apr	Globo TV
Norway 2	25 Feb	6 June	TV Norge
Poland 3	2 Mar	22 May	TVN
Mexico	3 Mar	16 June	Televisa Canal
Greece 2	8 Mar	30 June	Antenna
Australia 2	8 Apr	1 July	Channel 10
France 2	12 Apr	4 July	M6
Spain 3	4 Apr	14 July	Tele 5
Brazil 2	14 May	16 July	Globo TV
UK 3	24 May	26 July	Channel 4
USA 3	10 July	25 Sept	CBS
South Africa 2	28 July	12 Oct	M-Net
Holland 4	26 Aug	23 Dec	Yorin
Belgium 3	1 Sept	15 Dec	Kanaal 2

COUNTRY	START DATE	END DATE	BROADCASTER
Hungary	1 Sept	31 Dec	TV2
Spain 4	6 Oct	16 Jan	Tele 5
Argentina 3	15 Oct	16 Feb	Telefe
2003			
Brazil 3	14 Jan	4 Mar	Globo TV
Sweden 3	26 Jan	11 May	Kanal 5
Italy 3	30 Jan	8 May	Canale 5
Hungary 2	2 Feb	15 June	TV2
Mexico 2	2 Mar	29 June	Televisa Canal
Norway 3	8 Mar	15 May	TV Norge
Greece 3	10 Mar	30 June	Antenna
Ecuador	16 Mar	13 July	Ecuavisa
Romania	16 Mar	6 July	Prima TV
Germany 4	31 Mar	7 July	RTL2
Australia 3	27 Apr	21 July	Channel 10
UK 4	23 May	25 July	Channel 4
Pan-Africa	25 May	7 Sept	DSTV Channel 37
USA 4	8 July	19 Sept	CBS
Colombia	27 July	9 Nov	Caracol Televis
Belgium 4	31 Aug	14 Dec	Kanaal 2
Portugal 4	31 Aug	31 Dec	TV1
Denmark 3	21 Sept	27 Nov	TVDK2
Spain 5	21 Sept	11 Jan	Tele 5
2004			
Brazil 4	13 Jan	30 Apr	Globo TV
Italy 4	22 Jan	6 May	Canale 5
Sweden 4	27 Jan	9 May	Kanal 5
Middle East	21 Feb	29 Feb	MBC
Germany 5	4 Mar	28 Feb (2005)	RTL2
Romania 2	14 Mar	13 June	Prima TV
Australia 4	2 May	5 July	Channel 10

COUNTRY	START DATE	END DATE	BROADCASTER
UK 5	28 May	6 Aug	Channel 4
USA 5	6 July	30 Sept	CBS
Spain 6	5 Sept	23 Dec	Tele 5
Croatia	18 Sept	26 Dec	RTL
Italy 5	23 Sept	2 Dec	Canale 5
Bulgaria	18 Oct	1 Jan (2005)	NTV (Bulgaria)

2005			
Germany 6			RTL2
Serbia			RTS
Thailand			ITV
UK 6			Channel 4
USA 6			CBS
Australia 5			Channel 10
Brazil 5			Globo TV
Mexico 3			Televisa Canal
Norway 4			TV Norge

ACKNOWLEDGEMENTS

I would like to thank all those who gave me an interview, more than 160 in all. In particular I am grateful to John de Mol, Charlie Parsons and Paul Smith, who all spoke to me extensively, and Fiona Harris and Tom Phillips, who helped me research *Billion Dollar Game*. Thanks also to Tom Barnicoat, Mark Lucas, Robert McCrum, Ursula Mackenzie and Tim Whiting who all read the first draft. While not precisely agreeing with each other they all helped improve it. Some wished to remain anonymous. Everyone else who contributed, in one way or another, is named below:

Peter Abbott, Carla Affonso, Nabil Al Hamr, Sheikh Adel Al Maawada, Dr Mohammed Al Tabtabaie, Zain Al Thawadi, Mahmood Al Yousif, Piet Hein Bakker, Neil Balnaves, Anuska Ban, Marianella Bargilli, Hillary Barker, Mathias Barnekow, Marco Bassetti, Julia di Bello, Leigh Bennie, Arturo Bernardini, Bjarne Bo Berthelsen, Ulrike Beuys, Walther Boecker, Marco Borges, Borris Brandt, Charity Braun, Sarah Caplin, Gary Carter, Carlo Alberto Cavallo, Peter Cheshire, Mariano Chihade, Kathy Coleman, Marcelo Corazza, Stéphane Courbit, Solange Cristina Couto Maria, Analaura Daluso, Michael Davies, Christina Davis, Laurens Drillich, Phil Edgar-Jones, José Ramon Fernandez, Corina Fernández Giuliano, Sebastian Florek, Maria João Freitas, Andi Frick, Francesco Gaiardelli, Tim Gardam, Charlie Gardner, Emile Gaudreault, Fareed Ghazi,

Manuel Gilardi, Giorgio Girelli, Unico Glorie, David Goldberg, Rodrigo Gomez, Eleonora González, Marcos Gorban, Michael Gordon-Smith, Peter Grimsdale, Lurdes Guerreiro, Janan Habib, Lasse Hallberg, Ilsa Marie Hanekom, Adela Harnagea, Ruud Hendriks, Eduardo Clemesha Herrera, James Herring, Piers Hillier, Madeleine Holt, Hesther Jolly, Brett Kahr, Olivera Katic, Sheikh Mohammed Khalid, Marcelo Kohen, Martin Kweller, Gerry Lancaster, Peter Langenberg, Xuxo Lara, Rainer Laux, Catherine Lavenac, Joshua Levitt, David Liddiment, Mikolaj Lizut, John Makinson, Juan Maldonado, Karen Maldoy, Robert Minicozzi, Christian Möllman, Piers Morgan, Mike Morley, Jef Nassenstein, Hilary Newiss, Sverre Nordbø, Thomas Notermans, Juan Oke, J. B. Boninho de Oliveira, Joseanne de Oliveira, Jeferson de Oliveira Silva, Olivia Nuñez Orellano, Richard Osman, Leon Otto, Denisse Padilla, Howard Parker, José A. Bastón Patiño, Anna Pauli, Annabel Pearcey, Kleber de Paula Pedra, Olivio Petit, Francesco Porcelli, Rikkie Proost, Iyad Qasem, Peter Radnai, Sameera Rajab, Marc Rasmus, Marcellus Reynolds, Franc Roddam, Peggy Roeder, Paul Romer, Marie Rosholt, Douglas Ross, Claudia Rosencrantz, Abdul Nabi Salman, Gilda Santana, Dr Norbert Schneider, Aat Schouwenaar, Marc Schwinges, Floriana Secondi, Arnold Shapiro, Ben Silverman, Professor Michael A. Simpson, Vanessa Cristina Soares Dias, Salwa Soueid, Denis Spencer, Quentin Stafford-Fraser, Sven Steffensmeier, Sally Stockbridge, Errol Sullivan, Pedro Torres, Magdalena Tymorek, Sergio Vainman, Esther van den Brink, Astrid van der Knaap, Hummie van der Tonnekreek, Floor van Hofwegen, José Velasco, Luis Filipe Vera Portugal, Vasco Vilarinho, Liz Warner, Paul Watson, Jelle Weiringa, Fons von Westerloo, Dr Peter Widlok, Lauren Wiener, Megan Wilson, Don Wollman, Bradford Wood, Ruth Wrigley, Padricio Zambrano, Panos Zois, Herman van der Zwan.

BIBLIOGRAPHY

Brenton, Sam, and Reuben Cohen, *Shooting People* (Verso)

Brooks, Tim, and Earle Marsh, *The Complete Directory of Prime Time Network TV Shows* (Ballantine Books)

Cassidy, John, *Dot.Con* (Penguin Books)

Coleman, Stephen, *A Tale of Two Houses* (Hansard Society)

Gordon, Rick, *Digital Journalism: Emerging Media & Changing Horizons in Journalism* (Rowman & Littlefield)

Grant, Barry Keith, and Jeanette Sloniowski, eds, *Documenting the Documentary* (Wayne State University Press)

Guralnick, Peter, *Last Train to Memphis* (Abacus)

Hill, Annette, *Reality TV, Audiences and Popular Factual Television* (Routledge)

Hoggart, Richard, *The Uses of Literacy* (Penguin Books)

Johnson-Woods, Toni, *Big Brother* (University of Queensland Press)

Leavis, F. R., *Mass Civilisation and Minority Culture* (Cambridge University Press)

Lumby, C. and E. Probyn, *It Feels Real – Girls and Reality TV* (University of Sydney)

Mackay, Charles, *Extraordinary Popular Delusions and the Madness of Crowds* (Bentley)

Meijer, Irene Costera, and Maarten Reesink, *Reality Soap* (Boom)

Milski, Jürgen, *Jürgen Ich Sag's* (Verlag Donata Kinzelbach)

Munk, Nina, *Fools Rush In: Steve Case, Jerry Levin & the Unmaking of AOL Time Warner* (HarperCollins)

Murray, Susan, and Laurie Ouellette, eds, *Remaking Television Culture* (New York University Press)

Murray, Venetia, *High Society in the Regency Period, 1788–1830* (Penguin Books)

Negroponte, Nicholas, *Being Digital* (New York Times)

O'Loughlin, Dean, *Living in the Box* (The Gameford Files)

Ritchie, Jean, *Big Brother: The Official Unseen History* (Channel 4 Books)

——, *Inside Big Brother: Getting In & Staying In* (Channel 4 Books)

Ruoff, Jeffrey K., *An American Family: A Televised Life* (University of Minnesota Press)

Smith, Matthew, and Andrew Wood, eds, *Survivor Lessons: Essays on Communication & Reality Television* (McFarland & Co.)

Williams, Kate, *Emma Hamilton, England's Mistress* (Hutchinson)

Winston, Brian, *Claiming the Real* (British Film Institute)

——, *Lies Damned Lies & Documentaries* (British Film Institute)

Wolf, Gary, *Wired: The Book* (Random House)

INDEX

Abascal, Adriana, 173, 184, 212
Abbot, Peter, 241
Abby (*Big Brother* contestant), 246
ABC, 121–2; and *Big Brother*, 167,
  168, 169; and *Candid Camera*,
  21–2; and *Survivor*, 121; and
  *Who Wants to Be a
  Millionaire?*, 121–2, 123–5,
  139–41, 161, 283
ABN AMRO, 118, 195, 196, 197
Abril-Martorell, Fernando, 190–1
Absolutely Fabulous, 140
Africa: and *Big Brother*, 246–7,
  266–70
Airey, Dawn, 159
Ajram, Nancy, 253, 257
Al Asfoor, Sheikh Mohsin, 257–8
Alberti, Willeke, 7, 12
All You Need Is Love, 30–2, 34, 39,
  55
Allen, Woody, 22
Alli, Waheed, 80, 82, 120, 149, 204
Almunia, Joaquin, 190
America Online *see* AOL
American Family, An, 22
Andreessen, Marc, 44, 51
Anneveldt, Eelco, 131
Antenna 3, 65, 110, 206, 207
Antvelink, Gerard, 137–8
AOL (America Online), 59–60, 110;
  merger with Time Warner,
  160–1, 165, 166; purchase of
  Netscape, 110
Asmal, Kader, 246
Asociacion A Favor De La Mejor
  (The Silent Majority), 263–5
Association of Catholics in Business,
  177
Australia: and *Big Brother*, 241–2
Avesco, 71
AVRO, 11
Azcarraga, Emilio, 264–5
Aznar, José Maria, 8, 50, 65, 173,
  174, 175, 190

Bahrain: and *Big Brother*, 252–9
Baker, Noeline, 40
Bakker, Piet Hein, 248
Balnaves, Neil, 241
Ban, Anuska, 254, 256, 257
Banamex, 264
Banda, Chimunthu, 268–9
Barnicoat, Tom, 100, 147
Bart (*Big Brother* contestant),
  136–7, 152, 153, 154–5, 156,
  164, 177, 209, 280
Bassetti, Marco, 213–14, 215
Bassi, Leo, 210–11
Bateman, Nick, 226–9, 240–51, 280
Bauer, Frans, 32
Bauer, Ludwig, 116
BBC, 50; and *Big Brother*, 159

Beck, Kurt, 177
Becker, Christa, 177
Belgium: and *Big Brother*, 250
Bell Atlantic Corporation, 43
Bellamy, Julian, 231
Bergg, David, 96
Berlusconi, Silvio, 213
Berners-Lee, Tim, 44
Bertelsmann, 174
Betty 'Boob', 250
Big Breakfast, The, 82, 120
Big Brother, 73, 114–17, 180, 200;
    attempt to ban in Malawi, 266,
    267–70; attempt to get interest
    in and initial rejections, 112,
    114–16, 125–7, 126, 176;
    Australia, 241–2; Bahrain
    controversy, 252–9; Belgium,
    250; Brazil, 238–9
    Britain: (1), 217–18, 225–8; (2),
    247; (3), 229–30, 231–2; (5),
    233–5, 247; attempt to sell in,
    158–9; criticism of, 217–18,
    218, 230, 235; deal with
    Channel 4, 158–9
    'casting' of, 136–7, 152, 243;
    and Colombia, 247, 248–9,
    272–3; and Conservative Party,
    235–6; France, 260–1
    Germany: criticism of, 176–80,
    181–2, 201, 260; deal over,
    158, 176; first series and success
    of, 181–3, 200–4, 237–8, 240;
    initial failure in selling to,
    112–16, 176; second series,
    249–50
    Greece, 254
    Holland: criticism of, 130–4;
    first broadcast, 144–5, 152–6,
    164; and HMG/Veronica deal,
    126–9, 130; preparations for
    launch and construction of
    house, 135–9, 142–4; success
    of, 153–4, 156, 165
    and homosexuality, 247;
    Hungary, 250–1; international
    sales and success, 211, 213;
    Italy, 213–16, 239, 252; and
    legal action, 284; Mexico,
    263–6; numbers of voters, 273,
    284; opposition to and criticism
    of, 158, 232–3, 284; origin of
    idea 73–7 *see also Golden Cage,
    The*; 'pantomime villains',
    240–2; Parsons' legal dispute
    against, 84, 149–51, 169, 170,
    189, 204–6, 221, 283; Poland,
    274–7; and politics, 272–82;
    Portugal, 242–3, 247–8;
    postscript, 284; and
    psychologists, 242–3; 'reality'
    debate, 230; and sex, 245–52;
    South Africa, 245–6, 266–70,
    277–80; Spain, 206–11, 272;
    Sweden, 251–2; transmissions
    worldwide, 286–9; 'trash
    heroes', 237–41, 251
    South Africa: *Big Brother* (1),
    277–80; *Big Brother* (2), 246;
    Big Brother (3), 266–70
    Spain, 206–11, 272
    United States: (1), 216–17,
    218–20; (2), 242, 249; attempt
    to sell to networks, 162, 166–9;
    criticism of, 219, 220; deal with
    CBS, 168–72
    viewing figures, 153, 157, 165;
    web sites, 137–8, 144, 153,
    156, 165, 203–4, 225, 226,
    227, 284
Bijl, Arie-Willem, 131
Biosphere II, 74
Blue Peter, 52–3
Boland, Murray, 79–80
Boonstra, Cor, 198
Botella, Ana, 50

Bouchard, Sylvie, 88
Bragg, Melvyn, 231, 281
Brandt, Borris, 112–14, 115,
    116–17
Brazil, 284; and *Big Brother*, 238–9
Briggs, David, 56–7, 97
Brink, Nina, 138–9, 164, 192, 197,
    199
Brink, Robert ten, 31
Britain: and *Big Brother* see *Big
    Brother*; general election
    (2001), 273
Broadcast Communications, 100–1
Brusse, Kees, 24–5
Buena Vista, 82, 83, 124
Bunim, Mary-Ellis, 41
Burnett, Mark, 91–2, 121, 149, 188,
    216
Business Week, 59

Candid Camera, 21–2, 23, 88
Capital Radio, 57, 97
Carlton, 120
Carpenter, John, 161
Carrot, Jasper, 54
Carter, Gary, 83–5, 117, 146,
    147–8, 150, 162, 163, 166,
    167–9, 171–2, 206
Case, Steve, 59, 160, 165
Cash Mountain see *Who Wants to
    Be a Millionaire?*
Cass, Johnnie, 241–2
Castaway, 120, 149, 150
Catholic Association, 181
Cavallo, Carlo Alberto, 252
CBS, 121; and *Big Brother*, 168–72,
    189, 216–17; and *Survivor*,
    121, 149, 168, 189, 216, 220
Celador, 54–6, 72; and Avesco, 71;
    and Endemol, 55–6, 71; and
    *Who Wants to be a
    Millionaire?*, 57–9; *see also*
    Smith, Paul

celebrity culture, 239–40, 243–4
Centrefold, 25
Chakuamba, Gwanda, 268
Channel 4, 54, 80; and *Big Brother*,
    158–9
Channel 5, 159
Chen, Julie, 217
Chow, Stephen, 162–3, 167
Christopher, Sonja, 189
Clinton, President Bill, 138, 219
Coleman, Stephen, 281–2
Colombia: and *Big Brother*, 247,
    248–9, 272–3
Columbia Pictures, 27
Commercial Breakdown, 54
Conrad, Mark, 39
Conservative Party: and *Big Brother*,
    235–6
Coronation Street, 26
Courbit, Stéphane, 260–1, 262
Craig (*Big Brother* contestant), 280
Craxi, Bettino, 213
Croft, Annabel, 80
Cyrano de Bergerac, 48, 49

Da Costa, Rachel, 105, 106–8
Daniela (*Big Brother* contestant),
    250
Darnell, Mike (Fox Television), 166,
    168, 169, 170
Davies, Michael, 83, 122, 123–5,
    139, 140–1
Davies, William, 122
Davy, Gary, 15–16, 19
de Mol, John: becomes a freelance
    producer, 10–11; and *Big
    Brother*, 74–6, 94, 98, 111,
    112, 117, 125–6, 142–3,
    146–7, 153, 169, 170–2, 180;
    calls off merger negotiations
    with Pearson, 146–7, 163;
    challenging of social attitudes,
    31; character, 10; coining of

de Mol, John – *continued*
    phrase emotainment, 34–5;
    dislike of being head of public
    company, 70; Dutch television
    career, 8–9; Hendriks, Ruud,
    relationship with 44–5; love of
    deal-making, 14, 20, 40; pays
    off Endemol's losses personally,
    69; personal life, 7–8, 12, 26,
    191; postscript, 284–5;
    producer of TROS, 8–9, 10;
    public falling out with
    Telefonica, 285; rivalry with
    van den Ende, 8, 22–3, 48;
    setting up of John de Mol
    Productions, 11; and *Survivor*,
    286; social life, 19–20; and
    talent management, 13–14, 16,
    25; and Telefonica's offer for
    Endemol, 193; wanting to sell
    Endemol, 118; wealth of, 67;
    and women, 12, 19; *see also*
    Endemol; John de Mol
    Productions
de Mol, Johnnie (son), 12, 156–7
de Mol, Linda (sister), 15, 16, 19,
    33, 35, 38–9
de Nijs, Rob, 24
de Winter, Harry, 131–2
Deitmers, Hubert, 181, 192
Denmark: and *Big Brother*, 272
Denton, Andrew, 111
Denver, John, 10–11
Deutsche Bank, 178–80, 183, 185,
    189
Diana, Princess, 88
DJ Cat Show, 19
docu-soaps, 41, 72
Dolly Dots, 25
Double Your Money, 57
Drillich, Laurens, 265
Driving School, 72–3
DRTV, 150

Duncan Smith, Iain, 236
Durkin, Mary, 85
Dutch Football League, 68–9
Dyke, Greg, 129

Earth and Fire, 9
EastEnders, 26
Eco-Challenge, 91
Ed TV, 88–9, 111
Edgar-Jones, Phil, 231
Edwards, Billy and Antoinette, 9
Edwards, Blake, 53
Eisner, Michael, 122, 124–5, 140–1
Elwell, Graham, 104–5
Emma (*Big Brother* contestant), 233,
    235
emotainment, 34–5
Endemol, 109, 110; ambition to
    dominate European
    programming, 65–6; attempt to
    sell and suitors, 110, 111,
    118–20, 129–30, 163, 172–3,
    175, 178–9, 181, 183, 191–3;
    and Celador, 55–6, 71; creation
    of, 48–9; and *Cyrano de
    Bergerac*, 48, 49; deal with
    Dutch Football League over
    television rights and public
    outcry, 68–9; and European
    production companies, 100;
    falling of share price, 69–71,
    117; growth in television activity,
    70; headquarters (Hilversum),
    113–14; launching as IPO, 66–7;
    and *Loft Story*, 261–3; merger
    negotiations with Pearson and
    breaking off of by de Mol, 130,
    145, 146–7, 163; and output
    deal with HMG, 66; Parsons'
    legal dispute against *Big Brother*,
    84, 149–51, 169, 170, 189,
    204–6, 221, 283; programme
    hours produced, 48–9; rivalry

between shows, 156–7; share price rise, 164, 165, 171, 180, 183, 187, 195; and *Survive*, 84; Telefonica's negotiations over purchase, 175, 178–81, 183–5, 186–7, 189, 190–1, 192, 193–8, 212, 284–5; and telephone revenue, 63; turnover, 49; turns down *Who Wants to Be a Millionaire?*, 56, 117; under performance of theatre division, 48, 117–18; value of, 119

Endurance, 55

euthanasia, 26

Evans, Chris, 82

Evi (*Big Brother* contestant), 251

Expedition Robinson see *Survive (Expedition Robinson)*

'Family' documentaries (1970s), 22

Family Feud, 20–1, 26, 27

Family, The, 9, 40

Fischer, Carl, 111, 269

Five o'Clock Show, The, 29

Florek, Sebastian, 274–7, 280

Floriana (*Big Brother* contestant), 239

Fox, 87; and *Big Brother*, 166, 167, 168, 169

France: and *Big Brother*, 260–1; and *Loft Story*, 261–3; and *Survivor*, 262

Frequin, Willibrord, 157

Frere, Albert, 27

Full Service Network, 43

Funt, Allen, 21

Gabler, Neil, 220

Gaetano (*Big Brother* contestant), 246

Gardam, Tim, 158, 231, 232

Gates, Bill, 64

Gaudreault, Emile, 88

Geldof, Bob, 82, 120, 149, 204, 205, 206

General Electric, 64

Germany: and *Big Brother* see *Big Brother*: Germany

Gestmusic, 209

Gilbert, Craig, 9

Gillette, Pete, 80

Globe.com, The, 110

Glorie, Unico, 126–7, 128, 129, 137

Goes, Ronald, 126

Golden Cage, The, 93–4, 98–101, 110–11; establishing logistics and costing for, 92–4; name changed to *Big Brother*, 111; rejections of and detractors, 98–9, 100, 101; revision of format, 111; sales tape, 99–100; *see also Big Brother*

Good Times Bad Times, 156, 157

Goodson, Mark, 20, 27

Goodson organisation, 28

Goody, Jade, 229–30, 231, 232

Grade, Michael, 53

Granada, 72, 83, 147

Gray, Duncan, 147, 148

Greece: and *Big Brother*, 254

Green, Hughie, 57

Green, Michael, 120

Greer, Germaine, 231

Griffin, Merv, 21, 27

Grimsdale, Peter, 231

Guardian Media Group, The, 100

Gunya, Reverend Daniel, 267–8

Hamad, King of Bahrain, 253, 258

Al Hamr, Nabil, 255

Hayes, Mickey, 32–3

Hayward-Cole, Guy, 179, 180, 183, 184, 186, 190, 195

Hemd Van Je Lijf, 24–5

Hendriks, Ruud, 9, 170–1; attempt at buying John de Mol Productions, 44–5; attempt at selling Endemol, 129–30, 164, 192; and *Big Brother* idea, 76; and Celador, 55–6; and Dutch Football League deal, 68; ejected as a youth from studio by de Mol, 29; and Endemol's international expansion, 119; joins Endemol, 62–3; and Pearson merger negotiations, 130, 145, 147; and *The Price is Right*, 27–8; and Telefonica deal, 196

Hilversum, 33

HMG (Holland Media Group), 66, 70, 126–9

Holland: and *Big Brother* see *Big Brother*: Holland

House From Hell, 111

Hughes, Barry, 24

Hungary and *Big Brother*, 250–1

al-Ibrahim, Sheikh Walid, 252, 257, 258

I'm a Celebrity, Get Me Out of Here!, 283

Internet, 44, 50–1, 59–61, 63, 64, 89–90; and Jennicam, 60–2, 74, 89, 100; and 'the new paradigm', 64, 165; and voyeurism, 89–90

Isabella@home, 90

Italy: and *Big Brother*, 213–16, 239, 252

Itkin, Mark, 167

It'll Be Alright on the Night, 53–4, 56

ITV, 54; and *Survivor*, 92; turns down *Big Brother*, 158; and *Who Wants to be a Millionaire?*, 57–9, 71–2, 94–7

Janine (*Big Brother* contestant), 246

Jennicam, 60–2, 74, 89, 100

Jeopardy, 27

Jerry Springer Show, The, 87

John de Mol Productions, 13, 15, 16; and *All You Need Is Love*, 30–2, 34, 39, 55; attempt to sell programmes to America, 35; growth in output, 19; investment by van Kooten, 18–19; and *Love Letters*, 33–4, 35–6, 37, 38–9; merging with Joop van den Ende Productions to form Endemol, 45–9; output deal with RTL, 39–40; premises, 16; and *The Price Is Right* contract, 28–9; problems in early years, 13, 16–17; producing of chat show (*Hemd Van Je Lijf*), 24–5; productions of foreign formats, 20–1, 23, 26, 27, 28–9; rivalry with Joop Van Ende Productions, 22–3, 28; Sky contract, 15–16, 19, 26; value of, 45

Jones, Janet, 280–1

Jonkman, Martin, 152–3

Joop van den Ende Productions, 23, 28, 45–9

Jorge (*Big Brother* contestant), 208, 209

José, Marie, 208–10

Justin (*Big Brother* contestant), 249

Kahr, Brett, 228, 243

Kalff, Jan, 197

Kanal 5, 251

Karim (*Big Brother* contestant), 250

Kasonde, Chali, 246

Keenen Ivory Wayans Show, The, 91

Khalid, Sheikh Mohammed, 258

King, Allan, 9

Kirch, Leo, 37–9, 65, 112, 115

Kleber (*Big Brother* contestant), 238–9
Knight, Steve, 57
Kofler, Georg 112, 113, 115, 116
Kok, Wim, 68
Kornheiser, Tony, 142
KPN, 66, 197; bid for Endemol and failure,163, 175, 181, 183, 191, 192, 193, 194; failure of merger with Telefonica, 211–12
Krista (*Big Brother* contestant), 249
KRO, 73

Lankreijer, Ton, 130
Laux, Rainer, 114, 250
Lawson, Mark, 229, 230
Levin, Jerry, 43, 59, 160, 165
Liddiment, David, 92, 94, 95–7, 102, 103, 106, 158
Lizut, Mikolaj, 276
Loeff Claeys Verbeke, 148
Loft Story, 261–3
London Weekend Television (LWT), 53
Longwe, Ian, 267
Loud, Bill and Pat, 9
Love Letters, 33–4, 35–6, 37, 38–9
Luboto, Nsoto, 246–7
Lucent Technologies, 193–4
Luis (*Big Brother* contestant), 248–9
Luv, 12
Lycos, 211

McDonough, Blair, 241
MacInnes, Bruce, 179, 180, 183, 184, 186, 190, 195, 198
McKenna, Paul, 55, 72
McLuhan, Marshall, 42
Makabale, Cherise, 267
Makinson, John, 130, 145, 196
Malawi: and *Big Brother*, 266, 267–70
Maldonado, Juan, 273

Manchester United, 285
Mandela, Nelson, 267
Mansfield, Grant, 158
Manuela (*Big Brother* contestant), 240
Marco (*Big Brother* contestant), 247–8
Marga (*Big Brother* contestant), 12, 26
Marquard, Pia, 84, 86
Married Couple, A, 9
Marta (*Big Brother* contestant), 248
Martin, Quinn, 53
Maurits, 30–1
Al Maawada, Sheikh Adel, 253, 255, 257
May, Theresa, 235, 236
MBC (Middle East Broadcasting Company): and *Big Brother*, 252–3, 256, 258
Mbeki, President, 279–80
Mediaset, 213, 214, 215
Medical Centre West, 26, 39
Melin, Martin, 85, 86
Menten, Pieter, 191
Metcalfe, June, 42
Mexico: and *Big Brother*, 263–6
Microsoft, 64
Middle East: and *Big Brother*, 252–9
Middle East Broadcasting Company *see* MBC
Middlehof, Thomas, 174
Miller, Leszek, 275, 276
Milski, Jurgen, 201–2
Minahan, Daniel, 89
Mini Playback Show, The, 55
Mipcom, 84, 146
Mlanjira, Sam, 269–70
M-Net, 266, 269
Mole, The, 113
Monica (*Big Brother* contestant), 248–9

Moonves, Leslie, 121, 168–9, 171, 172, 217
Morley, Mike, 274
Mosaic, 44
M6, 260
MSNBC, 64
MTV, 41
Murdoch, Liz, 158
Murdoch, Rupert, 15, 68, 162
Murray, Jonathan, 41
Murray, Richard, 71

Nadia (*Big Brother* contestant), 247
Naik, Prash, 234
Namibia: and *Big Brother*, 267
NASDAQ, 14, 50, 64, 110, 164, 175, 186, 199
Nassenstein, Jef, 14, 15, 20, 21, 24, 26, 38, 40, 46–7, 76
NATPE, 163, 166–7
NBC, 54
Negroponte, Nicholas, 12–13, 42
Netcom, 50–1
Netherlands Institute of Psychologists, 132
Netscape, 51, 110
Network 7, 79, 80
News International, 15
Nieto, Juan José, 178, 179, 180, 184, 186
Nineteen Eighty-Four, 284
Nippon Television, 87
Notermans, Thomas, 132, 170, 171, 204
Nothale, Taylor, 268, 270
Now or Never, 55
Ntaba, Hetherwick, 270
Nujoma, Sam, 267

O'Brien, Simon, 80
Oliver, Elizabeth Ann, 90
Oostvogel, Alex, 192
Organisation Party, The, 278–9, 280

Parsons, Charlie, 78–85, 109, 117, 189; and *The Big Breakfast*, 82; court case against *I'm a Celebrity, Get Me Out of Here!*, 283; and John de Mol, 286; legal dispute against *Big Brother*, 84, 149–51, 169, 170, 189, 204–6, 221, 283; media career, 78–9; merging of 24 Productions to form Planet 24, 82; and *Network 7*, 79; postscript, 283–4; selling of Planet 24 to Carlton, 120; sets up own company (24 Productions), 80–1; and *Survive/Survivor*, 78, 80, 82–5, 91, 92, 120, 121, 149, 216, 284, 286; and *The Word*, 80–1
Pearson, 129–30, 158, 174; merger negotiations with Endemol and breaking off of by de Mol, 130, 145, 146–7, 163
Peeping Moe.com, 90
Persaud, Dr Raj, 242
Philbin, Regis, 139–40
Phillips, Craig, 226–7
PJ (*Big Brother* contestant), 231, 232
Planet 24, 82, 83, 85; selling of to Carlton, 120
Plantin, Marcus, 58, 71–2, 84, 92
Playboy magazine, 25
Poland: and *Big Brother*, 274–7
politics: and *Big Brother*, 272–82
Porsius, Pieter, 127–8, 129
Portugal: and *Big Brother*, 242–3, 247–8
Presley, Elvis, 235
Price Is Right, The, 27–9
ProSieben, 112, 113, 114–16, 125

Quattrone, Frank, 51
Quiz Show, 123

Raab, Stefan, 202, 237
Real World, The, 11, 41, 131
Rees, Maureen *(Driving School)*, 72–3
Renato *(Big Brother* contestant), 251
Rich *(Survivor* contestant), 242
Riggs, Conrad, 149
Ring, Professor Wolf-Dieter, 182
Ringley, Jennifer Kaye, 60–2, 100
Rios, José Antonio, 178–9, 180, 184, 186
Roddam, Franc, 40
Rolling Stone magazine, 60
Romania: and *Big Brother*, 250
Romer, Bart, 74, 75
Romer, Paul: and *Big Brother*, 74, 75, 76, 92–3, 94, 99, 127, 132–3, 136, 143, 145, 152, 178; and US *Big Brother*, 216–17
Rosencrantz, Claudia, 57–8, 94, 95, 102, 103
Roses From Your Ex, 113, 114
Rosetto, Louis, 42
Rossmann, Thorsten, 114–15, 116
Rothschilds, 118, 197
Routh, Jonathan, 22
RTL, 27–8, 179; and *Big Brother*, 158, 176, 260; decision not to purchase John de Mol Productions, 45; folding Dutch channels into Holland Media Group, 66, 126; and *Love Letters*, 35–6, 37, 39; output deal with John de Mol Productions, 39–40
RTL2: and *Big Brother*, 176, 177, 182, 203
RTL4, 44, 156; and *The Golden Cage*, 98; *The Price is Right*, 29
Rush, Frank, 142
Rushdie, Salman, 218

Sabine *(Big Brother* contestant), 137, 152, 153, 154–5, 156, 209, 280
Sat 1, 37, 176
Savija, Nermina, 86, 130–1
Savija, Sinisa, 85–6, 91, 127
SBS, 98, 125–6
Scalfari, Eugenio, 215
Scardino, Marjorie, 129–30, 145, 146, 174
Schily, Otto, 177
Schlesinger, Jeffrey, 120
Schneider, Dr Norbert, 177–8, 182
Scholtze, Patrick, 74, 75
Schouwenaar, Aat, 47, 49, 55, 76, 130, 145, 164, 192, 194
Schroder Investment Management, 117–18, 147, 196–7
Scott, Martin, 108
Sean Patrick Live!, 89–90
Sellers, Peter, 53
Sentana, Gilda, 208, 209
Series 7, 89
Servitje, Don Lorenzo, 264, 266
Sex Olympics, The, 9
Shaps, Simon, 72
Sharp, Pat, 19
Short, Chris, 226
Silverman, Ben, 124
Simpson, Professor Michael, 280
$64,000 Question, The, 57, 122–3
Sky, 15–16
Sky One, 158
Smit, Paul, 194
Smith, Paul: and Endemol, 55–6, 71; and *It'll Be Alright on the Night*, 52–4; later career, 283; sets up own production company (Celador), 54–5; television career, 52–3; and *Who Wants to Be a Millionaire?*, 52, 56, 57–9, 71–2, 94–7, 101–3, 104, 105, 108–9, 150, 283

Smith, Raymond, 42–3
soap operas, 26–7
Sony, 159
Soundmixshow, The, 23
South Africa: and *Big Brother* see
    Big Brother: South Africa
Spain: and *Big Brother* see *Big
    Brother*: Spain
Spargo, 13–14
Sport7, 68, 69, 70, 285
Stafford-Fraser, Quentin, 44
Star Academy, 253, 256
Stars in Their Eyes, 23
Street-Porter, Janet, 80
Strix, 84, 85, 86
Sun: and *Big Brother*, 226
Surprise Show, The, 23
Survive (Expedition Robinson),
    82–7, 91–2, 131, 149–51
Survivor, 78, 134, 172, 283, 284:
    attempt to sell, 120–1; first US
    production and success of,
    187–9, 216, 218, 220–1, 242;
    in France, 262; initial turn-
    down of by ITV, 92; legal
    dispute against *Big Brother*, 84,
    149–51, 169, 170, 189, 204–6,
    221, 283; origin of idea and
    Parsons' attempt to get started
    *see Survive (Expedition
    Robinson)*; sold to CBS, 121,
    149, 168
SVT, 84, 86, 91
Sweden: and *Big Brother*, 251–2
Sylvania Waters, 40–1

Talking Telephone Numbers, 55, 72
Talleda, Concha, 50
Talpa, 285
Tarrant, Chris, 57, 97, 103, 104,
    106
TCI, 43
Telecinco, 158, 206, 207, 211

Telefonica, 189–90, 206;
    controversial share options
    scheme, 174–5, 190;
    convergence deals, 65, 110; de
    Mol's falling out with, 285;
    failure in merger with KPN,
    211–12; negotiations with
    Endemol over purchase of and
    success, 175, 178–81, 183–5,
    186–7, 189, 190–1, 192,
    193–8, 212, 284–5; Villalonga
    leaves, 212; *see also* Villalonga,
    Juan
Telefonica Media, 179
Televisa, 263–6
Television Espanola, 207
Tembo, John, 269, 270
Terra, 179, 211, 225
TF1, 260, 261–2, 263
Thatcher, Margaret, 54
This Is Your Life, 22, 32
Thyes, Freddy, 45, 46
Time Warner, 43; and Endemol,
    119–20; merger with AOL,
    160–1, 165, 166
Tjia, Ton, 67
Tonini, Cardinal, 213–14
Torres, Pedro, 265
Toth, Sylvia, 66, 198
TROS, 8–9, 10, 33
Trouw, 128, 130
Truman Show, The, 87–8, 111, 215
TV Censored Bloopers, 54
24 Productions, 80–1, 82
Twenty-One, 123

United States: and *Big Brother* see
    Big Brother: United States; first
    Survivor series and success of,
    187–9, 216, 218, 220–1, 242;
    game show formats, 21–2; and
    *Who Wants to Be a
    Millionaire?*, 83, 121–2, 123–5,

139–41, 161, 283
Uribe, Alvaro, 272, 273
USA Networks, 162, 167

van den Ende, Joop, 28, 157, 194;
and *Big Brother* idea, 76–7; and
merging of company with de
Mol's, 45–9; paying off
Endemol's losses personally, 69;
retirement, 192–3, 196; rivalry
with de Mol, 8, 22–3, 48;
theatre division of Endemol
('Live Entertainment'), 117–18;
wealth of, 67
van der Tonnekreek, Hummie, 136,
137, 152, 155–6
van der Zwan, Herman, 25, 46–7
van Gundy, Doug, 141
van Klinken, Onno, 149
van Kooten, Willem, 18–19, 47,
67–8, 147
van Lange, Paul, 131
van Westerloo, Fons, 98–9, 125–6,
128
Vara, 21
Variety, 148
Velasco, José, 196, 206
Veronica, 29–30, 126, 144, 156, 157
Verwaayen, Ben, 66, 118–19, 175,
193–4, 198
Via Digital, 65, 207
Viacom, 43
Victor (*Big Brother* contestant), 233
Villalonga, Juan, 173–5, 285;
acquisitions, 211; allegations of
illegal share dealing, 212; and
Aznar, 8, 50, 65, 173, 174, 175;
background and career, 8,
49–50; downfall, 211, 212; and
Endemol deal, 178–9, 180,
184–5, 197–8, 206, 212; and
failure of Telefonica-KPN
merger, 211–12; leaves

Telefonica, 212; made
Chairman of Telefonica, 65;
and 'Operation Veronica', 179;
personal life, 173; successful
expansion of Telefonica, 212;
see also Telefonica
Villalonga, Ignacio, 8
VNU, 66
VoyeursDorm.com, 90

Warhol, Andy, 244
Warona (*Big Brother* contestant),
266
Watson, Paul, 40, 41
Wayans, Keenen, 91
Weintraub, Jerry, 10–11, 170
Weir, Peter, 88
Welch, Jack, 64
What's My Line?, 20
Wheel of Fortune, The, 20–1, 22–3,
27
Whitehill, Mike, 57
Who Wants to Be a Millionaire?,
134, 150
  Britain: audience figures, 108,
  109; broadcasting of first
  shows, 103–108; criticism of,
  142; development phase, 97–8;
  and ITV, 57–9, 71–2, 94–7;
  preparations for launch and set
  design, 101–3; and stripping
  show every day, 96–7; success
  of, 108–9, 117
  format, 95–6, 97–8;
  international success, 117, 148,
  221, 283; origins, 56–7;
  postscript, 283; turned down by
  Endemol, 56, 117; and United
  States, 83, 121–2, 123–25,
  139–41, 161, 283
Who Wants to Marry a Millionaire?,
20
Whose Line Is It Anyway?, 123

Wieringa, Jelle, 221
William Morris, 167
Williams, Sean Patrick, 89–90, 131
Winston, Brian, 230
Wired (magazine), 42
Wood, Brad, 277–80
Word, The, 80–1, 237
World Online, 138–9, 164, 175,
   181, 192, 198–9

World Wide Web *see* Internet
Wrigley, Ruth, 228

Yentob, Alan, 159
Your Big Break, 23

Zeppelin, 196, 206
Zlatko (*Big Brother* contestant),
   201–3, 237–8